INFIDELITY

INFIDELITY

A LOVE STORY

Ann Pearlman

Hodder & Stoughton

Copyright © 2000 by Ann Pearlman

First published in 2000 by MacAdam/Cage Publishing, USA
First published in Great Britain in 2001 by Hodder and Stoughton
A division of Hodder Headline

The right of Ann Pearlman to be identified as the Author of
the Work has been asserted by her in accordance with the
Copyright, Designs and Patents Act 1988.

10 9 8 7 6 5 4 3 2 1

A CIP catalogue record for this title
is available from the British Library.

ISBN 0 340 81934 0

Printed and bound in Great Britain by
Mackays of Chatham plc, Chatham, Kent

Hodder and Stoughton
A division of Hodder Headline
338 Euston Road
London NW1 3BH

ACKNOWLEDGMENTS

Several people aided the birth of this book. Throughout the years, Susan Miller has been my writing sister and read drafts of nearly everything I've written. Her wisdom and criticism have been bolstering as well as pointed. She has never told me merely pretty lies. For that I am indebted. Michael Harper encouraged me to coalesce a mess of pages into a consistent work. Samuel Horowitz's relentless dissection and questioning challenged me to reach further, deeper, wider. Dennis Dieckman provided encouragement and support as well as valuable suggestions. As always I relied on Gail Farley and Linda Sherby's insights and acumen.

I am especially appreciative of the contribution of my agent, Jodie Rhodes, who saw my dream of this book and whose intuitive vision of its entirety helped me hone my story. Truly, without her belief and spectacular persistence, this book in this form would not have come to be. Then she found for me an extraordinary and enthusiastic editor, Pat Walsh, whose devotion to writing and books midwifed my manuscript into its final form.

Gratitude and love beyond reckoning is for Bump and Rena, who dealt with these events and my telling them in only a loving way, and Woozie, who is as proud of her mother as her mother is of her daughter. My ex-husband has always made sacrifices and been generous in the support of all art regardless of costs. For that I am thankful.

For my brother...

Although we come together,
Nothing will come of us. But we would not give
It up, for death is beaten...
We have done it again we are
Still living. Sit up and smile...

"Adultery" — *James Dickey*

CHAPTER 1

David is eleven months old and sits on the floor, not yet able to walk. His toys are helter-skelter around him. Toys that were once mine. I am three and I hate him.

He plays happily with a duck that flaps its wings when he rolls it back and forth. He is oblivious to me and the pain he brings. I stayed with my grandmother, Lala, when he was born. Disobedient and uncontrollable as I was, I rocked back and forth on the dining room chair, hit my head against the corner of the sideboard, and had thirty-six stitches to sew my head together.

When David was brought home from the hospital, the adults surrounded his lacy cradle, crowding each other for a glimpse. Even Daddy stood and watched him. They *oohed* and *aahed* over his plump knees and dimpled cheeks. Gasped with delight almost in unison when he opened his eyes. What a treasure he must be, I thought, what a prize. I walked to the cradle when they left. His eyes were closed. He was immobile. I waited. He did nothing. He did not move. What was the thrill to this creature? I poked him. He waved his arms helplessly and then settled back into his sleep. Boring. Not fun. I didn't get what they saw in him.

I tried to knock him off my mother's breast with my elbow. I pinched his foot dangling from underneath Daddy's arms and heard him howl.

Now David shoves the duck back and forth, back and forth, his brows brought together, watching its wings flutter as he rolls. He is happy, but I no longer am and I despise him.

Then I remember the soft spot my mother warns me not to touch. It throbs on top of his head while he nurses from Mother. MY mother. Never, never touch the baby there. Never. Underneath the pulsing is his brain.

I go to him now and I see the indentation. There. Soon it will be covered with bones like mine is. Hard. I have asked my mother endless questions. Soon it will be too late. He will be safe. Now he reaches for a block. His arm is chubby, his elbow dimpled. The adults love his dimples. He scoots forward to the blue wooden block, his fingers outstretched. It used to be my block. Now it is not. I stand above him and touch the spot. It is like paper. There is no warmth to it.

I press down. He stops reaching. I press harder. He is motionless. How hard do I have to push to make him go away. How hard do I have to press for my fingers to enter his brain. Kill him. How hard?

He moves his arm close to his body. He tries to raise his head. He cries.

I push. Crush. I do not remember the feeling of my fingers pressing his soft spot.

He screams louder. Louder than I've ever heard. But I persist. He yells. His face is red. He screeches. Red almost purple. His tiny fists clench. He screams his life out. His arms are raised. He howls in terror.

My heart pounds. When will this work?

The yells stop. His mouth works like a dying fish. And then a piercing yowl.

I jerk my hand away.

He howls in waves, gasps for air in between screams.

His open purple mouth, his swollen, shut eyes, his scarlet cheeks. His screams fill me.

His mouth opens and closes. His fists open and close, tremble. I tremble, too, feeling the terror.

My mother who is fixing lunch comes running. She gathers the howling baby in her arms and keens, "What's wrong? What's wrong?" while running hurried fingers over his arms, legs, face, torso, head. She turns over his arms, peels open his fingers to check his hands. She presses his palm to her lips. I stand off to the side and watch. She does not accuse me. She does not question me. She does not acknowledge me. She hugs David, rocks him, holds him close. Croons "Ah, ah, baby. Ah, ah, baby." My song.

Her singing halts his cries. He returns to playing, the flush leaves his cheeks.

He sits on his high chair, happily smearing saliva-soaked zwieback into his mouth while I toy with my lunch. "Eat your carrots. They'll make your hair curly," Mother says. But a queasy feeling fills my stomach and there is no room for food.

Later, while we wait for Daddy and dinner, I push the duck in front of David and he watches, claps his hands, all suspicion gone. I help him build a tower. Mother comes in, unaccustomed to the quiet. "Oh my, what nicely playing children I have." She bends down and kisses the top of my head. Where my soft spot used to be. My face burns at her compliment.

After dinner, after our baths, she rocks David to sleep, singing "Nita, Juanita, gently blow the early winds," and then her endless "Ah, ah, baby." I lie on the floor and listen while I color in my coloring book. When I think of what I did, I get sick. I used to be a good girl. I want my mother to pick me up and hold me close to her like she does with David. I want her to love me like she used to before he was born.

CHAPTER 2

The horses in my parent's bedroom hang on a wall next to their bed. I hear them panting. I smell the musk of them. Side by side they rear in a stark whiteness that shines from black green foliage. Their front hoofs paw the air. Each muscle is flexed. A vein arrows down a nose to disappear in the darkness of a flared nostril. Vigorous tendons and cartilage join limb to torso. When they finish rearing, they will race through the jungle. Together. Bound side by side, they are about to soar.

I am five. World War II is over and we have moved from Washington D.C. to a small court in Chicago, apartment buildings on each side. Bars over the windows. The court and our apartment is my world. David and I share a bedroom. David and I spend our time with Mother. We walk to shops and bring the bags of groceries back in David's baby buggy. A darter, Mother has him on a leash. I am embarrassed that he is walked like a dog.

I color with the yellow crayon, absorbed in the strokes the color makes over red. Just lightly, shading it in gently. The beautiful sun. The syrup smell of the wax. David sees it and grabs it. "No." I grab it back. His eyes darken and he picks up my drawing and crumples it. I scream. He kicks me and I reach to hit him. He gets up and starts running. I chase him, raining wild blows on his back.

"Children, children. Children. What are you doing. Bad children. Hitting each other. Kicking each other. Chasing." Mother's dismay makes her voice quaver. Her eyes are wet. "Brothers and sisters do not fight. Hear me. Do not. Do not. Must not fight." She punctuates each "do not" with a punch in the air. She shakes her head sadly. "I have never never seen such." She searches for the word. "Such turmoil. Such violence."

The orange sun is crumpled under David's foot.

"Into your bedroom."

We go into our bedroom. We are the only brother and sister in the world who fight. I hear the door lock. I hear her walk away. It is quiet. I try the door, but she has locked us in. There is something still wrong with me that I get so angry, so passionately furious with David. I believe my mother. I remember my crime. But we cannot seem to stop squabbling. I am angry at Mother now. Locking us in.

"Let's get out of here."

"Yeah."

"Run away. Make her sorry." We try to figure out how to escape our jail. We will disappear into the city. Hide out in the coal mine in the Science and Industry Museum, play with the train set at night. She will never find us. When we're gone, she'll be sorry. We push together against the bars in the window, each of us pulls the bars apart. Did we do it? Maybe just a little. We are each pulling with all our strength. My arms are sore. We try to skim through them, but we are too big already. We try to file through one with a nail file, but give up with weary arms, the bars stronger than us, the metallic taste of iron in my mouth.

As soon as we are sufficiently quiet, she lets us out. This is family ritual that cements David and me.

. . .

Summers we go to Pittsburgh and spend long weeks with Lala, my grandmother, and Docie, my grandfather. Lala is a landscape architect and Docie is a physician, a roentgenologist. I do not understand this. I only know that my grandfather is a doctor who takes x-rays. X-rays are like those machines where you wiggle your toes in the shoe store to make sure your shoes fit. I only know that Lala's garden is a sheltered world of outdoor rooms. A brick patio with soft moss, a pool with slow-moving orange fish, a stone brother and sister carrying a basket laden with grapes, a forest path lined with bleeding hearts and jack-in-the-pulpit, columbine, and a flower garden of tiger lilies, tulips, Shasta daisies, delphinium, hollyhocks.

Faith and Penny are my aunts who are nine and eleven years older. I watch these two girls carefully, copy how Penny eats her dinner in a circle, eating one bite of each item around the edge of her plate. Faith points her napkin with her finger and pushes it in the corner of her lips before blotting her mouth. Faith spends the summer playing tennis, reading women's magazines. She wears rolled-up jeans and sneakers and cardigans buttoned up the back. Faith's dark eyes contrast with her pale skin. A freckle is placed perfectly at each point of her cupid bow. She is beautiful, but nonchalant about it. I know she is the most beautiful woman in the family. Faith and Penny are my aunts, but also my cousins. This is how it happened: Lala's adored sister, Cassie, died shortly after giving birth to Faith. Lala adopted the two motherless girls, first Faith and then her older sister, Penny. I know, and later Lala makes no bones about it, that Faith is Lala's favorite child.

Penny tells me stories of hot water bottles talking to clocks that climb trees to gather grapes grown wild. We walk to the Giant Eagle and bring home groceries for Lala. Laddy, a runty border collie, comes with us. As Lala cooks, I sit on the stairs near the French doors that open onto the patio and bury my nose in the dog's sun-warmed fur. He gently licks my fingers. Mother lies in the sun lazily reading a book while watching David play in the garden.

Lala's mother, Mum, her fingers webbed with creases and blue veins, sits silent. She is either disapproving or so old she has no interest anymore. I cannot tell. Nor does she seem interested in me, her first great-grandchild, except that she makes me exquisitely stitched doll clothes with seed pearl buttons and crocheted purses that open. They're so elegant and fragile, I don't play with them. Mum speaks German and occasionally this language flies between Lala and Mum and we are excluded. I know their German is war German. Is Nazi German. I know that my father, my grandfather, and I are Jewish. I know that Faith and Penny are not and that a condition of their adoption was that they be taken to church and maintain their father's Christian last name. They attend the Protestant church on the corner of Forbes and Murray, gray stone and always a cool moistness inside, candlelight ceremonies on Christmas Eve, sometimes with Mum, never with Lala.

But this summer day is a lazy day of long cooking. The house contains only women, except for David. Docie is working as always late into the evening at the hospital and Daddy is on the road selling, still in Chicago. So it is four generations of six females and one little boy, a toddler smashing Lala's flowers and pulling Laddy's tail and digging in her garden. Faith teaches me how to play checkers and we play on the patio. Afterward, she flips through a magazine, but I cannot maintain much interest in the fashions, though I pretend and for awhile turn the pages. Lying with Laddy on the still warm earth, smelling his aroma, I fall asleep.

Then it is almost time for dinner. I churn up ice cream with globs of peaches in it. At first it is easy, then the ice cream begins to freeze. My arms tire and I slow.

Lala says, "That was my job when I was your age." She watches me churn and says, "That's how I helped my family in Pup's, your great grandfather's, bakery. We lived in the back. Summer meant ice cream. I stirred it till my arms got strong."

I push as hard as I can. "Is it ready yet?"

Lala opens the lid and shakes her head. "No complaints from you. I did this every day." She pokes her fork into a pot of boiling potatoes. "We never sat down to a meal together. Always jumping up because someone would enter the bakery and we'd have to serve them. Always ate standing."

Now Lala strains the potatoes and forces them through a ricer. The flesh on her arms shakes with her motions. "Probably why now I like it when we eat sitting in the dining room with cloth napkins." My mother whips oil into eggs for mayonnaise. Faith snaps the points off green beans. Penny wipes the counters. I shake my arms and return to my churn. We gently bump into each other as we complete our tasks. Finally it's frozen. We'll eat on the patio. It will be cooler there.

Carefully, I set the silverware, the napkins, the plates. Not the good plates since we'll be outside. The sky is pink turning purple; the forest and its path already hidden in the gloaming.

Dinner is timed to Docie's arrival. He smoothes his napkin over his skinny thighs, Lala brings him a plate of dry toast to eat with his meal, and the food is passed. I am complimented on my ice cream. Docie retires to the living room to finish reading the Pittsburgh Post Gazette.

We are back in the kitchen. I clear the table. Faith washes, Penny dries. They laugh about some boy down the block. Faith teases Penny. "Always look your best, you never know when you'll meet Prince Charming."

"And wear clean underwear. You'll never know when you'll get in an accident." Penny mimics Lala's voice.

They giggle. I grab a rag and wipe the counter. We go back outside. Now the shadows are purple, the forest disappears except for white flowers. Fireflies blink. Mother lies on a chaise, David at last asleep in the attic bedroom. I see a flash of match, Mother's face is illuminated as she sucks on her cigarette. Then the red glow moves to the arm of the chaise.

"Look. The moon is full," Lala says. The moon smiles with a familiar face at me. Lightning bugs, the glowing cigarette tip, the silver moon. Darkness is alive with light. The world blinks off and on.

Faith leaves the patio and I lie on the chaise cuddling with Mother, listening to adults talk in hushed tones. The flickering fireflies illuminate a lily, the pond, the rhododendron, the grass, the stone girl's face.

Faith calls, "Ann."

I walk into the kitchen. The moon shines through the window over the sink.

"Do you know what happens when the moon is full in summer?" Faith asks.

"No." My brows move together.

"Well. I'm going to tell you a secret." She moves her head close to mine and lowers her voice. "You have to promise not to tell anyone. Ever."

"I promise." I will be given a gift. Maybe an adult gift.

"When the moon is full in summer the water changes."

"Huh?'

"The water changes to lemonade. No one knows how the moon does this." Faith shakes her head slowly.

She is serious and sincere. Yet, water is always just water.

"I just tested it and it's lemonade now."

"Really?"

Faith nods. "You want to try it?"

"Yeah."

Faith places a glass under the spigot and turns the handle. Clear liquid rushes out the nozzle, bubbles into the glass. She turns to me, smiles. "Here. Try it."

I look at the glass of water, search her face.

"Taste it. See if it's still lemonade."

I sip. Tart sweetness. Lemonade. I try some more. "It is. It's lemonade."

"See. Told you. You can have it. "

I drink the lemonade and it is the finest lemonade I've ever tasted.

Perfectly tart. Perfect amount of sweetness.

I look at the glass and her and the moon and the chrome spigot. So ordinary. Just like when we were washing dishes and rinsing lettuce and filling up the pitcher for our dinner water.

"The moon does it. It's magic."

I swallow the last drop and lick my upper lip. "Can I have some more?"

Faith smiles and shakes her head. "Nope. We've probably used it all up for this month. We have to wait till next month. When the moon is full."

That made sense. Precious things are hard to come by and vanish quickly. Like birthdays, candy. Hugs.

"Don't forget. It's our secret."

I go out to the adults. The moon still smiles. Blue and warm in the thick sky. The red glow from Mother's cigarette lights my way to her. I place my cheek on her soft stomach, lay on the chaise as she strokes my hair. The lemonade. I guess it is sort of like Santa Claus, special and magical.

The next morning, I'm sprawled on the living room carpet cutting out pictures. Lala crouches down beside me, and then sits cross-legged, settling into the oriental carpet. She wears a soft dress, dark, always dark, with small flowers on it. A cameo of a woman and child prancing among sprays of flowers is pinned to the collar, the face of the woman worn off. She takes a piece of paper and folds it, picks up my scissors and cuts, dipping and slicing with precision. "Look," she says.

There is a girl with saucy braids and a skirt, her arms reaching out to each side. "Look." Lala slowly pulls the edge and the girl's hands hold another girl, and another girl. A chain of girls each one exactly like the other. Lala points to the middle girl with a finger that is gnarled and twisted at the tip.

"This one is you." She moves her finger to the next one. "This one is your mother. This one is me. This one is Mum. This one is my grandmother. Born on Christmas, too. My grandmother and my granddaughter born on the same day. Women stretch all the way back to the dawn of time. To the primordial past."

I am used to her fancy words and she uses them liberally with me. Primordial. It's how she describes the white plants that lived before the dinosaurs.

Her finger returns to the middle girl, me. And she says. "Remember? This one is you." Her finger moves to the left. "This one is your daughter, and this one is your granddaughter. All the way into the infinite future. Beyond imagining."

She folds her hands together for a moment, resting them on the mound that is her yielding stomach. And then she clasps me to her and hugs me hard, kissing my temple. Rocks me for a moment. I smell her lavender, her sugary maple smell. "The whole scheme of evolution. Each of us a new evolutionary try." Then she releases me and dangles the paper dolls. "Here. They're yours now."

After dinner, when the moon glows round in the kitchen window, I try the faucet. But it is not lemonade. It is only water. Cool from the earth. And clear.

On the train back to Chicago, Mother, David and I snuggle in a bed which appears from the wall and covers the entire compartment. The train rocks us into each other and then apart. I search for the moon out the window, but all I see is black sky and flashing pinpoints of lights from faraway houses. Not even fireflies.

"Is the moon full?"

"I don't know," Mother says, her voice already husky with sleep.

"Where is it?"

"I'm not sure. We can get a book from the library and find out."

"I'll miss it."

"There's a moon in Chicago, too. And it comes and goes. A crescent, then half full, full, and then back down to a crescent and finally no moon at all. And then it starts all over again."

I snuggle close to her.

"We'll find it in Chicago, too."

But it's hard to see the moon from our little court. Hard to see through the bars on our windows. And after awhile I forget. I see it when we're driving on Lake Shore Drive along Lake Michigan. It is reflected in the lake. I am surprised and then reassured. Two moons.

CHAPTER 3

My father gets promoted and we move to a larger apartment on Hyde Park Boulevard. My own bedroom is decorated with reddish furniture, heavy curtains on the windows. The horses still rear, plunge, pant, and paw the air in my parents' bedroom. There is a wrought iron balcony behind French doors overlooking the backyard's meager grass. The living room windows have wide sills on which my mother places African violets and little orange trees. Cars whiz on the boulevard. I must stay far away from the curb.

There's an orphanage on the corner. I can't play with the kids. They march in and out quietly, unobtrusive in the neighborhood. Daddy teaches me how to write my name in Hebrew and I am proud of my unusual skill. Mother shows me how to recognize letters. I start first grade and I hide in the closet reading my old books.

I am aware for the first time that my mother's life is not all mine and David's. She is always home when we are home, but at school I see her talking with the principal, the principal bending toward her to listen. I glance up from my desk and, through the glass window in the door, see her strolling down the hall, her arm crooked to hold a clipboard and notebook. My mother is important to other people, too.

I do not know it then, but Mother was a union organizer before she married; during my elementary school years she becomes president of the PTA and works in the Woodlawn Project attempting to organize a neighborhood to guide its own destiny. But when we are home, she is home, building her life around us.

My brother climbs up the three-story fire escape and balances on our building's roof. Mother stands below, her apron fluttering in the breeze, one hand to the base of her throat, the other shielding her eyes, as he walks along the edge of the roof. And then he descends the fire escape. Her yellow, checked apron flutters, her hair ruffles in the constant Chicago wind; but otherwise she is frozen like a rabbit in her own fear.

Some time later, my parents buy a swingset and install it in the backyard. Our backyard becomes the gathering place for neighborhood children. My brother climbs to the top and swings across the railing.

My mother cooks laborious meals — raspberry and cherry pies, meat loaf and mashed potatoes, chicken with tarragon and wine sauce, chicken livers sautéed with green peppers and onion in champagne over egg noodles.

We are clean for dinner, hands and faces washed, fresh clothes on, but we must wait. The smells and sounds from the kitchen make my stomach hurt with hunger. "When are we going to eat?" I want to know.

"When Daddy gets home."

I try to distract myself with drawing.

"When's Daddy getting home?"

"When he gets here."

I am tenacious. "When'll that be?"

"We'll wait for your father." Mother's voice is clipped.

I start to ask how long, but know it will be no use. She doesn't know.

I move a philodendron vine meandering along the wide window sill and sit there to watch the boulevard below. The cars swish by. Rich, from upstairs, already finished with dinner, is outside throwing a ball against the side of the building. Daddy's bus lets him off across from the orphanage, but I can't see the bus stop from my window. I know he walks down the sidewalk, his briefcase swinging with each long stride, his hat at a rakish angle. Clothed, as I remember, always in a taupe or gray suit.

For a while I count the cars. And then I begin chanting, "Come, Daddy. Come. Come, Daddy. Come." The words hum in my mouth, it's almost a song. I rock as I croon, "Come, Daddy. Come." As if my incantation will magically bring him, "Come, Daddy. Come." I rock on the window sill, "Come, Daddy. Come." I watch stragglers below as I chant.

Mother peers at me, a wooden spoon in her hand. I see her out of the corner of my eye, but I have soothed my hunger with my mantra, my rocking. Until I see him suddenly pivot to climb the stairs to the door and enter our building. I hear him climb, the door opens, and I run into his arms. My mother and I reach him for kisses simultaneously. My chanting works to bring him home.

CHAPTER 4

The restaurant is hushed. Shades are drawn and peculiar spiky plants lines the sills. This is my first restaurant meal with my father. I am between Daddy and Mother, David across from me. I finger the thickness of the coarse white tablecloth and clink the empty glass with my fork. Mother frowns and shakes her head. The waitress' white uniform reminds me of a doctor's office. I am impressed with the paper menu, the various items in separate categories: appetizers, desserts. Some are new words: Entrée, à la carte. The waitress, her dark hair a shining helmet, moves behind us to pour water. The ice clinks as it slides with the liquid. She spills a drop when she pours Daddy's, which seeps slowly on the cloth.

"Oh, pardon me. I'll get that right up." She dabs it with a napkin.

I study the menu. Ice cream. Coca-Cola. Hamburgers. Liver and onions. Pot roast. Malted milks. I am eight. I can easily read the menu. I can order anything I want.

She returns and stands between Daddy and me. She smells of roses and grease. Her fingers are poised around her pencil, pink nails curve at the ends.

"Ready to order?" She winks at David. I pull the white napkin from under my fork and spread it over my thighs. I know what I will order: turkey and mashed potatoes, cranberry sauce. A meal fit for Thanksgiving.

When she approaches my father, her voice slides down just a little.

"What did you think of the White Sox?" he asks her. "Catch any night games?" He flashes her a broad smile.

"Whenever I can." Her laugh is slow and throaty and doesn't match her gentle voice. Daddy's eyes sweep her hips as she walks away. Her slip makes a slight sound as she sways, her nylon-clad legs brush each other with each step. I see him watching her. And he looks away.

14

Her belt rests easily below her waist. She goes to another table and then sashays from the kitchen handing plates of crispy brown potatoes and hamburgers for a young couple.

She has a slender, tight body, while Mother's is lush. Mother fusses with David's napkin. He is five and wiggles the napkin to the floor.

The waitress returns with our salads, iceberg lettuce and a limp tomato shellacked with lumps of dressing.

"So did you catch the game Friday?" Daddy asks.

Mother silently cuts David's salad and I fish the tomato out. "Yuck," I squinch up my face, the tomato lays bent and dripping on the tine of my fork.

"No negative comments. It's impolite," Mother warns.

I delicately place the tomato on the rim of my plate.

"If you can't say something nice, don't say anything at all," Daddy says to me and turns back to the waitress.

She wets her lips. "Yeah. Well, I was supposed to go with my boyfriend, but…" She taps her pencil point against her pad and raises her eyes to the ceiling.

"But?" Daddy pursues.

"He was rained out."

He laughs. "I have some tickets for tomorrow night's game."

"Lucky you." She raises one eyebrow. "Well, can I get you anything else?"

"No. We're fine for now," Mother replies.

And then a voice from the kitchen calls, "Polly." As she turns, her skirt brushes my father.

Polly returns with our plates, sets down my turkey, the gravy with a grease slick on top. She slides Daddy's steak and potato from her arm. She bends at the knees to do it, leans closely over him.

"That was quick, Polly," he says.

"How did you know my name?"

Daddy jerks his head to the kitchen. "The cook told me."

"Well, I try to serve my customers well." Her voice is low and she says her words slowly.

I poke my fork into the mashed potatoes and slide it across them, turn the fork to make checkerboard stripes. Mother cuts David's meat and reminds him to eat his carrots. The cranberry sauce slides off my fork onto the white table cloth. No one has noticed. I hide the sauce with my napkin and slowly push it to my hand and sneak it back to my plate. Good. Mother and Daddy are busy talking about meeting friends at Blue Orchid Jazz. I move my napkin. A red smear streaks the cloth.

Polly takes the order of a sour-faced couple and then returns, "Everything okey-dokey here? Get you all anything?"

"I might be able to get you some tickets to a night game. Sales meeting so I can't go. Might have some right here." Daddy pats his gray suit pocket, checking inside his jacket. He pierces Polly with his black eyes, scans her. He is aware of her every movement, turn of phrase.

"Oh, yeah. My girlfriend loves the Sox, too." Polly flashes a smile. Her lips glisten a soft pink. "Oh, my next order's up." She winks at him. His charm has won her over.

I twist up my face. I am brave after my trick with the cranberry sauce.

"It's nice to be nice."

I play with my potatoes.

Daddy rests his hand on Mother's arm. His blunt tan fingers and sparse hairs are at home on her pale blue sweater. "Might as well make things fun," he says.

Mother flashes her casual smile and for a moment I too am swallowed by her warmth, and then she moves her arm from under Daddy's fingers to cut David's hamburger with the edge of a fork.

"Ah. My family," Daddy says.

I cut my meat, the fork makes a screeching sound that curls my spine. My brother kicks me under the table.

"Ow. Stop it."

"Stop hurting my ears."

"Children." Mother's voice has her stern edge.

Polly returns with coffee for my parents and cherry pie for David and me. The globs of cherries, glistening under the crust, divert David from nudging me. Mother methodically stirs sugar into her coffee, gazing with soft green eyes at my father. He leans back and pats his tummy. He has dumped out the potato's insides and has eaten only its skin.

"I'm still the same weight I was in college," he announces.

My mother pulls out a cigarette and my father strikes a match with one hand and then shakes the book until the flame is extinguished.

Polly removes our plates and leaves the check.

Daddy pays the bill and enters the men's room. Mother smokes and enjoys her coffee, then nods at the plants on the window sill. "Those are called mother-in-law tongues. Called that because they contain a slight poison that numbs the tongue. Peculiar for a restaurant," she muses.

David squirms off his chair and heads for the exit, his chubby legs like pistons. His arms shift determinedly. Lickety-split he is on the street. Mother grabs her purse and rushes after him.

Just before I push open the door to follow, I turn to see Daddy stroll toward the waitress. He presses money into Polly's hand and says something to her.

She opens her hand and along with the folded soft money are the skinny tickets and a slip of white paper. She reads, tilts her head, smiles. She says something so quiet I can't hear, but I see her lips move slowly. Then she raises one eyebrow.

I sense how much can be pressed into a hand along with money.

Mother races after David on the street, grabs his hand and he twists and turns at the end of her arm. Daddy strides toward them, toward me. Hat tilted to one side, cigarette slanted from the side of his mouth, eyes on the distance. He is the lone hunter.

I long for him. But I turn away, running to reach Mother, relinquishing Daddy. Protecting myself.

CHAPTER 5

I skipped first grade at Kozminsky School and am now in third grade. The teacher sends me to the library, where I read whatever book I choose. I am in a Kate Seredy-mode, reading about flying white stags and children living in Sweden. I love school and hate vacations. Now I run home until I get the ache in my side, then slow to a walk, picking leaves from the tall privets lining the yards. I crunch the leaves between my fingers. They make a crisp sound and smell of freshness and sun.

David is in kindergarten and hates school. He covers his ears and hides under the piano when the other kids sing. He walks along the top of the jungle gym. He fights with the other kids on the playground. He refuses to sit at his desk. He is sent to the University of Chicago for testing. He is brilliant, my mother is told. Brilliant. I.Q. off the charts. He is bored with school.

I sing:
A chicken in the car
And the car can't go
And that's how you spell
Chicago

. . .

I twist my hips with the rhythm and crunch a privet leaf at each go. The sun warms my hair. I round the street across from the orphanage and pull out my yellow comb, curling a strand in a spiral around my finger. The carrots I obediently ate have not worked. My hair is stick straight and mousy brown. Sometimes I set it in socks and the curls last half a day. I am hoping if I comb and wind it enough my hair will be trained in a curl. At least one.

Once, my mother sent me to the beauty parlor. Under the dryer, the beautician kept checking my hair; but it was still damp. The other customers finished, paid their bills and departed. My cheeks were flushed. The other beauticians left. The lights were shut off and the closed sign posted on the door. My hair was still damp. Finally, she took me out and unwound my hair. At last, long ringlets of brown hair down past my shoulders. I ran all the way home to show Mother, but by the time I got there, my hair had been pulled straight by my speed and its dampness.

Now I cut through the alley next to my house and see David in the backyard gym and start skipping again. My comb flies out of my hand and down an open manhole. "Oh, no." I drop to my hands and knees and see the yellow comb floating on top of the sewage. I smell the fermented shit and gag. My comb is gone. I cry as though the loss of the comb is the end of beautiful curls.

And then beside me is David. "I'll get it."

Lickety-split he flips over the side of the hole and climbs down the ladder. He hangs from one arm and reaches for the comb floating on top of the sewage. His hand is in the disgust. He touches the comb and sends it scooting away from him. And then he is in it, his head visible. He grabs the comb, holds it above his head. "I got it. I got it." He dog-paddles to the ladder and climbs out of the hole. He stands before me. Wide smile and chubby cheeks. Triumphant. He hands me the comb. He is drenched and dirty and smelly. I'm reluctant to take the comb, but he is so proud, I clasp it and we go home.

When Mother sees him, she orders, "Take your clothes off right there." She shuts the door in his face and runs bath water. He is exposed in the hall. He holds back tears at the possibility of public nakedness. She puts his clothes in a paper bag and shoves it down the chute to be burned. He stands in the hall, covering his penis, a confused look on his face. Mother does not praise him for his heroism. I feel his humiliation. While he takes his bath, I rinse the comb. It doesn't smell. It looks good as new, but I'm afraid to use it. I put it in a drawer and stop wishing for ringlets and curls.

. . .

School is out and the other kids sing and shout with joy at their freedom. I am sad. I know David and I are going to camp, the South

19

Side Day Camp for Girls and Boys. Morning time, beach time at camp, I rake through sand looking for spiral shells and put them with my paste emeralds and rubies in a subdivided clear plastic box. After lunch is rest period. The girls practice embroidery. I do not need to rest. I've given up naps long ago and in fact hate sleeping at all. I tell my counselor that my brother needs me, I see him crying. David and I escape into the woods. We walk along the path next to the creek turning up rocks looking for salamanders and catch toads which pee on us. We find a deer print and a wolf print. We think it's a wolf. We can see the claws pressed into the mud, and it is bigger than my palm.

We show David's counselor and he teaches us to make a cast of the print. It's probably a dog. Wolves are long gone from Chicago, he tells us. The deer's sharp hoofs, the rounded pads and pointed claws of the dog set now forever in white plaster.

. . .

I'm in fourth grade, David wins second place in a raffle and chooses a doll for me as his prize.

I still rock and wait on the window sill repeating "Come, Daddy. Come" sometimes to myself, sometimes out loud. He is always late. I am always hungry for dinner. We wait for dinner. We wait for him. Often he is away on the road. When he gets home, he brings excitement with him. He brings me wrapped bars of soap from his hotel.

The next year in school, I make the honor roll. I am proud of my name, Ann Pearlman, one of three written on the board. The bell rings and we wait in a line before we can go home. We all must be lined up. We all must be quiet. We all must be standing at attention. I wait. I whisper. The teacher catches me whispering and makes me erase my name from the honor roll. The next day she seats me at the back of the class in a seat where I am alone. "I'm going to teach you to stop talking," she says.

I finish my work and am more bored than ever. I bring other books to read. I draw elaborate drawings on my book reports and color them in with crayons. I get back on the honor roll. "See," she says, her dark etched eyebrows wiggling at me. "See what you get when you don't talk. When you obey my rules."

But it's not worth it.

Right after that, in the middle of my fifth grade, we move back to

Pittsburgh. "Back home," Mother calls it. Pittsburgh means Squirrel Hill. Pittsburgh means a large family on both sides. Pittsburgh means a new school, Whitman Elementary. Daddy is starting a new business with his brother, Uncle Isaac.

"I'm an entrepreneur," he tells me. He sells everything we own and we move to the attic of Lala and Docie's large house on Bartlett Street. Penny is away at Carnegie Institute. Faith, still at Allderdice High, stays in her bedroom and studies. If she keeps up her grades, she'll be valedictorian. Mum has had a stroke and lays in her bedroom on the second floor. She can talk, but she can't move. She looks like a child under the sheets, her legs and arms fade into the mattress. Her blue eyes are colorless behind her glasses. Only her white hair is lively. I visit her as little as possible.

After we women have done the dinner dishes, we join Docie and Daddy in the living room. I grab the comics to read the Jackson Twins, a habit that has followed me from Chicago. When Lala sits down, Laddy licks her toes. Her fourth toe crosses over her third toe and by the end of the day, her foot hurts, because she wore tight, narrow shoes when she was a girl. Trying to be beautiful. Trying to be fashionable. It's because her family was too poor to buy new shoes every year. It is because she is too fat. It is because she stands on her feet too much. Every time I ask her, she gives me a different answer. Laddy responds to her pain and his licking soothes her.

Before I crawl into bed I smooth Heinz Honey and Almond Lotion on my face, inhaling the sweetness of bitter almond. My skin is soft and smooth. The sheets are ironed. Car lights travel across the roses on the wallpaper, there is a hush to the tires on the streets. So different from the boulevard in Hyde Park. Here, each car is distinct. I can't hear the voices of the adults below. David is sound asleep in the next bed. Mum is still inert under her comforter. The lights, the gathering then ebbing sound of the cars, become my company. And the Jackson Twins. They are not alone since they have each other.

I tell everyone in school that I have an identical twin sister named Jan. She attends Ellis School. She looks just like me except she's prettier and makes better grades. For awhile the kids are fascinated and I am guaranteed celebrity. But then they talk with their friends at Ellis School and stop believing my story. They walk past me and hold their noses and say "P.U. You stink." A few weeks later they decide to be nice to me. Finally one tells me that they have decided I live in an orphanage. Lala and Docie's house is huge and has children of diverse ages. Can't be one family. I turn this over and over in my mind. This is just my family. My aunt, Faith, who I guess is not really my aunt, but a second cousin, is only nine years older than me.

My father is one of seven children, five sisters and a brother, all of whom still live in Pittsburgh. His mother is already dead. Zaida, my grandfather, is outgoing and fun. Uncle Isaac and his wife, Aunt Mildred, have us over on Friday nights for Sabbath. After we bless and break the bread and eat the meal, all the cousins — there are eight of us within five years of each other — talk, tease, torment and play.

Mildred and Isaac's daughter, Sara, is one grade behind me at Whitman. Her mother tells me Sara can already play Grieg, Gershwin. I covet her thick wavy hair and flashing dark eyes. Her boyfriend Teddy Miller is in my grade. I haven't had a boyfriend yet. Aunt Mildred is an actress. She and my mother have been best friends since they went to Allderdice together and, after going to Bucknell together, married two brothers. Sara is the only girl cousin my age. Instead of going home for lunch we walk to Solly's delicatessen. We squeeze ketchup into a paper bag of French fries, add salt, and shake it up. Friday nights, we escape into her bedroom and whisper, pretend to each other our bodies are more developed than they are.

I make a new friend, Susie, and we spend hours playing with her Toni doll, giving her a permanent wave, and sharing crushes on boys. My father picks us up from a matinee movie at the Warner Theater. When he finds out her name, he sings,

If you knew Susie,
Like I knew Susie.
Oh.
Oh. Oh what a girl.

· · ·

Next time I see Susie, she says, "Ooooh. Your father is soooo good looking. I can't imagine that he's even a father. He's not like a father at all, but some movie star." When she comes over after that, she stands next to my father's chair reading the book over his shoulder. I stop inviting her to my house.

Slowly I relinquish my loyalty to the White Sox and accept the

Pirates. Slowly Whitman becomes my school. I take the street car downtown to Jenkins Arcade for medical appointments. I buy pralines with pecans from the candy shop at the street car stop and let each small bite melt in my mouth on the bumpy ride home, sucking the nuts until they are limp. I look forward to the family Friday nights and festivals, I relax in Lala's cooking and warmth, the wet sound of Laddy licking her toes.

CHAPTER 6

Daddy and Uncle Isaac strike it rich selling TVs in the surge of consumer goods that sweep America. Their stores, House of Television, spring up across the area — Monroeville, Uniontown, Reading, Philadelphia, Wheeling, Johnstown, Youngstown, Erie, Sharon, Harrisburg. I hear advertisements over the radio, see them in the newspaper. My father rides the crest of his salesmanship, America's lust for merchandise, his good looks.

We are firmly established in an eighteen-room house across from a golf course. Our garden is landscaped by Lala and I watch the workers lay bricks for a retaining wall, dig a pool, and put in a stone patio. Above the half-moon-shaped pool is a statue of a woman and then cherry trees pruned to twist together, like lovers. Mother redecorates the inside of the house: marble foyer, architectural wallpaper, a curving staircase, French doors, black and pink kitchen.

My cousins call Daddy "The Great Rich Uncle Jake." He has no false modesty and laughs, hooks a thumb in his belt whenever he hears his new name. He comes home for dinner later and later. We wait. The cook, Beatrice, leans over the marble kitchen table flipping the pages of a magazine, impatient to get home to her daughter. My mother sits at her bird's-eye-maple desk with a secret compartment, talking on the phone. She has become active in the National Council of Jewish Women and is helping to start a day hospital for the emotionally disturbed. She doodles as she talks, makes up lists of things to do, people to call. David and I appease our hunger with Lebanon bologna and Swiss cheese sandwiches as we watch TV in a darkened room. The steak and potatoes turn cold, marbled with white grease. The angel food cake, frosted with bits of peppermint, hardens.

In junior high, my body develops. My pubic hair darkens, then curls. My breasts grow into small mounds, not as lush as Mother's. I get my period. I've been waiting for it. When I tell Mother, she hands me the equipment she has purchased. I slowly tread down the curved staircase learning how to walk with thickness between my legs. A woman. Mother senses my mood and says, "Proud of yourself, aren't you?"

I glance at her open, damp eyes and shy smile and realize she's proud. I blush and then grin. It's a passage for her, too.

. . .

Mother and I shop for a new suit for the occasion of my eighth grade graduation lunch with Daddy. We buy it at Adele's, where the clothes are hidden and the saleslady brings those she thinks will interest me to my dressing room. We choose a red and white check with a mandarin collar and large black buttons. A black silk carnation is pinned on the lapel. Mother finishes my outfit with white gloves and my first pair of stockings held up by a panty girdle with cruel hooks and rubber knobs. The hooks are not as harsh as the metal barbs of my sanitary belt which rub red sores on my stomach and the crack of my butt.

Pittsburgh's renaissance is in full swing. The steel mills only occasionally now arch fire into the sky. Daddy and I are going to the Point where the Monongahela, bordered by the city's mills, and the tamed Allegheny merge to form the Ohio, slowly moving south and west. Gateway Plaza it is called. Once gateway to the west, to the frontier.

A sleek expanse of glass reveals bridges to the far side and houses clinging to the mountain. I have two hours with my father, the longest time I have spent with him alone. The restaurant is quiet and cool. The other diners confer in hushed tones. We talk easily enough as I eat my Maurice salad, a more sophisticated order than hamburger or even turkey club. Fascinated by mummies and archaeology, I have been reading the *Egyptian Book of the Dead*. Now I describe in exquisite detail exactly how the brain is drawn out of the corpse's nose with a special tool, careful not to mar the face or skull.

He listens, sucking his Camels incessantly. Smoke travels up into his nose when he inhales and wafts around him in a fuzzy halo. He tells me about Freud's Interpretation of Dreams, paints the concept of objects being more than what they seem, symbols, gauzy layers of meaning. An icy pecan ball covered with caramel sauce chills my mouth while he explains that ties and hats are penises, cats and tunnels are vaginas, water is the womb, and ladders are sex.

He flirts with the waitress, of course. I am used to it. I am involved with my conversation with Daddy. So adult. So knowledgeable. And then he leans toward me. His eyes pin me. "You can be anything you want, you know. Whatever you want. You're smart – in the top half of one percent. Healthy. Beautiful. Energetic. We can give you whatever you need. Education. Equipment. Classes. Whatever, we can give it to you. Always beside you to support and comfort you. We can bring the world to you."

"David's smarter."

"Doesn't matter. You're smart enough. You just need to work hard. And want it enough."

I ponder this. Egyptologist? Ballerina? Movie star? Scientist? I ask, "Anything?"

"Dream your dreams, darling. You can be whatever you want. If you want it bad enough and work hard enough for it. I promise you."

. . .

We walk into a sunny June day, not so hot as to be sticky, but with the customary fog of Pittsburgh which I assume is the atmosphere of the planet. Around the restaurant is a broad cement plaza. A fountain plays in a rectangular dish. Saplings struggle in cement boxes. Beyond the plaza are construction sites — the continuing building of the Golden Triangle. The sun shines warm on my hair. I unbutton my jacket and inhale free air. What a radiant day. What a beautiful lunch. High school. It will be easy. Life will be easy. I can be anything I want.

Under the scattered shade of a sapling, a group of women talk and laugh. All are tall and blonde and immaculately groomed, not in the fashion of my mother and her friends, but in the fashion of Vogue, nudging but not crossing the line into garish.

One of them notices us and I sense her inspection as we stroll toward her. Me on the brim of womanhood with my darkly handsome father. Her frosted hair is in a French knot, her angular arms crossed, her pelvis slightly tilted. She wears a baby blue dress and jacket. When we approach her, she lifts her chin, laughs a slow pleased chuckle, and says, "Why, hello, Jake."

Daddy nods.

"I knew you liked 'em young, but isn't she too young? Even for you?"

His stride picks up, his eyes straight ahead.

Red creeps up my face, matches the checks in my suit. "She thinks we're on a date," I say, feeling simultaneously embarrassed and proud.

"She's just a friend," Daddy says to me, out of the side of his mouth.

"You like 'em young?" My voice is sharp. And then I am silent.

"A casual acquaintance. A client."

He walks so fast, my new shoes rub blisters.

"Casual?" I'm not pushing him, not cornering him. I'm confused.

"Now I know what you're thinking. That's just one of my customers."

I work to match his stride. I think my heel is bleeding. I don't know what to say.

"An old friend who was making a joke. I don't know her really."

"Slow down. I can't keep up with you in these shoes."

"I just happened to sell her some furniture and then here she is... and she's teasing me."

"Teasing you?"

"Yeah." And then we're out of the Golden Triangle and reach the Lincoln convertible, black and shiny. The sun seems to have disappeared. "I guess you're looking pretty grown-up."

I replay the conversation all the way home. Look out the window as we pass the J & L mill, silent black towers and sooty forms, the Monongahela visible beyond it. I don't say anything through the Boulevard of the Allies. When we pass the Carnegie Museum, I realize his defensive protest blankets his guilt. I feel his distress. He clenches the steering wheel, a cigarette dangling out of his mouth. In the confined space of the car, I smell his cologne, lemony with just a suggestion of musk. I couple his coil of smoke now and her crossed arms, her low chuckle. Recognize her brief casual jealousy of me. I know she knew him sexually. Am certain without question. I feel my father's lie as hot as I feel the sun now blazing through the car window and the blisters on my heel.

CHAPTER 7

In my high school classes, the boys' pants pleat when they stand to answer a question. A fold of fabric covers a zipper, a crease is formed where hip joins thigh. Between classes, I walk behind a boy in chinos. He moves easily down the stairs, his legs stretch out in angles. I have never seen a man naked. Not even David, since he was five. I do not understand how men are packaged. Do their thighs hit their penis, flopping it from side to side as they descend stairs? I try to imagine the boy without his chinos. My father never crosses his legs at his thighs like I do, curling one leg around the other. He crosses ankle over knee. Is that because he would crush his testicles?

All the marble statues at the museum have fig leaves. The calm, pale stone bulges with muscles, a vein traces down an arm. Our art books on Michaelangelo, Picasso occasionally contain paintings of nude men, but their genitalia are abstracted, their immobile bodies give nothing away.

A boy in my geometry class has a thick neck which comes down straight from his ears, his shoulders stretch his madras shirt tight. I concentrate on the proofs, flip my protractor and compass to form figures. Girls aren't supposed to feel this way. Girls are supposed to remain virgins till they're married. If you go too far with a boy, he'll lose respect for you. Pregnancy ruins your life. Of course, you hear about girls having abortions, or going away and giving the baby up for adoption. Those are the alternatives and, in any case, no nice boy will have you after that. Being an unwed mother is out of the question. Not an option. Lala tells me, "When it's hard, he's soft. When it's soft, he's hard." I think to myself, maybe I won't get married. But I'm going to have a baby. I'll get myself pregnant, move to another town and say I'm a widow. Nice women don't even get divorced.

Boys though are allowed to like sex. In fact, sexual experience boosts a boy's reputation and boys brag whenever they can, making up stories if necessary. Boys can go to the prostitutes in Wheeling, Steubenville, or the Hill. They can go as far as they want with as many girls as possible. Just then the boy in madras walks to the blackboard to present his proof. He draws the familiar T and I see a muscle in his forearm move. At night, sometime in the morning I touch myself. I am sure I am the only girl who does this. No one even talks about it. Boys masturbate. But not girls. I envy boys their sexual freedom.

My mother puts makeup on in her dressing room. She is getting ready to chair a meeting of fundraisers for her halfway house. Preparing her face is part of the ritual. I lay sprawled on my parents' king-size bed flipping the pages of *Seventeen*. Forcing nonchalance in my voice I ask, "Do you think a girl should be a virgin when she marries?" Girls are supposed to lose their virginity on their wedding night. What if I hate sex and I'm married to someone forever and have to do this thing which seems so disgusting, so intimate for the rest of my life. Doomed.

Mother concentrates on smearing her Erno Laszlo lotion on her cheeks. The black and white bottles decorate her dresser. Drawers of underwear and closets of dresses surround her. "I think that's a question you get to decide yourself." Her voice is measured.

I hold my breath and riffle more pages. "Were you?" I'm looking for guidance, but not sure how to get it.

She glosses her eyelids with a soft peach. "My decision was my decision. Your decision must be your decision. Weigh the pros and cons."

I roll over on my back and stare at the ceiling. "Well, reasons not to be." I hold up a hand in the air and pull out one finger and say, "First, you get to try it out to find out if you like it before you're stuck doing it the rest of your life. That's one." I think longer. I can't think of another.

The velvet sweetness of Mother's Joy perfume floats from her dressing room.

"Pros. You won't get pregnant before you're married. You're sure the guy loves you. You don't lose his respect. Your reputation is intact." I'm done.

Mother smears rouge on with her index finger, staring at her own reflection in the lighted mirror. The peach eye shadow makes her eyes appear clear green. The fact her mouth tilts on her face is more obvious when she is unmoving and reflected. Usually, she is smiling, talking, smoking. Just then she lights a cigarette and the smell of smoke obliterates the Joy.

"I guess I'll be a virgin."

. . .

Browsing through our library, I discover *Sex and Temperament in Primitive Tribes*. The picture on the cover is of a man and woman naked from the waist up. Maybe this book will answer my questions. God, I wish I lived in Tahiti. I try to imagine how the couple join kneeling, facing each other. I am more confused than ever. Girls feel sexual, too. At least the girls on the Pacific Islands. I discover the Kinsey report on *Sexual Behavior in the Human Female* and race through the charts and graphs — ages of onset of adolescence, techniques in pre-adolescent sex play by education level, masturbation by age and marital status. Ah, this one. The graphs aren't even in percentages. But some weird number code I don't understand. But it's clear. Other girls masturbate. I'm not the only one.

Lala's blueprints cover the dining room table. She leans on her thick elbows, her flesh quivers as she sketches in shrubs, trees. It's a bird's-eye view, yet I can see which rounded lines are deciduous shrubs, which angles are the dwarf Alberta spruces fooling the eye to a distant point. "This garden was inspired by Monet's garden in Giverny," she tells me. She stands up, her hands on the small of her back, her broad belly poked out. Her glasses slide down her nose and she scans her drawing. She nods her head in approval. "Enough for now. Come."

We are in the parlor. A portrait of Faith as a child, watery brown eyes and soft auburn ringlets, is on the upright piano lid as though the piano waits for her. A glass-topped table contains a collection of amethyst crystals, rose quartz, petrified wood, a fossil dinosaur bone, and garnets still encased in dirt. Lala brings coffee with lots of cream and sugar in it. "When I was a girl, even as young as six, Pup would let me have coffee with him. Like this. Just a drop of coffee. You're not six though. Not by a long shot. Getting to be a woman." She blows on the coffee. "I guess your mother won't scold me."

Laddy ignores my attempt to caress his soft ears but laps Lala's toes. "Oh, God. All day on these poor feet."

I have stopped off at Lala's house on my walk home from

Allderdice. My arms are tired. I have a lump on my third finger from writing and my arms are flat from carrying four books, stacked two on top of each other on top of a zippered notebook. School changes my body.

"Take the chill off anyway."

I can't imagine her in high school. But then, she was already working and in nursing school when my age. I look over at her. "How did you meet Docie?"

She takes her glasses off and places them on the glass table top. She doesn't need to see for this. She leans back on the sofa, hands on her lap. Motionless for once. And to the sound of Laddy's incessant licking her toes she says, "I met him at the Montefiore. I was just eighteen and I saw him, the young doctor, rounding the hall, tall, his white coat flapping around his knees. And, I know this sounds corny, my heart stood still.

"Well, he was working day and night and I watched for him. See his jet black hair from the distance. Always in a hurry. Always rushing. Learned the sound of that white coat flapping. Got to know his rounds and made sure I'd be walking where he might be. And then finally we bumped into each other. Yes. He walked right into me. In such a hurry. He dumped my tray of surgical tools, newly sterilized. Scattered them every which way in the hall. Click clang, clatter, clatter, skidding along the waxed floor. He picked them up."

She smoothes her dress over her knees. "Anyway, we got to talking and talking. And he took me out to dinner to apologize for all the extra work he made for me. You have to remember, I know it's hard to imagine now, but I was considered a beautiful young woman. Petite. With fine bones and thick glossy hair. Bright eyes. A coquettish smile. And Mum made me beautiful clothes. And then I took him home and Cassie fell in love with him, too. She was just six then. And he loved her. I think she was almost as important to him as she was to me. When I saw how good he was to her, I knew I would marry him. He'd be a good father." She sips coffee. "Sort of a new way to drop a handkerchief, eh?" She laughs at herself.

"Do you know what? He gave Cassie a ring for me, emerald with a diamond on each side. It was to be my Christmas present and she was to hold onto it until the morning. But of course she couldn't keep a secret and told me as soon as he left. So I got my present from him on

Christmas eve. Just a minute."

She pushes herself off the couch and slowly climbs the stairs. "Stay there. Be right back."

When she returns, she says, "Oh, this old house and all those stairs." She is breathless when she sits down and places a hand on her chest and inhales heavily. "Here, give me your hand." She slides the ring on my finger. "Fits just like I knew it would. Doesn't fit these clumped up fingers anymore." She stretches out a knobby hand. "Suits you. So it's yours. Anyway, next day, he asked me to marry him, got down on one knee and pleaded with me and I said yes."

"So that's the story."

"It's not like fairy tales, living happily ever after. It's not the end, just a beginning of another chapter. On the night before my wedding, Mum was ironing my wedding dress crying big blotches all over it, and saying, 'If you had to marry a Jew, you could have at least married a rich one.'"

Lala twists the thin gold band on her finger, imbedded in the pads of tissue. "God, how I loved that man." Her cheeks are flushed. Her forehead damp.

I have my opening. "So you were a virgin?"

"Your grandfather believed in sports for young men. He played football. Sports and cold showers. When we met, we both were virgins."

I squint up my face. " Oyh."

"He was a wonderful lover. Wonderful." Her face has softened, her tongue wets her lips. "For ten years I gave myself completely and totally to him. Like I never knew I could."

I am embarrassed by the glimpse of passion. "Being a virgin with a virgin. Jeez. What if you don't like it?"

"When you love each other, it brings you closer. It was wonderful." And then she laughs. "I was so dumb though. So damn dumb. After a few months when I wasn't pregnant, I started worrying about myself, something was wrong with me. My grandmother came to visit and saw my red eyes and said, 'Laura, what's a matter?' 'There's something wrong with me,' I told her. 'I can't have babies.'

" 'No. no.' She patted my hand. 'It's only been a few months. You can't know that yet. Besides, maybe The Doctor', she always called him the doctor, 'is taking care.' She explained about birth control to me.

And I asked him and sure enough, he was taking care — using condoms. I thought I knew everything, being a nurse and all, but I was so dumb. Naive."

"So. It's okay?"

She nods and says, "But my mother, she took a bath with her clothes on. I swear. I still can't imagine that she ever had sex. And yet there were four of us — and Cassie the surprise. So who knows."

Lala clasps me to her. "You'll be all right. I guess we're all made that way. Made to like sex so we keep reproducing the species. In spite of the pain of birth. Mother Earth arranged it."

Outside, the streets are streams of gold and red leaves. I kick the jewels as I walk and enjoy the crunching as I stomp. The books no longer press as heavy on my arms. The emerald and diamond ring is light on my finger. I remember what my mother said, that she couldn't imagine Lala and Docie having sex, or enjoying it. But I could imagine her and Daddy — though I didn't like to think about it and was, when I was younger, sure they must have only done it because they really really wanted me. I guess it's hard for kids to imagine their parents enjoying sex. But maybe Lala is right. Mother Earth has made it so we do. Maple trees arch over Darlington Road and curve toward me as I stroll down the middle since there's no sidewalk. The leaves rearrange themselves with each step.

CHAPTER 8

I am a sophomore at Allderdice High School. My life is my own, separate from my parents. Yet family serves as a safety net, a refuge from the teenage worries of appearance, popularity, dances, boys, and sex. We kids do not worry about grades much. It is before Sputnik and we will go to college because our parents can afford it. Besides, girls go to college to find husbands.

That is not true for me. Mother has told me to beware of the three D's — Death, Divorce, Desertion. I must always be able to support myself and my children. She insists, never be financially dependent on a man. And yet, she is financially dependent on Daddy. How could she support us? She can type ninety words a minute. I guess she could be a secretary again. I struggle with the inconsistency of her message to me and her own life.

Who you marry is the most important decision you make in your life, Daddy says. I read about foot binding in China, clitorectomy in Africa, female infanticide in the Arctic, child brides in India and suttee. I know that for women, even in America, the quality of life is determined first by her father and then by her husband.

I pore over plays by O'Neill and the books of Erich Fromm. Friends see me carrying *The Art of Loving* and want to see the pictures. After school, we walk to the soda fountain and have french fries and then separate to our different homes.

Docie shares my interest in archeology and we join an archeology group that meets at the Carnegie Museum. After laboriously translating part of the *Egyptian Book of the Dead*, I walk into the office of the Director of Archaeology, my handwritten manuscript in my arms for proof, and ask for a job. "I want to be an Egyptologist. I'm willing to work for nothing."

The curator, shock of white hair and cherubic face, looks up from his desk, puts his pen down. "Do I have a job for you," he announces.

He takes me through the American Indian exhibit, unlocks a thick, wide door in the hall. It's a storage room of American Indian artifacts. "Here, you can retag the items."

I skip school and sit in the library reading, or retreat to the room of shelved musty artifacts. Baskets, beaded bags, feathered headdresses. I rewrite numbers on a linen tag and tie it to the artifact.

. . .

Because of our prosperity and Mother's love of shopping, I have more clothes than I know what to do with. My mother and I go to Adelle's, Linton's, the Tweed Shop to buy me six-gored tweed skirts, a thick mahogany belt, flowered dresses, cashmere sweaters.

Cashmere sweaters are the high school status symbol and I hear the other girls bragging about how many they have. Linda got five for Chanukah. Risa says in her snootiest voice, "Well, I have ten."

At home, I count mine. I have 40. I don't tell anyone. I have so many summer dresses I cannot wear them all during the spring school season. I am not growing, but Mother buys as though I need to be completely outfitted four times a year. As though scads of clothes will make me popular. As though scads of clothes will make me beautiful.

Daddy and I are playing chess in the sunroom, the French doors tightly closed against the cold. This is a rare day, Daddy home even on a Sunday. He pays Pennsylvania blue law fines for each store in Pennsylvania so that it can remain open on Sunday. People shop on Sunday. But this Sunday, he is home and we concentrate on the clutter of black and white.

I castle and he studies the board. Outside, snow falls in soft flakes, melting into the pool, cloaking the statue, crusting the cherry trees and evergreens. Occasionally, I beat him. I am not a serious chess player. Rather, it is one way to be close to him. I have been told I look like him. I sense we have the same restlessness. I enjoy his charisma, his extroversion. Mother's shyness is often mistaken for snobbery. He makes a move and says check. And then pauses. I study my king's escape, but find none. My castling has given him his opportunity. His knight and a bishop block me in. "I think that's mate," I say.

He nods.

. . .

A fire blazes in the living room. Daddy sits in the Queen Anne chair, the arms carved into swans. Smoke clots around him. Volume Two of Jones' biography of Freud is open on his knee. I sprawl on the gray silk sofa, eating rye bread toast smothered with cream cheese, reading *Mourning Becomes Electra* by O'Neill. I feel the presence of my family. Mother broods at her desk, rubbing small circles in her scalp as she details financing for her halfway house. "It's a whole new way to deal with the mentally ill. They will be close to their families and able to obtain emotional support. Not stuck off in a hospital, but more community oriented." David weaves patterns on his Indian bead loom. Fire blazes warm orange. Snow blankets the house in an unruffled calm.

Later that evening, we go to Uncle Isaac's and Aunt Mildred's for dinner. All of the cousins are there, except for Rob and Danny away at prep school. Sara and I giggle in her bedroom over her latest boyfriend. Sara as a teenager is as sensual as her girlhood promised. She dates and discards the junior boys, Steve's, her brother's, peers. We giggle over her brother's friends. Steve is the school golden boy. I am a mouse, a school fixture by comparison. After dinner, we watch *The Hit Parade*. "Get a Job" is on the Top 10, but Snooky Lanson can't capture the beat.

Mark is Mildred's brother. Tall and dark with a baby face, he still possesses the body of the football star that he was in high school. He has worked occasionally as an actor. Occasionally selling story ideas to movies. Occasionally as a sales executive. Occasionally in advertising. He is divorced with two daughters my age. I find out later, much later, that he brought prostitutes home and forced his wife to serve them breakfast in bed. I find out later, much later that he has an illegitimate daughter who will graduate from Allderdice High School in the same class as his younger daughter.

The black-and-white TV flickers a gray glow on our faces. Mark comes behind me and begins to tickle the back of my neck. He does this with gentle fingertips until I feel goosebumps rise on my neck, my shoulders, my breasts, my arms. I am enflamed. And then he moves away. The Lucky Strike ad comes on and I go to Daddy who stands, arms crossed, by the fire. I rain kisses on his face and, when I retreat back to the darkened TV room and the Hit Parade, I hear him say, "Wow, she's going to be something."

I discharge my feelings on the safest man I know.

CHAPTER 9

Daddy and Isaac, Mother is told by Isaac, were eating in the Webster Hotel restaurant when my father became ill. It was indigestion, he thought. He checked into the hotel, intending to drive home when he felt able. He didn't feel better and entered the Montefiore Hospital.

Mother is called to the hospital. Jake has had a heart attack. Myocardial infarction. He is critically ill, but alive. He has round-the-clock nurses. Mother can only visit him for five minutes at a time. David and I are not allowed at all. His heart is damaged. Mother is relieved he is still alive, still her husband. All else recedes in significance.

"Your father is ill." Her face is white, her eyes light green, her lipstick worn off. Her words are measured and her voice even. "He is in the Montefiore Hospital and has the best doctors possible."

I frown. I am sixteen. My life has been sheltered and predictable. In our new house, the horses no longer rear and plunge on my parents' bedroom wall. "What are you talking about?"

"Your father has had a heart attack, and will spend some time recovering, but he'll be OK."

He is thirty-eight. His heart attack has no reality to me. He looks twenty-eight, brushed with youthful good looks and dark intensity. He is too young to have a heart attack. Too alive. He is off on a long business trip.

He can't smoke anymore. He must change his diet. No eggs. Not so much steak and Roquefort cheese. More chicken and vegetables. "But I'm still the same weight I was in college," he protests.

Not so much tension.

He rolls his eyes and holds his hands palms up. "No tension? Oh, God. How do you live without tension? It's inevitable. Like rain." Gray circles deepen his eyes.

I ask and ask. "How did he have a heart attack?" As though he has done something which made this happen, some extra added stress, a virus maybe, something terrible he ate. Mother tries to explain the medical facts, but the details clarify nothing.

She tells me what happened to him in Webster's Restaurant. But it's clear she doesn't believe the story. Even I know that when you feel sick you check into a hospital, not a hotel. Mother learns the truth from Aunt Mildred. I hear the story much later from Mother, how she pieced it together. Daddy was with a woman in the Webster Hotel when the elephant sat on his chest. I wonder if Daddy and this woman, who I picture with dark hair and a Maidenform bra spiraling her breasts into bullets, have just finished, just started, or in the middle. I wonder about her fear. In his agony and panic, he calls Isaac, calls the hotel doctor. When Isaac arrives, the woman is still there. The hospital doctor calls an ambulance. When Daddy recovers enough to speak, he tells Mother the restaurant story.

He stays in the hospital. After he's been there a month, I am allowed to visit once a week. Even seeing him, gray and pale, the heart attack doesn't seem real.

When Daddy returns home, he is installed in my bedroom. It seems incongruous, him sleeping under my curved canopy surrounded by dotted Swiss and lace. There are dark circles under his eyes. He slowly moves down the curved stairway, his black hair hangs lank over his forehead, both hands press into the mahogany banister. His untied bathrobe sways from his shoulders, the belt sags by his knees. I can't watch him.

I am moved to the third floor. I have the entire floor for myself — three empty rooms, two storage rooms and two bathrooms. I spend the dwindling days of summer sunbathing nude on the roof, smearing my body with baby oil, luxuriating in the sugar hyacinth smell and glistening oil on my browning breasts, stomach. I draw and paint murals of wispy ballerinas dancing with huge tulips, stamens and pistils revealed and trembling. I lose myself in the bright colors splashing and then absorbed by the plaster, sucked and muted.

I walk through Schenely Park to the Carnegie Museum, sit in the musty room lined with cases of American Native artifacts. Using india ink, I painstakingly rewrite their catalogue numbers on linen tags and tie it to a basket or a feathered headdress or a deerskin doll or a beaded moccasin. I run my fingers over the tiny stitches, the closely beaded flowers and swirls. I try to imagine the woman, sitting in a teepee, warmed by a fluctuating fire, bending toward the light as she worked. What was she thinking? Was she nursing a baby, mourning a husband, hungry? Or did she concentrate solely on the colors of the bead, the rhythm of her needle? I translate a monograph on the Jivaro from Spanish to English and learn how to shrink heads, stew the skin, soak it in poisoned sand, and embellish eyelids and lips.

. . .

Daddy is upstairs reading. He climbs down the stairway only for dinner. David is in the TV room. Mother and I are in the kitchen. Faith and her three daughters have spent the day with us. They crashed into a Moroccan screen in the sunroom, sent its tiny carved pieces off their moorings. Mother's eyes reveal how disturbed she is, but she says, "At least no one is hurt." Now, Faith has taken her children to Lala and Docie's house and returned. It is Sunday, Beatrice's night off. We have finished the dinner dishes and sit around the marble kitchen table.

"I need help," Faith says. The freckles on her cupid bow are dark in her wan skin. "I don't know what to do anymore." She talks in a whisper. Her husband, scion of a wealthy retailing family, has gambled away the fortune inherited from his grandfather. "This is far different than Docie's poker playing. And you know what that did to Lala."

Mother nods. I listen.

"I can't tell you what living with the fear is like. Every time the phone rang. Bill collectors. Making up stories and telling lies. And then silence. Because the phone's been turned off. Then the heat. Then the electricity. Me and the girls in the dark and cold. Waiting. Every time the doorbell rang. Scared who it would be. And then three men came and told me they would hurt him. I thought, maybe they'd hurt Elaine, Libby, or Pam. That's when I called his father." Herb's father paid off his debts. "I thought it was over. I thought he learned his lesson. But. But. Already he disappears and returns stinking of booze and smoke. Hiding his eyes."

Faith and Herb live in the perfectly neat and clean house. Adorable and well dressed daughters. As though ordered drawers and perfectly folded towels can protect.

"I can't live with the insecurity. The mistrust. The fear. The goons."

Mother's eyes are damp. She places her hand over her sister's. "Will you leave?"

Faith bites her lower lip. Shrugs. "I don't know what to do. I haven't told you, but it's been years."

"Stay with us. You could move up to the third floor with me." My suggestion is not attended to.

"I talked with Lala and Docie," Faith says. "Docie will help me get my old job back at the hospital."

Mother says, "He could join Gamblers Anonymous. Maybe you both could do couple counseling. Maybe you'll get through this, the two of you."

"How can I support three small children on an x-ray technician's salary?"

"Maybe you could take control of the money and give him an allowance. Remove his name from all the accounts," Mother says.

"I still love him." Faith turns her head away from us.

"Love him harder. He must have a huge void inside he's trying to fill with this excitement. You fill it with your love. Heal him." Mother leans close to her, her hand on Faith's arm.

"I do that. I can't imagine loving him more. Maybe it doesn't work. Maybe it won't work. Love. Simply love."

There is quiet.

Mother reaches for the rest of the raspberry pie she made for dinner. The aluminum strikes a chord against the table. She walks to the cutlery drawer and withdraws a knife.

"Why can't they just move here?" I insist. I turn to Faith. "Move here and finish college. Then you'll be able to support the girls."

Faith answers, "There's too much going on."

I think she means Daddy's heart attack.

Faith looks at me. "Learn from this. Always be able to support yourself and your children. Always."

"I know. I know. Death, divorce, desertion." I think she could do it. We could help her. We could all live together. It seems like a simple solution.

Faith shrugs, "Shit. At least it's not other women." And then she presses her lips together. Mother's mouth twitches and she leans over the table, knife in hand. She slices the pie. "It's an addiction. Like alcohol. Drugs. His gambling is an addiction. Like Jake's Don Juanism."

The knife cuts through the soft pie and the sound of scraping fills the room. A thrill as shrill as the metal against metal runs through me. My father's behavior is explained by a name.

CHAPTER 10

Daddy's business goes bankrupt. Store managers had skimmed cash off the till. Uncle Isaac had installed a woman in every city where there was a store, paid for by the business accounts. My father, carried on the crest of his omnipotence, didn't pay attention to details. The House of Television, 21 stores in three states, is a house of cards that tumbles down around us.

"Did he know this before his heart attack?" I ask Mother.

"He was trying to figure out a way to recover, rescue Isaac and Mildred. Juggle stuff."

"Is there?" It was beginning to make some sense. Daddy's heart attack.

"We'll be okay. Don't worry. We have each other and our love."

. . .

And we are OK. Daddy walks up and down the stairs, though he doesn't bounce as he used to. The stores have huge liquidation sales. At breakfast, Mother doesn't put an extra egg yolk in his scrambled eggs. He buys a sun lamp and covers his sallowness with tan. The circles disappear under his eyes. He moves back into the king-size bed in his and Mother's room. I am almost relieved when I catch him smoking. Everything is back to normal.

It's my senior year at Allderdice High School. Mother and Daddy sell the house across from the golf course. Then they sell everything in the house, my canopy bed, Mother's bird's-eye maple desk with the secret compartment, the piano, David's bed, the sun parlor furniture, the dining room furniture, rococo Daddy called it. I say good-bye to the empty house with the long corridors winding. I say good-bye to the cherry trees entwined over the looking pool, dropping their blossoms on my waiting lips. The herb garden with the sundial. The patio furniture and purple chaise lounges. I say good-bye to the skinny ballerinas dancing on my walls. I say good-bye to the tulips and thyme Lala planted. We take the marble kitchen table and the woman who looks into the pool with us. We move into an apartment for my senior year at Allderdice.

We no longer go to Uncle Isaac's and Aunt Mildred's. Mildred takes a job at the Tweed Shop selling clothes. On my way home from school, I stop to see her. Uncle Isaac has set up an office in the garage. He translates the Talmud from Hebrew, to Greek, to Latin to English, then back to Hebrew checking to see if he got it right. An endless circle trying to find answers, guideposts, morality. We never know what he finds. He watches fish swim circles in his fish tank. He shows David the joy of mesmerism, of simple peace. I learn later that my parents have covered Isaac's debts.

The sale of our house starts Oxxford Furniture Galleries in Dormont. We move to Mt. Lebanon to lessen Daddy's commute. Mt. Lebanon is the blond suburbs. Everyone looks alike. We buy a small house backed by the forest. Mother plants mignonette. She wants to smell something sweet. David raises miniature roses. He catches possums in a Havahart trap hoping to make a pet. I dress in black tights and huge Italian sweaters, line my eyes with thick black and wipe my lips with white lipstick. Tease my hair.

. . .

Sara is in Montefiore with hepatitis. She is so thin she is only luminous brown eyes and tan skin, a pouty mouth and as always glossy hair. As though her illness has uncovered a glowing sun inside her. Our fathers are the only men we don't talk about.

Before she got sick, she was collecting jazz greats as they swung through Pittsburgh on their tours. Now all she can do is listen to their records. She nods her head at a record player on the floor of her hospital room. She hates being cramped in this small room. Hates eating the terrible food. Her mother rarely comes. Her father has only come once. He never leaves the house anymore. But something good is happening. A new love affair. And I'll never guess who. He was so kind to her. There for her, holding her hand and talking to her. When she was all alone. His name is Dan and he's her internist.

Dan comes in while we are talking, a pudgy man with kinky reddish hair. The start of a beard.

When he leaves, Sara whispers, "He wants to marry me. We do it right here." She pats the bed. "He locks the door. He is a great lover, he gives me vaginal orgasms." Then she quotes her bilirubin rate and tells me facts and figures about her disease.

I am still a virgin. "God, Sara. You are so lucky." Even sick, even fevered she captures men.

"You're the lucky one. Your mother is so loving, so caring. Mildred," she calls her mother by her first name, "is interested only in herself. She's not interested really in being a mother. "

I don't see Mildred that way. "Really? She's always so warm to me."

"Easy enough once or twice a month. "

I wish they were still friends, Mother and Mildred.

"She thinks I should marry him. Get me out of the way. And he's a doctor. But she doesn't tell me. She just leaves us alone and doesn't visit."

Steve, Sara's brother, graduated valedictorian of Allderdice, now at Princeton, is home for the summer.

"Steve's having an affair with Liz Levin."

My eyebrows go up. My mouth opens. I know my astonishment is apparent on my face. "The accountant?"

"Yep, our family accountant." Sara shrugs and lights a cigarette. "She's a real slut. Dad fucked her too."

I mull this over in my mind. Steve and his father have both slept with the same woman. I wonder if Steve did it out of anger.

"Isn't that sort of like incest?"

Sara frowns, "How so? She's not related to either of them."

"Well, once removed." I am uncomfortable and take one of Sara's cigarettes, light it from the lit one in the ashtray. "Did Steve know?"

Sara inhales on her cigarette, "Suppose so, if I did."

"Well, do you think you'll do it?"

"Marry Dan?"

Sara throws her head back and laughs. For a moment we are girls in Squirrel Hill taking a bubble bath together. "Not till I get outa here. Not till I see what he's like outa this puke green shithole. Then we'll see. But I think I'd rather go to Antioch."

. . .

I wind home through downtown, the Golden Triangle off to my right. I mull over Sara's freedom with admiration. It's not yet rush hour so I zip through the tunnel choking from gasoline fumes to get back to Mt. Lebanon. I guess Steve and Sara are both angry at Isaac.

Daddy is on the gray silk sofa, now worn at the arms, reading, drinking a martini, and smoking a pipe. He hopes the pipe will help him cut down on cigarettes, but a cigarette burns in a large wooden ashtray next to him. Mother is in the kitchen cooking chicken breasts in sherry, garlic, and mushrooms with rice pilaf for dinner. David draws pictures of cars with flames on their fins. I wish we could be close with Steve and Sara and Aunt Mildred and Uncle Isaac again. I bring it up at dinner, but the subject falls flat. When I tell them that Sara might marry her doctor Mother just says, "We'll see." And eats her chicken. David tells Daddy he's breathing too loud. Daddy doesn't say a word. I can hardly wait for autumn and college to start.

CHAPTER 11

I'm living in the dorm at University of Pittsburgh when Daddy starts playing poker Friday nights on a friend's yacht gliding the Allegheny. There's no phone. Some nights, he falls asleep in the ship's La-Z-Boy recliner. "I'm so tired. I just sit on it and next thing I know it's morning. They keep playing," he says on Saturday when he returns home to shower and shave before driving back to Oxxford's. "And let me sleep."

I roll my eyes.

Mother lights a cigarette and says, "Maybe we should buy one. If they're so comfortable, I mean."

In winter she receives calls from an anonymous woman warning her that her husband is having an affair. With Donna, the store's new designer. They're seen all over town.

I'm home for the weekend.

"Should I ask him?" she wonders. Dusk has gathered, but she hasn't turned the lights on. We sit in the twilight living room. The pinpoint glow of her cigarette is the sole spark. I smell brisket cooking in the oven, long and slow. "Do I just ignore it?"

"I don't know."

She ignores it. She's busy with her halfway house for the mentally ill; it has become a prototype for a new kind of treatment. Busy also with efforts to desegregate Southern schools.

The calls stop.

It's early spring when she tells me the calls have started again. She asked Daddy about it. "All he did is shrug, concentrate on his pipe," she says. She reclines on my bed, now a studio bed with a brass headboard.

I'm at my desk studying. I put down my pen, swivel in my chair to her, and draw on my cigarette.

"He said they were probably having a business lunch with customers. The calls are nonsense. Someone with nothing in her life — a busybody. How could I even take that seriously?"

I believe the caller. Somehow, without words I feel Daddy. I sense how his mouth sets on one side, I sense how he curls his thumb into his palm when he's lying. I sense before the calls who he plays poker with on Friday nights. Who he pokes. The knowledge turns my stomach, crawls up my spine. I want my intuition to be wrong. I want Mother's hopes to be true. We are what we seem, an ordinary family.

I mindlessly ruffle the pages in my book.

Mother's lips are parted, her eyes wet, watching the poplars tremble in the breeze through the window over my desk.

She'll believe what she needs to believe. She floats on the water of her denial, occasionally being sucked into the depths of her anxiety. She buys more clothes. She is also president of the National Council of Jewish Women. She is involved with more meetings, flying to Washington for conferences.

David works at the Oxxford Gallery weekends, in the summer delivering furniture with Bobby and Oliver. They are friends of our laundress. Bobby is a tall skinny black guy with processed hair, Oliver, black also, is husky with an easy smile and a wide gold wedding band.

David tells me this in June. "You father be cool, be *the man,*" Bobby says to David. His front tooth is half chipped, but it doesn't make his smile less friendly. "Cool cat, that man." He winks at my brother. "You got the touch, too?"

David doesn't understand.

"Got this little piece, you know. Some extra action. Some side action. That Donna, a fox. Got tits on her... see 'em comin' round the corner half block before she do."

David has been replaying the conversation. Trying to make it come out different. Trying not to think of Mother. He tells me all this during a TV commercial, gray patches flickering on his face. "That's all they talk about. Daddy having sex with Donna." David rubs his belly. He's lifting weights and watching his diet, turning the pudginess that earned him the nickname Otto Smedlack in camp into hardness.

"Maybe Bobby wants her."

"Should I tell Mother?"

I tell David about the calls. I tell him that Daddy says they're working together, planning window display, deciding about inventory.

"Makes me sick. And Bobby thinks it's so cool."

Donna comes to the house so Daddy can sign some papers. I notice her pointy breasts. She doesn't sweat in the summer. We are almost the same age, but with a world between us. I admire her grooming, elegant hair, glossed fingernails. She is without thighs, she is without hips, she is only legs stretching down from breasts. I am surprised at David's shock.

Bobby doesn't let it go. They're moving furniture from the basement of the store. Bobby says, "They fuck on that bed. When there's no customers."

I wonder if Bobby has walked in on them, does he watch them?

"Your father has 'em all," Bobby says, "Customers, working girls, you name 'em, he gets 'em." Bobby itemizes.

David tells him, "I don't want to hear that shit."

Bobby calls him a sissy, a mama's boy. Oliver says, leave the kid alone and help with the dresser.

Donna moves to an apartment near Oxxford's.

David starts following Daddy.

"Why?" I ask.

"To prove Bobby wrong," he tells me.

"You want Daddy to be faithful?"

"Mother deserves that." He inhales a cigarette.

But David sees Daddy's Buick parked in front of Donna's apartment on Wednesday afternoon, on Friday nights when he's "playing poker." The Buick is next to her VW Beetle at Locante's for long lunches.

We're meeting in the dark TV room. Shades drawn to prevent glare. "Mother deserves better. I'd be a better husband."

I nod. "I hope so."

David decides to take pictures of them doing it and then blackmail Daddy for a new Corvette for his sixteenth birthday. He'll climb the tree outside of her apartment and take a picture. The tree forks just below the second floor, he can shimmy up the right-hand branch. It should hold him. He can perch there and snap the picture. He holds an invisible camera in his hand and squints one eye. But maybe the flash will give him away, warn them.

The TV program changes to a western. He knows just the kind of Corvette he'll get. Daddy will buy him the car to keep him from showing Mother the photos. David knows just how he'll detail the fins. He brings me his drawings of the fins, the headlights, the hubcaps, the flames arching across the car doors. He draws with sharply pointed pencils, thin as needles.

. . .

Summer passes, it's fall and I return to Pitt. I delve into Plato's *Symposium* and *Dr. Faustus,* into Hegel and Engels. I come home one Friday evening. Daddy is away playing poker. Of course, I say. David is at a high school dance. I have brought my laundry home. Mother and I sit around the marble table in the dining area of the kitchen.

"The calls have increased. Now she's irate because I haven't stopped the affair."

I pick celery and onions out of the wooden salad bowl. Remnants of baked potato and green beans and broiled chicken are smeared on our plates. "It's always the same person?"

Mother eats a long green bean with her fingers.

"Maybe it's just some nut." I push the potato skin with my fork.

"He keeps saying, it's nonsense. I should scream at her to stop calling." Mother lights a cigarette. "I asked him if he wanted a divorce."

"What'd he say?" My heart pounds.

"I said, 'If you want to go be with her you can. I'll give you a divorce.'" Mother pulls on her cigarette. "He said, 'What're you talking about? You must have another man. I don't want a divorce.'"

A strong offense is the best defense, I think.

"Maybe they're not having an affair," Mother says. "Maybe it's just some nut."

I shrug and light a cigarette. Each of us smokes three packs a day. We go through cartons of Camels. I stand up to get us some coffee, come back with half-and-half for Mother.

Mother replays their conversation again. Saying it all again. Just like David going over what Bobby said, going over the tree outside Donna's apartment, the Corvette. Both of them going over and over conversations hunting for hidden meanings, the slight signals of lies. Drifting between reality and wishes not sure which is which. She is baffled, hurt, and yet her eyes are dry, her lipstick freshly applied.

I consider and then draw on my cigarette and say, "Bobby says Daddy's having an affair with Donna. David told me."

"David knows?"

"Yeah. David doesn't really believe Bobby. Thinks Bobby likes to tease him."

"Oh God." She watches the cream curl pale swirls in the coffee and stirs them all away. "How do I do this?" She shudders.

For Mother this is family. This is secret. She can tell me because her shame is our shame. And she has to tell someone. But I am not fully able to grasp the depth of her pain. The wife's pain. I blow on the hot coffee. I only know I will not marry a man like my father. In spite of his appeal, his charisma, his brilliance and wealth. I will not. I will not get myself stuck like this. I am only able to listen. Only able to witness her worry away the problem.

"Well, maybe he is sleeping with her. Fucking her." The word explodes. I have never heard her say that word before. As a child, she washed out my mouth for saying "shit."

She lights a new cigarette with the ember of the last one. "He can have her if he wants to. She must be a dalliance. He must want me more."

Mother has offered Donna to Daddy on the platter of divorce, like John the Baptist's head on a charger. "He chose me." Mother stretches the word "chose." It lasts as long as a breath. It is almost a moan.

"Yes," I say. "He chose you." I have a sudden memory from my childhood. I walked into the kitchen and there, in front of the sink, my father presses my mother to him. He has just come home from work, his hat still on. He kisses her, his hands rub large circles on her hips, her arms are tight around him, pressing him closer, closer to her. Their mouths are open and then I hear Mother sigh deep and soft. They hear me and part. I am embarrassed, but secure.

"You know what? I think I'll go back to college. Finish up my degree," Mother says.

. . .

I thumb through the *Sexual Behavior of the Human Male*. According to Kinsey, as far as I can tell, only sixty percent of men ever commit adultery. Good, I think as I close the book. It is possible.

INFIDELITY

I can't imagine, can't picture how to be me as an extension of an entitled ambitious man. A man like my father. I am determined not to redo my mother's marriage.

CHAPTER 12

It's 1961, and the National Council of Jewish Women's annual conference is going to take place in Pittsburgh. As president and a resident of Pittsburgh, Mother will give the welcoming address right after the Mayor and the Governor. Thrilled by this, the culmination of decades of work, she is nonetheless terrified of speaking on a stage, behind a podium, using a microphone, to hundreds of people. She writes her speech on notecards, the words blocked out in different colors, red words to remind her to smile, green words to speak loudly and clearly, capital letters for emphasis. She stands in front of her bathroom mirror nightly for weeks repeating her speech.

She rehearses it for David and me in the living room. "One more time," she says. "I can do it better, I'm sure." I don't hear the difference, but say, "Yes. You're getting better." In truth the words and the ideas are fine. She has to relax in the delivery. In the speech, she welcomes the national community to the city of Pittsburgh. She impresses upon them the crucial gifts and impact that Jewish women can make in the '60s. The privilege of serving and forging new directions for the community, the ill, minorities. Healing the wounds of the Holocaust.

None of us are there to hear her speech. She spends the conference at the Pittsburgh-Hilton Hotel near the Point. The morning after her speech, my task is to drive David to an appointment using Daddy's gray Buick. I wake up, get dressed, brew coffee, but there is no car in the driveway. I go to their bedroom, but the bedspread is smooth with a sharp crease under the pillows. I call Oxxford's. No answer. I wait. I listen to the ringing, endless and empty. I cannot figure out how to complete my assignment. Call a cab? Do I have enough cash to cover the fare into the city? The ringing now seems like breaths. Do I call and cancel David's appointment?

I am startled by the sound of the other phone ringing. I pick it up and it is Daddy.

"Where are you? Where the hell are you?"

"At the store."

"You know I have to drive David to Cuden's, right?"

"I'm on my way."

"Hurry. We'll be late with rush hour and all."

David is already dressed, dabbing his hair with Brylcreme when Daddy returns.

I narrow my eyes at Daddy and inhale. "You weren't at the store." How could he do this on Mother's big night? "I had the store on the other line and there was no answer." My cheeks burn. A vein in my neck pounds.

Daddy smokes his cigarette, and skims through the mail on the table. "I was speaking metaphorically." He brings his cigarette to his mouth and uses his thumb to tear open an envelope. "I was at the White Castle on the corner getting coffee."

"I don't believe that." I move in front of him, forcing his eyes away from the letter he's reading. "You were out all night. On Mother's big night." We are a foot away from each other, hissing in furious stage whispers. I grab the keys, still warm from his pocket, off the table.

He has taught me to meet a stare unblinking. To never look away. My eyes burn.

"Don't tell your mother. She doesn't need to know."

CHAPTER 13

I am the last virgin I know. I am dating several men, but no one is crazy about me. I want to be desired, I want to desire. My girlfriend, Judy, has more men than she knows what to do with. I go out with her surplus dates.

"It's simple," she tells me. "You have to pretend you have a secret. Maybe a secret life, or a secret sorrow. Stare off into space until the man becomes alarmed. And then blink as though you were on a long journey. When he asks, shrug and look sad. Or smile slowly and say, 'I'll tell you sometime... Maybe.' Stare off again and then meet his eyes. Act a little nuts. But don't do anything crazy. Men like to feel big and powerful. The damsel in distress routine works every time."

I must look unconvinced, because Judy's red hair bobs as she says, "Really. Believe me. It works."

I decide to test Judy's theory. Hank and I have been seeing each other for eight months or so. There's no compelling zing between us so I'm not sure I want him, but we like each other and I'm sure I don't want another woman to have him. We neck in the prop room, backstage in between scenes. He's going to school on the GI Bill after doing a four-year stint in Germany. He is an actor and an artist who grew up poor and rough on the Hill until his home was razed to make way for Three Rivers Stadium. He cooks huge pots of pasta on an electric coil and serves it as lunch for all the artsy/beatnik crowd at the university. He fries salami and eggs and that's our dinner. He's turned the prop room into a meeting place. His expansiveness is boundless.

My parents don't like him. Daddy says he's too old. He's the son of a bookie and what man who takes his responsibilities seriously would support his family through an illegal activity. Mother shakes her head in agreement.

"Hey. He's Jewish," I retort.

They aren't impressed.

Hank and I are at a bar drinking shots and beers and eating hard-boiled eggs dotted red with Tabasco. The place is dark and grimy. Sticky from dancing, we sit in a burgundy vinyl booth downing boilermakers and laughing with friends. Quotes from the last play — *My Three Angels* — fly with new meaning. Hank won an actor of the year award for his performance.

I stare into a dark corner. Paneled and as grimy as the rest of the bar. Dim overhead lights cast shadows until the corner recedes into the gloom. Clouds of blue smoke curl around the ceiling. The laughter recedes. My eyes burn and I slowly blink.

"Ann. Annie," Hank calls.

I notice there's a stool in the corner. Empty.

"Annie?"

I patch a new self together from characters out of books — the spacey aesthete, Lillith. The helpless girl child from *Tender Is the Night*. *Lolita,* ripe with sleeping sexuality. I am available, but untouchable. Obtainable, but unconquerable. I sew a persona from many patches in a quilt and stitch the pieces with a dreamy wistfulness.

He touches my arm. "Annie?"

I turn slowly to him and blink and then meet his eyes as my father has taught me. "Why would someone sit alone, in a corner, at a bar? Like making yourself a dunce," I say.

"Are you okay?"

I shrug and act as though I'm trying to participate in the conversation. Then I'm dragged into staring at the stool again, pondering the life of the person who would sit alone in a bar's hidden corner. Might as well just drink at home. Then I realize the answer. "Oh. It's a way to get away from home," I say. I almost believe my act.

Hank wraps his arm, heavy around my shoulder. "Come on. Let's go."

The streets are cool from early fall, crunching leaves echo in the dark. My skin is now dry, but my skirt, damp from dancing and the vinyl, sticks to my thighs.

"What's up?" he asks.

I shrug. I haven't made up my story yet. What is my secret? I could tell him I'm pregnant. Then I'd need to be rescued for sure. His hands are slung into pockets of his leather jacket. "Come on, I'll take you for a ride," he says when we reach his Vespa.

I wrap myself behind him and smell the leather of his jacket, feel the warmth of his back on my chest, the inside of my arms. The wind of the city whips my hair into my face. We fly across the river and climb the Southside hill. He turns off the cycle and below us twinkles Pittsburgh. Shimmering lights capture my breath. The air is black. Not even stars. I feel heated by the fast ride, his warm back, my legs spread around him, my crotch pressed against his ass. The game I play.

I light a cigarette and the red tip glows as I inhale.

He waits for me, his arm around my shoulder. Warm. He takes his jacket off and covers us both with it. I concentrate on my cigarette and on the lights.

"You're not yourself."

Here we go. "Yes, I am. I'm just letting you see it."

He thinks this over.

"I get scared sometimes, or feel like going away inside my own head and being alone," I tell him. "Sometimes, all the voices and people are too much chaos for me." My lie is thick now. I love the people, there's never too much action or wildness for me. Like the motorcycle ride, part of me wants to go faster, longer, harder. I pull on my cigarette and I am mesmerized, no act now, by the lights. "So I long for the quiet and I've learned to go inside myself to find it. And then I go, I don't know where. To the moon or someplace inside that's like this." I gesture toward the black river carving through the mountain of white lights beneath us. I gesture to the streams of twinkling snakes crawling around the hills. He pulls me to him and kisses me.

"I feel so close to you."

I snuggle into the warmth of his chest, the smell of him, his soft black hair. And I sigh.

"Will you marry me, Annie. Marry me. "

This works faster than I imagined.

"After I get back from Europe, will you marry me?"

"Yes," I say.

. . .

When I tell my mother that I'm engaged to Hank she moves to the stove to take out rock Cornish hens stuffed with wild rice and glazed with cranberry jelly. She sits down facing me and picks up her cigarette shedding soft ash and says, "Are you in love with him?"

I nod.

Her green eyes are on mine as she inhales the cigarette. "Have you slept with him yet?"

"No."

She shakes her head. "How can you marry a man you haven't made love with? Don't you think you should make sure that part is okay before you're stuck with him for life?"

"We just haven't gotten there yet."

"You don't seem like a woman in love. You seem like a girl who wants to belong."

. . .

Hank takes me for the first time in the prop room. We lie on a mountain of velvet curtains and he kisses me and touches me and he enters me and I remember to push myself down on him to ease the pain just like my parents' marriage manuals suggest. "Spread your legs wider," he says. But they seem spread as wide as I can get them and it hurts, but I like the ride. Afterwards, I soar. I've done it. I liked it. I am empowered.

The next time we make love, he takes his time with me and I come and the time after that, we come together. And I think, this is easy. Why did the books make it sound difficult?

"Annie, my love," he calls me. "You're the best."

We make love in the prop room and the storage room and in his bedroom and in his friend's apartment. He shows me everything he knows from his years of experience and everything he learned in Europe and all the tenderness and giving and generosity that he has. I am the eager learner, wanting to try out every position, to let him lead me to his every fantasy and thereby discover my own. And I love the dancing, riding of sex and I love the communication that accompanies it and the knowledge you gain about the other person.

I slowly drop the act, but continue to defer to his greater experience, age and knowledge.

And I realize I do have a secret. It's my father's secret and I share that, my one secret with him.

In January, he goes off to Europe on a grant. And I kiss him with tears running down my face and we promise to write every day and we promise undying love, faithfulness. And I will see him in London.

But, by March, I realize I cannot marry this man. He does not know me. He has fallen in love with a character I invented. Not me. My apparently helpless persona entitled him to authority and power over me that I am coming to resent. I have no desire to be rescued the rest of my life.

He is returning to be a graduate student at the University of Pittsburgh. I apply to Big 10 schools with good anthropology departments.

. . .

Robert is a hunk. Rich, suave, and popular. Smart and prep-school educated. When I get into his bed, I smell the sex of other women. And I learn you can have too much of a good thing — he is so large and thick, sex is only uncomfortable. And I learn there are two kinds of men. Men who put their energy into making the sale. And men who put their energy into pleasing a woman.

I know my father is into making as many sales as possible.

However, my interlude with Robert seals Hank's fate. I will not marry a man I've been unfaithful to. My infidelity is the final proof of the inadvisability of this commitment.

CHAPTER 14

.

I am aboard the *Bremenhoffen* steaming to England. I'm going to work in a settlement house for the B'nai Brith. The gray sea under a clotted gray sky create a nothingness that seems like security.

My fellow passengers are German students and families returning home, Americans going overseas. Strangers. I am not traveling first class; my round-trip ticket costs $432. The sea rocks me, the library with its sparse collection of books and solitude seduces me.

My assigned dining companions in the second seating are a German family. The son is in his mid-twenties. His parents rambled around the U.S. before returning home with him. His dark good looks and chiseled features initially add interest to the meal, but he is withdrawn and without intensity or intrigue. Only the horseradish in the salad dressing adds pungency to the meal. The remainder of the food is not as good as Lala's.

Days stretch across the gray Atlantic. Lazy reading in the musty library, walking circles on the deck, gazing at the endless horizon as the wind agitates the sea. I have a shipboard romance with an architect working with Mies Van Der Rohe. Nights of dancing, drinking, and singing German ditties that sound suspiciously nationalistic.

Meals last for hours. What began as leisure degenerates into weariness. I am bored by my tablemates' small talk and the silences. I welcome their lapse into German so that I can escape into my own mind.

To entertain myself, I talk about the Anasazi culture and an archeological expedition to the Southwest that I had been on. The family attends to me. "The Si Papo hole in the kivas, the ceremonial chamber, is where the soul arrives on earth... I found a thousand-year-old potsherd with a fingerprint on it. Immortality for an anonymous artist who lived millennia ago. My index finger where her index finger was." They listen intently. They want more.

In ancient Egypt, the soul was weighed by the gods and goddesses. I tell them about monotheism in ancient Egypt and the realistic art movement it ushered in, quoting Freud's *Moses and Monotheism* and Frazier's *The Golden Bough*. They ask questions. They want more, even more. I am amazed. The Ten Commandments are rephrased promises from the *Egyptian Book of the Dead*. I am captured by my own fluidity, charm. I don't care about them other than their attention. These adults are held in thrall. I flip a switch inside me and turn on this other self, a blithe charmer that lay awaiting my summons. It is my father, the salesman.

As the meals continue, my stories become more exotic. They hear about gangs in my high school, girls early pregnant. They are shocked, but thrilled. Everyone is excited by sexual impropriety, even this staid family, I note. I describe how the Jivaro Indians shrink heads.

They talk now, too. Our voices become louder. The son tells interesting stories of laboratory errors and strange cell behavior. We are the liveliest table in the sedate dining room.

I look at the parents' middle-aged faces and want to ask about the war. Twenty years ago were they fighting? Were they hiding? We touch on the topic of concentration camps. The son tells me they were the threat of his boyhood, the bogeyman when he was naughty. Everyone knew about them.

On the deck, they drag chaises and blankets to talk with me. I use my promiscuous reading, I use my father's lust to make a sale, I use my father's licentious ability to entertain. My father and I share lots of traits: extroversion, a relentless curiosity and wanton joy of life, sometimes self-destructive adventure-seeking. But this faculty to charm seems somehow foreign, not me. It requires I flip into my father waiting inside of me. There when I need it, it is his gift to me. Knowing the psychological thrill he receives, I become more tolerant of his compulsion.

When I get off the train in London, I see Hank. He stands against a pillar, wearing a black and red checked shirt and khakis, carrying a bouquet. His face brightens when he sees me. My unease grows as we chat about my boat trip across the Atlantic, his trip from Paris to London, the room he found for us. He is like he used to be. He is unaware that I have changed. I feel unreal, as though I am at a distance watching the two of us in the twisted, black channels of the train station.

I can't bear any more illusions between us. He is quiet as I tell him I can't marry him. "I'm too young," I tell him. "I pretended to be someone I wasn't and I'm not sure who you love."

The flowers droop in his hand.

"I've been with another man."

He is polite. He helps me get to Stepney Green and the hostel I'll be living at while working.

A few days later, we walk around the East End, eating fish and chips greasy in paper. He feeds me a French fry dipped in vinegar and salted. "I like ketchup better," I say. He takes me into the subway and explains the system and we ride rushing cars into Soho. We are delicate with each other, as though tender new friends. As we stand in a line to buy tickets for *Hamlet,* we talk of friends in Pittsburgh and his new friends in Paris. I am relieved by the possibility of our friendship. I push the sick feeling away.

He asks, "Annie. Do you think you have to do this because you've been with another man? Because I don't feel that way. I love you."

I inhale and bury my head in his chest, smelling him, and the faint smell of plasticine clay. I blink tears away. He wraps his arms around me and we stand in the middle of a London street, Englishman in trench coats, bowlers, and umbrellas stepping around us.

"Annie, my love." He whispers in my ear. "What do you think? Can we go forward?"

I inhale and move closer to him. He mistakes the gesture as agreement when it is simply great sorrow.

"I'm still prepared to spend the rest of my life with you."

"I want to fool around some more. I'm sorry. So sorry. The guy was the symptom, not the cause." I think, I'll always be grateful that Hank introduced me to lovemaking. I think, I might never be able to be faithful to any man. Not ever.

I think, I am my father's daughter.

Hank's warm arms surround me, I feel his generous acceptance and know what I've given away.

CHAPTER 15

I am in the Café Select with Bora, a Yugoslavian expatriate, a boxer, a poet and my lover. He has the most beautiful smile in the world. We sit with Peter, my friend from London, who had been one of the Hungarian student revolutionaries. Peter gave me Bora's name when I left London for Paris. Tasha, a white blond, high-cheekboned Yugoslavian, had been married to a black American before she was Bora's lover and is now with Louie, a model and sometime gigolo. Louie leans away from the table, scanning the crowd. His sculpted good looks and perfect grooming are almost boring. A face seen in every magazine has turned him into an icon. Dehumanized him somehow. Jeanette tightly holds Ahmed's hand as though she'll never leave him. Her leg is draped over his lap. But in spite of her clingy affection she does not define herself as Ahmed's woman. She'll leave for Columbia University to get a Ph.D. in English. When I ask her about Ahmed, she shrugs one shoulder and blows away a lock of bang and says, "Men. Don't they have them in the U.S.?"

They speak a flash dash of French, English, Yugoslavian, Russian, and Italian. There is no one language we all speak. Now, they argue politics of the Hungarian revolution in accented French. Peter is a Trotskyite and Bora hates all communism. "C'est fascism," he exclaims. Peter leans forward earnestly. His French is quiet, but quick. I pick up something about Stalinism, a distinction he's making between Lenin and Trotsky.

I have been with Bora living this floating Parisian life for almost two weeks. I arrived in Paris after working for six months in Jewish Settlement House in Stepney Green, London. I saw numbers tattooed on the arms of friends. Abandoned children of American G.I.s and the kids orphaned by the war. I met the reality of war-torn lives. In Paris, we spend evenings in the Café Select, or in Tasha's and Louie's apartment overlooking the Champs. We explore the soft gray towers, gargoyles, and groomed parks of the city.

I don't want to go home. I want to go to the Sorbonne, to the London School of Economics, to Tel Aviv. America seems so materialistic, so stifling, so boring. A fluffy white dog at the next table licks bits of pâté from his mistress's red-tipped fingers. "C'est magnifique! Trés adorable," she exclaims to him and then a rush of more adoring French, more high-pitched doggie love. A fiddler in a red shirt and yellow tie and hat with a purple flower plays *Volare* and *Finiculi, Finicula* when people toss him coins. The violinist prances to the frivolous music. Bora and Peter continue their intense discussion, voices rising now, about European communism.

I unwrap the paper hospital corners enclosing a sugar cube and dip it in my espresso, suck it until it's white again. I light a Galloise, the acrid smoke fills my lungs like nothing since Pittsburgh.

. . .

The next day, Bora and I buy a bag of blue grapes for a nickel and eat them on the banks of the Seine. Chagall's stained-glass windows bathe us in colored light. Blue stripes his angular nose. Pink glow covers his forearm. The windows are going to Israel. That night, we smoke pot and eat eggs in Les Halles at three in the morning. And then make love in the adhesive heat of his garret apartment with its view of myriad chimneys. Over and over we make love, falling asleep as light bleaches the roofs. We lay shellacked with sweat and semen and smelling of wine. His gentle cradling while we sleep is paternal.

The next morning, Bora turns on the radio. The French is fast and furious, the announcer's voice rises and falls in a strident cadence. Bora paces, lights a cigarette, and puffs on it rapidly. He turns the radio up. I try to make sense of the piercing French, but catch only a word or two.

"What is it?"

He shakes his head. "La guerre. La guerre."

War.

Bora's fast strides cover the room. His face is red.

"What's happened?"

He puts a finger over his lips. "Shh," he hisses.

Bora dials a phone. The radio screeches on. Something about Berlin and Etats Unis and Russia. Kennedy and Khruschev.

Bora screams over the phone in Yugoslavian.

The shrill announcer keeps saying "la guerre," but I cannot translate the other words.

War? Now? In France? In England? What if I'm trapped in Paris? I remember the Holocaust. Suddenly war, which had been just history, was close. Here. What if I can't get back to the U.S.? I check my passport. There in my purse, my earnest face smiles complacently, one lock of my hair out of place. The American seal forms a comforting relief in the paper. Home. Pittsburgh and America. When before, it seemed so hypocritical; suddenly, it seems so safe

"They built a wall in Berlin."

"They?"

"The fucking East Germans, the Russkies. A wall. Kennedy moving troops to East Germany. All Europe holding breaths. Might be World War Three."

"No war yet?"

Bora shook his head. "No. Just wait and see."

I have time to get home. Maybe, just maybe. I look out of Bora's window. Shafts of sunlight nudge rectangles down the building onto the street. A housewife marches; a long baguette points out of her net bag. A child trudges with a wagon loaded with grocery bags. The street seems customarily quiet next to the raging radio, my beating heart.

"Kennedy scream at Khruschev. Can't tell bluff and show. Or if war." Bora shrugs, his arm muscles clench with the motion. "Politics or fighting."

He smiles at me, his eyes appreciative and walks to me. "I ask you stay in Paris, but." He opens empty hands. "In a week, a month, a year, three years, You'd be with another. I another. This no city for girl like you. You could last Paris. But your good would fight against her. Go home. Fight your badness instead of your goodness."

I'm ahead of him. I have tickets to sail on the *Queen Mary* in less than a week. "Think I'll be trapped here?"

Bora holds me, "You make it. Lucky girl. Be in Etats Unis and safe from Europe merde. French and Germans. Slavs and Croats. Russians and Poles. Trotsky and Lenin. Always little tribe fighting. Back in room where you were as little girl."

College. I can hardly wait to get back.

CHAPTER 16

Iowa is so vacant and clean it hurts. Cobalt skies and vast emptiness stretch everywhere. Always a blue shelter renews the land. No tall buildings rise like cliffs on either side to screen the space. No smoke. No belching fire.

Back from Europe, I'm still carrying Galloise cigarettes and Deux Magots matches in my jeans when I first see Tyrone. We pass each other walking down Clinton Avenue in front of the Airliner Tavern. He is brown skin and bulging muscles, wearing his letter jacket, black with a yellow I, his black leather arms crossed over his chest. Solid muscle and power. A thick neck. I come up to his shoulder. He looks at me without moving a muscle, just slides black eyes to the corners. Taking me all in. My stomach spins.

Tyrone and I pass each other for a few months. Each time I'm more aware of him. Our eyes hold on a little longer, our mouths open, but we don't speak. I pass the Airliner at the same hour hoping he keeps a regular schedule and afraid he does. I don't know what to do with my feelings. He's scary, but exciting. I had seen interracial couples in Europe. No big deal. I had friends who had been involved with black men. But here interracial couples mostly slip and slide to each other under cover of night. Hardly my style.

I answer a telephone call to my roommate from a classmate asking her about an assignment in Earth Science. When will she be back and am I taking Earth Science, by any chance? a soft voice asks. We start talking about classes. He's an art major, and he talks about colors and forms and design. A sweet helpful guy. Easy. A voice you could melt to.

After we talk for twenty minutes, he says, "Well, I'll see her in class." The next night, he calls again. Again I answer the phone. We talk about our families, we talk about our dreams. We talk all night. I know he's black — colored then — and figure he must be a football player since all the black guys in Iowa City are athletes.

So Tyrone keeps calling and we keep talking. We fall asleep with phones pressed to our ears, wake up to talk more.

Ty and I talk our lives. Talk our families. He tells me that his father moved up north because he didn't move to the back of the bus quick enough and the bus driver held a gun to his head. His mother left one day without telling Ty. She was just gone when he got back from nursery school. Gone to be with his father. Hurt her too bad to say good-bye. Nine months later Ty was put on a train with his two brothers and arrived in Michigan.

I tell him how the kids tormented me because I wore a black patch over my eye to correct a weak muscle. I tell him how I ran across the street following Faith and got hit by a car. Thought the car had run over my neck.

Ty's my friend. It's his senior year. Iowa's football team is number one in the nation. He's co-captain. I read about him in the newspapers, he tells me he's swamped by kids after the game. Stopped on the street by fans to comment on a good play. "My name is no name. I have no claim to fame," he says. "No matter what I do in my painting, I probably won't be as famous as I am right now."

I don't like football. Have only gone to one game. Ty feels safe.

We finally meet at the River Room. When I see he's the guy in front of the Airliner, my heart pounds. Too sexy to merely be my friend. When we dance, he moves like a cat across the floor but with the African beat to his hips and the power of 270 pounds of muscle. He teaches me to stroll, to twist. We tease each other as we come close, turn around and slid away. We gather a crowd.

At dusk, we walk along the river bank. Leaves are tipped with red and yellow. The wind whips my face promising winter. "This is my favorite place, right here on this bridge. When I was a freshman, I spent all winter here, listening to the ice. Alone on the bridge," Ty says. "Ice was my only friend. It cracks like there's an animal trying to get out. In the spring, it moans. I'd stand on the bridge and talk to the ice like it was my mother." His hands are hard, broad. The fingers wide. When we place our palms together, my fingertips approach the place where his fingers start. We weave our fingers together, his dark brown, my light beige. At first it surprises me. The pink under his nails, the brown lines etching his palms.

We are each to the other a victory waiting to be won, a dream waiting to be realized.

After Christmas, he touches me so softly sometimes I hardly knows he's there and then with such force it's as if he wants to gather all of me up in his hands. Lying close, close, closer. Talking together. Moving together. I try to breathe with him, but his breath is so fast, I am breathless and starved for air. I don't know how he does it, how he lives breathing like that. We make love as though to claim each other, as though to learn each orifice, each possibility of each other's bodies. As though to reinvent the world.

All that winter we lay in each others' arms, talking, kissing, licking, loving. The snow piles up against the windows, drifts catch in the panes. The wind roams across the white covered plains, across beige bristles of corn stubble. It wails through his house on West Harrison, serenading us, a solitary note. His paintings surround us. Our perfect place.

I want to be inside him and see the world through his eyes, experience his history with him, know him completely. We tell each other secrets we have never shared, ease away vulnerabilities. The racial, religious, class difference are a source of fascination. We cannot get enough of each other. We cannot give enough of ourselves. I know I could be faithful to this man. I know he will be faithful to me. We are the first lovers in the world. I can make this happen. I can make this work.

"See that star out there?" He points to a star caught in the window next to his bed.

"Want to make a wish?"

"No. Serious now. See that star alone in the dark night sky? See it shining all by itself? That's how we'll be if you stay with me."

"Shining stars?"

"No. Alone."

"Alone. Together." It's fine with me. Safe. Our communication, our love and union will bridge any gap. I'm convinced. Fill any need. I'm sure.

Ty slides his eyes, wet and black, over to the corners. His mouth is still and then it trembles ever so slightly. "I love you." His voice vibrates inside me.

. . .

Ty fries up some steaks and I brush bread with garlic, thyme, and melted butter.

"I can't imagine life without you," I say. "When I think of not being with you, I feel empty. Like when I was a child and thought about my parents dying and being an orphan. Chilled and abandoned without you."

"It's like a game we play, you and I, close to the edge of the world," he whispers to me after making love.

I no longer envision my life without him.

. . .

A black-and-white poster of Ty is in the window of the barber shop. He stands in the three-point position ready to charge. His head up, there is a fierce expression on his face. His fingers are spread and the veins in his hand stand in sharp relief and trace up to his forearm. At the end of the season, Ty was most valuable player, All Big Ten, coach's All-American. Football teams called and he negotiated, listening to advice from Flora, Burns, and Evashevski, his coaches. He was drafted by the Dallas Cowboys and the Texans. He was approached by the Winnipeg Blue Bombers.

Now, the photo is a source of pain. His image as the football hero is used to capture clients. He is an easy male discussion point while hair is being buzzed and cut and combed and shampooed. The barber bragged that he knew Ty. And he did. When Ty was a freshman, he tried to get his hair cut in the shop, but was refused. "We don't know how to cut your hair," he was told. "Weren't taught that in school."

There's a civil rights protest for the freedom riders and Ty has decided to march. He is one of few blacks, the only one with a high profile. He wears pale green corduroys, a baby blue short-sleeved button-down shirt. He does not wear his letter jacket. He wears, instead, a sport jacket. I march behind him. Although there's tension in the air, thick as the spring pollen, Ty's walk is easy and smooth. He carries his sign with one hand as though it is scarcely a burden.

Then he slows to walk with me. He motions to a white guy he knows vaguely. "He thinks he is doing something for us." His mouth barely moves, and I lean toward him to hear his words. "We're supposed to be indebted to him 'cause he's doing this thing, showing how great he with his unpredjudiced ways." Ty swallows and clears his throat. "Never before has he spoken in public. Never before a sign of recognition." Ty shakes his head.

"How true is the white man? Can't trust him even though he puts forth an effort, tries to cover up the previous mistakes."

I wonder, what about me? How do I fit in this?

Ty reads my mind. "Women are different. In a way, white women are white men's victims, too."

We have made a complete loop of the campus. There are now crowds of onlookers. "Hey, isn't that the football player?" I hear one ask.

We walk slow as he whispers to me. "They picket for the sake of picketing. To say, 'Gee what fun, Mom and Dad *wouldn't* be proud of me.' So I must be tolerant to fill their needs? Because they can't escape themselves?"

Then, ahead of us, there's a flurry among the onlookers. A group gathers with their backs to us surrounding a man who is shoveling. As we approach, the group parts. There's a sign, tilted in the grass, which says, "Go home outsiders." Ty's upper lip trembles in a rage he tries to control. He breaks ranks with the marchers and saunters smoothly toward the crowd. There is no anger in his amble. As he approaches, the crowd retreats.

He doesn't touch their sign. He grasps his, raises his arm and in one fast motion plunges it into the ground. The earth groans with the force of being abruptly opened. His sign is in the ground, in front of the other sign. "Freedom for all" it says.

Then he walks away, crosses campus, crosses the main street, and I see him enter the barber shop.

. . .

I smell the turpentine and oil as I walk into his apartment. Miles Davis blows his horn, lonesome and jarring. Red drips from the sky onto the chained bodies of a black man and woman. The man's arm is raised as though to threaten the sky.

Ty says, "That was my first and last protest. I'm not nonviolent." He dabs more purple tones on the woman's flesh.

I put my hand on his head. "Got him to cut it, uh?"

" 'Bout time." He stabs the brush into the turpentine.

He leans back and says, "I'm tired. I'm tired of this life of stupidity. This shit doesn't become me."

I feel alarm in my chest as he grabs me to him.

. . .

That night we go to the River Room to dance. By now I am good, by now Ty has taught me everything he knows. I can twist and jerk and fly and slide and subway. The music thumps in my heart, in my hips and sends me soaring. There is nothing but my response to the music and my playful lust with Ty. I can mash potatoes. My hips are the beat of the music. Our love making has improved our dancing and we play and push each other in the game at the edge of the world. We laugh as we twist toward each other and then ebb away, teasing. Then, a new tune plays on the juke box.

Ty's friend joins and we pretend we are a baseball team, winding up and pitching, making a slow hit and then tagging out. All the time, our hips are moving. Our laughter is the ripple of water over stones and merriment devoid of hostility or shame. His pitch is the jerk and then the release of the ball is the twist. I catch it with a monkey and pretend to run to first base and then Ty mashes over to me and tags me out. We are laughing and wet.

A slow song starts and Ty pulls me close, both arms around me. I feel the sheen of his skin and smell his aftershave, turpentine, our sex, and the musk smell of his sweat that is so dear to me now. His back, his hips tense with the movement of his thighs, his joint slightly erect against my stomach. We sway close and he sings, whispers the words in my ear, singing in a soft voice.

He pulls me even closer and whispers, "It's true. Just stay with me."

. . .

My curfew is near. We walk out of the River Room, through the cafeteria and into the Student Union. I notice a small boy. Blond, he wears shorts and a jacket and he climbs the stairs alone as though he knows where he is going. He still focuses on the mastery of his muscles as he places each foot on the stair.

"What a cute kid." His concentration touches me.

"That's the kind of boy you want," Ty says.

I jerk away. He imagines that he is merely a strange interlude in my life, soon to be obliterated by a return to the safe white world. "No. I want your child. One with black curly hair and coffee skin. You bastard."

I do not know then, do not sense then his insecurity. But regardless, he has his answer.

The next day he tells me, he's made his football decision. He can't imagine our relationship will survive him being in Texas, which is still the Deep South and dangerous for a black guy let alone an interracial couple. Besides, Winnipeg has offered him a larger bonus to sign and the coach, Bud Grant, seems excellent. "So I'll be off to Winnipeg when the term is over, when you go back to Pittsburgh."

My eyes fill with tears at the thought of our parting.

"I'm doing this for us."

CHAPTER 17

Docie has several strokes that force him to a walker. At first his speech is not impaired and then after another stroke his face no longer has his smile, his words. Then he falls in the bathroom and breaks his hip. He dies in Montefiore Hospital surrounded by his card buddies who joke about his lousy gin rummy as though he is already dead.

In Lala's garden, the late tulips are in bloom. Purple Jewel, Red Emperors, and Dutch Yellow flower in bouquets. They will be replaced by tiger lilies. When I was little, living in Chicago, Lala froze a tiger lily in a block of ice so I could see it in the winter. The flower, colors still brilliant, wavered under the crackling ice. As it melted, the edges of the flower turned brown, and when it was released from its frozen cage, the limp flower folded into itself. It had two deaths.

It is uncharacteristically warm. I can sunbathe in May. Her fountain gurgles softly. Lala's gnarled hands lie open on her ample lap. Always we eat. Conversation without food is like a plant without light. This time: cold salmon poached in white wine and capers, Stilton cheese with English biscuits.

Her thick glasses rest on the ball of her nose. She has been gardening and wears a worn supple dress. I can ask her anything and she will tell me. She gives me everything she has learned, everything she knows, all her speculations about life. She'll rip open old wounds if it informs me. I am her favorite grandchild. This is how she loves me.

This time we talk about my mother and father. This time she makes a veiled reference to my father as a ladies' man. It is oblique enough that I am not sure if she is referring to his affairs or the fact that women like him.

I do not know what Mother has told Lala. I have no interest in exposing her betrayal, but I also have no stake in keeping secrets. I tell

Lala about Donna.

Lala's hands remain open and still on her lap, her eyes follow as a goldfinch flits in the peach tree.

"David knows, one of Daddy's workmen told him. Mother has offered him a divorce, but he turns the offer around — says she must have a man."

Bees feed on the tulips, the tree. And then Lala says, "You know a few years ago, one of my women clients said to me, 'Your daughter, Nora, I don't know how she puts up with that Jake. With him screwin' everyone in town, everyone. But there she is with her head high, chin up as though nothing is going on. Smooth. Unruffled. There she is as though he is the most faithful husband in Pittsburgh.' I was furious." Lala's forehead shines with sweat. "That she would say that to me. Me, her mother. In my house. I wanted to ask that woman to leave, but before I could say a word, she said, 'Your daughter, Nora, has more pride and class than any of us. You got to hand it to her.' So after that, what did I need to say?" Lala shrugged.

Now it is my turn to watch the bees and the goldfinch. I am not surprised that he is promiscuous. I just didn't know he was famous for it. "Yeah. Can't help the flirting. Even my girlfriends. I remember when he met my friend Susie, we were children and he starts singing, *'If you knew Susie like I knew Susie, oh, oh oh, what a girl.'* I could have died. Susie was thrilled. Had a huge crush on him after that."

Neither Lala nor I laugh. It's not funny any more.

I switch into silence. "I don't see Mother's silence as pride. It's pain and confusion."

"She doesn't tell me. She doesn't tell anyone."

"Faith?"

Lala brings up a shoulder in a small jerk, a gesture that says she doesn't know.

I had not realize until now the full burden of Mother's shame.

"I remember your father's mother, Fanny," Lala says. "Such a quiet, unassuming woman. Always so proper with her white gloves, small handbag. From Russia. Her daughters surpassed her in understanding America. She stood in their shadows more and more. Helpless to tell them what to do."

"I only have one memory of her. Trying to have a party for us grandkids. Got scads of toys. Cake. Ice cream. And then she just stood and watched."

"Actually, your grandmother was sick, weak. After your father was born, what was it nine births, seven still living? She may have said 'Enough!' Supposedly, your grandfather was involved with the housekeeper." The goldfinch lands on the fountain. It sweeps through a sprinkle of water and then ruffles its feathers. We watch it dart to and fro under the spray.

"Does Mother know all this?"

"She keeps her own counsel. I thought she didn't know about Jake, or was pretending," Lala says.

"Daddy's denial, I guess, allows Mother to go back and forth between the illusion of his fidelity and her knowledge of him as a Don Juan. Keeps her hanging."

"Maybe she's decided to wait him out." Lala passes me the poached salmon. The table is glass and our feet, wavy like heat on a road, are visible. We are both shoeless. Laddy is dead. Lala's crossed toes are dry, but no longer painful. Her body has finally accommodated itself to them. Lala's eyes are wet. She inhales a gasp of air that sucks in the sorrows of the garden. "My poor baby," she says.

Something fractures inside me. My father's infidelity is no longer a drama, a game. I feel my mother's sorrow. I feel Lala's yearning to keep her daughter safe. I wipe my eyes with the cloth napkin.

"Love. I married Docie for great love. I know now this is so, for I continued to love him years after he had ceased to be romantically in love with me. During the depression your grandfather began a relationship." Lala shakes her head again. And sips from some ice tea. "Ruth." She says the name as though she is amazed she can say the word without clouds gathering and lightening striking.

I eat my salmon. It is everywhere, I think.

"It was worse than his gambling. You know, for ten years, I gave myself to him. All of myself. Every corner. Completely and without question. More than I knew I even could or had. Or probably should have. He opened doors in me I did not know were there." Lala's eyes fill with tears. "A long time ago. A long, long time ago. God what's it been? A half a century."

"Anyway. And then the card playing. He played with our extra money. So," Lala shrugs. "I did what I had to. Worked. And then Ruth. She was his best friend, he told me. They worked together, he told me.

Colleagues at the hospital." Lala turns to me for an aside. "She was a social worker. The first one there. He talked to her on the phone. At night. They met at the Waldorf for dinner. They walked around Schenley Park. He denied the affair. Denied it."

Lala's rolled-down stockings make a soft sausage bulge above her knees. Her hands rest on this bulge now. "I imagined her young. Thin." She gestures to her stomach. "Imagined that was why he wanted her. She was slim. Beautiful. This woman who had taken him from me, from our family. I went to the hospital to take a look at her. She was fatter than me. Not so young. Younger, but not so young. She was merely Jewish. That's all." Lala stops, the fountain gurgles, the bees hum their song. "Men always are little boys. They never grow up. Never. They eventually go home to Mama. One way or the other."

My grandfather? My Docie. So precise. So cool. Eating his toast with each meal in small bites. His mustache trimmed. Blue veins knot the back of his hands, trace up his arms under translucent skin.

"It was the depression." Lala stops. Time for a history lesson. Her voice shifts, from the tear-clotted deep register, up several notes. "During the depression, your grandfather had to sell his practice. Pup was fired from the bus company six months before his thirty-years retirement. So Pup and Mum came to live with us. After Cassie died, we had Faith and Penny. Then Docie's parents and sister came to live with us and your mother came home from Bucknell to work at the DPW. So there were twelve in this house." The goldfinch finishes his bath and smoothes his bright feathers with his beak. He watches us from the peach tree. "The ladies next door burned all their furniture one winter to stay warm. Couldn't afford coal and too proud to tell anyone.

"Anyway, all through this ordeal, Docie regularly disappeared with her. For long Sunday afternoons at the Phipps Conservatory, or the Carnegie Museum. He kept saying they were friends. Just friends. She was his best friend. They were not sexually involved. But it didn't matter. They were always together. I was dismal in my feeling about him, about us. After Cassie's death, and Docie's surgery — the stomach operation where it was touch and go for months. And now this. The depression. This affair? I cried at the drop of a hat. I was beside myself with grief. Beside myself. Almost mad, I think, with anguish." She closes her eyes tight and clenches her fists. "Oh God. Oh God. Still working, taking care of everybody. And Faith and Penny. Then this. What we endure. What we can endure."

Lala shifts in her chair. Her cheeks are wet. She takes her glasses off and wipes her cheeks with her napkin. Sips some tea. Begins talking again. "Finally, I went to Ruth's parents. I told them their daughter was involved with my husband. That they were the talk of the hospital. I had been getting warning calls. They were seen having lunch, taking walks. It was damaging both their reputations. My husband was the support of five children, two sets of parents. They had to control their daughter. So they arranged a marriage for Ruth and she left for New York." Lala spreads a cracker with Stilton cheese. It cracks like fire when she bites it.

I gaze at the pond of grass as though it is a stretching, yawning sea. For a moment we are ladies at a lawn party.

"I don't know. Maybe I didn't love him enough. Too busy missing Cassie and taking care of her babies. Maybe I just didn't love him hard enough."

"I can't imagine you not loving enough," I say.

"It didn't matter. I mean, she was in New York, but they wrote. She was his friend. 'We're going to write.' He informed me." Lala punctuates each word with a jerk of her head imitating Docie. "What could I do?" She shrugs. "Nothing. At first those damn letters came every week. Then every month. So every month, for all those years, amongst the mail, I'd see that turquoise spider writing on an envelope. I'd leave it under the chime clock just like all the other mail. He'd pick it up, disappear to his desk and then spend the evening reading. Rereading. Poring over her letter and writing her back. So what did I stop?" She pauses.

"Then on his deathbed, just about the last thing, he says is, 'Laura, tell Ruth. Please. Tell Ruth. Make sure she knows.' He held my hand tight as though for dear life and talked about her."

CHAPTER 18

I am back at the University of Pittsburgh for my senior year. Mother is finishing up her undergraduate degree, also at Pitt. We drive to school together. Mother is galvanized by her studies. "Listen to this," she interrupts my reading, "Listen to what Goffman says about institutionalization."

The Friday night poker games have stopped. Night after night, my father reads with his socks off, playing with his toes. He reads Thomas Mann and Jules Romain, working his way through the entire *Men of Good Will*. He collects first editions of Freud's books and stacks them next to Hemingway and Faulkner and Sandburg and Theodore White. Smoke curdles around him. Bach comes from the stereo. Outside our windows, the forest, silent and cool, beckons. He swings open the patio door. "It's a singing day," he flings his arms wide. "It's a singing day." He inhales as though to gather sun, sky, forest into his lungs and then closes his eyes, memorizing the images.

David no longer talks of blackmailing him. He roams the city looking to get laid and then goes off to college.

My parents disapprove of Ty. It is 1962. No one is ready for this but me and him. Ty is playing Canadian football and we are usually separated. He will be unfaithful, my father warns. He will pimp me and have me walking the streets.

Daddy threatens to have Ty and his family investigated. This will prove his infidelity. It will at least prove what terrible credit they have. Nothing comes of this. Their credit is excellent. They are a salt-of-the-earth working-class family. My father knows I am not my mother. I would not stay with an unfaithful man. I would not stay with a man if I were unfaithful.

Between work and school and studying and reading, there is dinner. We gather in the dining area and sit in our customary places.

Daddy and Mother drink martinis. One night at dinner, I describe a monograph I am reading for primate anthropology class on the social organization of gibbons. I put down my fork and announce, "Gibbons are monogamous."

"Can't be. No primate is monogamous," Daddy says and then launches into a discussion of estrus cycles.

"Well, this guy sat in trees somewhere and spent years watching gibbons. He should know."

"During the time he observed." Daddy works on his steak, his sharp knife slices red meat in neat cubes.

"They're monogamous. In nuclear family units." I stop eating. We sit across from each other, identical brown eyes glaring.

"Do these gibbons have estrus? Yes. of course. In *Civilization and Its Discontents,* Freud says that originally all mankind lived in herds, all the males fought over the females. The sons, cannibal savages that they were, killed and then devoured the herd leader, the father."

Steak, barely warm at the center, bleeds on my plate.

My father holds his knife and fork. "They did this to gain sexual access to the females — their own mothers and sisters. This proves our basic promiscuous nature. Human males lust after every female, even mother and sister."

"Help yourself to some salad." Mother holds the wooden salad bowl across the table to me.

And daughter? I wonder but do not dare say out loud.

Daddy's lemony cologne mixes with the tartness from the salad dressing, the greasy smell of the meat.

"The human female has no heat," I counter. "This distinguishes us from the other mammals. Makes continual sex necessary for reproduction. Lucky us. Besides, Freud is not modern, scientific anthropology." I use tongs to place lettuce on my plate, ignoring the meat.

"Thereby the birth of the incest taboo," Daddy concludes.

The next night the argument continues. I buttress my point with additional primate monographs, he pulls in more Freud.

He rationalizes his behavior, I think. But I say, "Even Kinsey says at least forty percent of men, men right here in America now, are faithful."

"So far. They are faithful so far and that's what they tell the researcher." He pins me with his eyes unflinching, his dark eyes deep and sad and lonely and loving as he claims his sovereign right. "Men are unfaithful." He inhales. And waits.

I blink at what he has admitted.

His fingertips are on the table edge as though he will push himself away. He is frantic to protect me, to keep from the hostile, malevolent society I determinedly stroll toward. For months, we have trod on the edge of this and he has just walked off the cliff.

"Just because you are, just because men in this family are, doesn't mean all men are."

"Believe me, my darling daughter. Gibbons may be monogamous, men aren't. Satisfy this sexual itch you have. But marry well. You can love lots of men." His voice is soft.

CHAPTER 19

Ty writes: *All is sorrow at your parting. The heavens in sympathy shed tears and the ground is as wet as my heart. I wanted to tell you many things that time would not allow and they passed unspoken, trapped in the maze of my mind. Now far from their original context, I want to tell you.*

I am lonely. I ache all over. I want to cry, but can't even though my whole body and heart are sobbing. As you left for the airport, you looked so well, so lovely. A brief kiss before you went. Your head high, proud, strong. You entered the plane. My heart sang come back. It screamed, but there was silence. You were gone.

I don't want to lose you. There is something within me driving me to you. Not because you're white, not even because you're a woman. But because I love you deeply, love without limits, love with nods of understanding. I doubt that there is a hate strong enough to creep into our hearts and break the bond of friendship we have. The ghost of our lost love, lost desire would haunt us both forever. We would think of what is and what could have been. We would have cheated ourselves. Our lives would never be quite fulfilled. Things familiar will be only endurable.

When you found me, I was crippled. Now I'm free. Free with myself. Free in your arms.

After the Argonaut football game, he comes to town, and we meet in the Ellis Hotel. The bar near the lobby is dark, smells of scotch and stale cigarettes. Our room contains only a bed and sunlight. We buy grapes and cheese and crackers and make love, talk, eat, make love. Ty pours wine on my stomach and laps it up and we are close, closer, closer. It has been so long since I've been with him that our lust is fierce. We plunge into each other. Try to scoop each other up, possess each other, get him deeper and deeper inside me. Become one.

That night, we leave our hotel, eat ribs and white bread, then go to Crawford's Bar and Grill. We sit there drinking screwdrivers and listening to Art Blakey.

Later that night, after he enters me, Ty sings, *a love supreme, a love supreme*... and rides with the cadence of the music until we drift away into sleep. We're still connected as if glued by sweat to each other. The next day, he is gone.

I write: *I have just returned from being with you — being part woman, part animal, part challenger, part challenged. You make me feel beautiful. No other man has done that. With you, I'm a different person. Savage, perhaps, but I want you so badly that savagery, violence seems to pull me closer to you. It seems to transform me into the raw me. Not the good me, or the gentle me, but the raw me. Hair prickling, nerves showing. And yet you make me feel gentle and kind and I like me like that. You rekindle me. You destroy my self-illusion... and show me a me I can truly love and give to you.*

Why does love want the impossible? I want to crawl inside you and feel what it feels like when you swallow milk, when crusty bread hurts your mouth, when you touch me. I want to hear Blakey's beats with your ears, see the blue of your blue sky, see what I look like, what the snow looks like. Why does love want the impossible? No other man can have me. Not as you have me now.

CHAPTER 20

Uncle Isaac dies of a heart attack. He is forty-eight. An earlier attack, six months before, left him weak, blue, whispering, gasping for air. Daddy and he reconciled and we visited his apartment where Isaac sat, his books and papers surrounding him, fish swimming in endless circles beside him. The funeral is over. Tears are cold on our faces. My father's sisters, a chorus of dark specters, whispered about their bodies and picked at their food. Aunt Mildred was drunk. Isaac's son, Steve, flew home from Oxford and his Rhodes Scholarship, hair below his ears. He wore Levi's and carried a glass filled with Cutty Sark, neat. Sara, home from Antioch, whispered of her affair with the current jazz star.

On the way to the car, I say to Mother, "His life is erased. Like that." I snap my fingers. "Everyone just talked about their own mundane lives. Their own bullshit."

"That's what the funeral is for. To remind us of life," Mother says. Daddy walks hunched over, keys already in his hand, to the car.

On the drive home, rain drops diamonds on the windshield, a soft tattoo on the roof. I am in the back, cocooned from the black night. Daddy drives. "I wish Mildred hadn't told him," his voice is heavy. "Isaac was sick, dying."

"She was mending their relationship. Trying to get close to him, to finally have a modicum of honesty and truth." Mother's voice is even. In the dark, they have forgotten I am in the back seat of the rushing car.

"You don't confess affairs to your dying husband. She broke his heart. Literally. Just broke his heart."

"She was haunted, Jake. All those woman in all those cities. Look what it did. To them." I hear her inhale. "To us." I smell Mother's flowery Joy perfume.

"Should have denied it to the end. It's always better not to know," he says.

"It is?" Mother asks.

The swishing of the wipers reveal a wavy world lost to the pointillism of raindrops.

"There're all neurasthenic. My family. Neurasthenic."

No one knows what to say to this pronouncement. This welling of disappointment. We drive through blackness while lights make tunnels for us to follow.

. . .

Later that night, vomit gushes out of Daddy's mouth. It heaves in great forceful streams, splashes over the floor, walls, ceiling as he rushes to the toilet.

"Let me take you to the hospital," Mother says.

"Don't be silly. It's something I ate. That fish at the funeral."

CHAPTER 21

Ty plays a game in Montreal, gets the next two days off, and drives to Pittsburgh. It's three in the morning when we meet in a friend's apartment, fall into each other's arms, smother each other with kisses, shed clothes on the way to the bedroom, and make love till our bodies glisten. In the morning, I throw on a pair of jeans and a T shirt, still smelling of his sweat and sex. We relax at a dinette table in front of a window of the apartment, drink coffee and eat toast and jam. My body is mellow from making love, from the close coziness of sleeping together. Sunlight burnishes our held hands in irregular patches. We'll spend our day together at the Carnegie Art Museum.

Bang. A sharp punch to the door.

We extricate our hands. Bolt upright in our chairs.

Bang. It reverberates. Booms around the room. The door trembles on its hinges.

Ty pushes his chair back; the legs scrape the floor.

Bang.

Ty stands, bent forward slightly, ready to spring.

"Open up. It's the police." Words thunder.

The police?

Ty strides to the door, unbolts the lock, and opens it. There are two policemen and my father. They enter the apartment as though it is theirs. My heart beats in my ears.

One policeman, portly enough to stretch the fabric on his blue uniform, says, "We're checking out what's going on here." His words crash around the walls of the close apartment.

"We're having toast and coffee." My voice cracks. My God. They're here to arrest Ty. Arrest me.

Ty's upper lip trembles, his hand is clenched.

My father is pale. He hasn't acknowledged me or Ty. He stands as though removed, but curious.

No one screams, but it feels as if we are all screaming.

Ty could be hauled off to a jail cell. Not able to return to his football team. My heart pounds. Taken to the station and beaten. Bloody. Images evoked by the civil rights movement hit my mind. Black men beaten, killed, castrated. Lynched. My heart feels as if it's roaring around my chest, pounding my ribs.

"What's the problem here? No one is doing anything illegal." Ty's voice is even, too even. He speaks gently and wets his lips with his tongue.

"We've had complaints from the neighbors. Wondering what was going on," says the other policemen. His glasses smeared with grease.

Ty nods. "We've been quiet, officer."

"Well. A Negro man in this neighborhood... They don't come in this neighborhood." The fat officer rubs his hand through black hair.

The other officer pushes his glasses up his nose. "There's the Mann Act. Transporting across state lines for immoral purposes."

Now I know about the Mann Act. It was used to arrest Chuck Berry for his romances with young white girls.

I'm confused. "I don't get it. You're accusing me?" My throat is parched as I try to swallow. They're going to arrest me. Daddy is going to arrest me.

The fat policemen looks down, shuffles a clipboard of papers one hand to the other, and then glances to my father.

"I didn't transport her across any state lines." Ty's voice is deliberate, nonthreatening. That of the artist, not the football player. Then Ty notices my father. He is gray. Blue circles under his eyes. He stands mutely, his arms hanging. Shifting from foot to foot.

"Daddy?" He looks sick. What if he has another heart attack?

"Mr. Pearlman? Are you okay?" Ty asks.

I am frozen. My fury at my father is dwarfed by fear of losing him.

Ty drags a chair from the table and puts it behind him. "Here. Sit down. You need to sit down."

Daddy stands and wipes his forehead and shakes his head no. He places his hand on his chest.

"Please, Mr. Pearlman. There's a chair now. You can sit," Ty leans toward him.

Daddy sits. He inhales deeply.

"We all need to calm down," Ty says. "Let me get you some water." He brings him a glass of water. "Maybe you'll feel better."

My father takes a sip of water and then places it on the floor. He hunts in his pocket and takes some medicine.

The light is clear and white. Everything is slow. My father drinks the water, his Adam's apple slides with each swallow, the knot of his tie bobs. His hands with the familiar crumbled nail and sparse hairs fumble with the lid to his medicine. I try to grab some air. I watch the policemen stand mutely, the fat one's mouth opens and then closes. The other's glasses blur his eyes. Ty's upper lip is still. He waits. My father loosens his tie.

Daddy sits in the chair, still blue. Ty and I and the two policeman stand.

"Daddy, are you okay?" My voice shakes, cracks.

"Too much excitement," Ty states.

"I'm fine." Daddy brushes us all away with a wave of his hand.

Good. He's okay. He sits alone in the middle of the room, while the rest of us stand.

The policeman with glasses says, "I want to talk to you." He points to Ty.

The policemen take Ty outside. Their voices are muffled by the door. I cannot make out their words. My father and I are alone. "How could you do this?"

He sips the water Ty brought for him.

"Are you all right?"

"Fine. Fine." He stands. "Too much melodrama. What parents do for their children." He lets the phrase stand complete and shoots me a displeased look. "You don't know, can't imagine how I love you."

This doesn't seem like love to me, I think. Something else, but not love.

The policemen and Ty reenter the apartment. "Mr. Pearlman."

They leave. Suddenly I'm in Ty's arms and crying. "I'm so scared," I whisper. "This is unreal. I can't believe it and we're in it." I wipe my tears away on his shirt. I feel him trembling. I feel the flexing of his shoulder muscles, his forearms around me. "Are you okay?"

"I told the police I love you. You love me. I haven't done anything wrong. You're almost twenty-one. Two adults. This will be okay. Just sit tight." His words are so different than his heart pounding in my chest. My heart pulsing in my neck.

"What do you mean? This happened."

"Your father's upset."

When they return, I'm still in Ty's arms. My head deep in his chest, his arms calming me.

"We should all have dinner tomorrow night. Talk this over. You, me, Ty and your mother," Daddy says. "But now, you're coming with me."

Ty whispers, "Go. He loves you. I'll see you, talk to you tomorrow."

I am reluctant to leave Ty's protecting arms.

On the way home, my father tells me that the police couldn't do anything to me. They couldn't activate the Mann Act because I hadn't left the state; they couldn't arrest Ty for statutory rape because of my age. It is obvious Ty and I love each other. They were sorry, but there was nothing they could do. They understood my father's pain and concern.

"Even those fucking cops see the love Ty and I have for each other. Why can't you?" I maximize my victory. But then my concern for him wipes away my triumph.

CHAPTER 22

The next night, Ty drives to our house in the forest. The trees have not completely relinquished their leaves. When he arrives, sunlight drifts in the west windows to gild the remaining leaves. My father and mother drink Martinis. They offer Ty one, but he declines.

I've fried up chicken to eat with fresh string beans, salad, potato. We serve the meal in the dining room, not around the kitchen table. As we eat, my mother asks Ty, "What does your father do?"

"He works in the GM foundry. Been working there almost twenty years. When he first came up north, he didn't have a car and he used to get up at four in the morning and walk to the foundry to do his shift. He also sells furniture in a friend's store some evenings and weekends."

He didn't tell the story about the Ku Klux Klan threatening him so his father had to move up north. I push my string beans around on my plate. I don't know what to say and see exactly what my parents are doing.

Ty tells them about the importance of church to his family, the fact the church added to his scholarship when he left for college.

I nibble on a chicken back, listen to Ty's careful answers, my parents' relentless questioning. I try to think of a way to help him out, but he's doing fine. He has nothing to hide but the thing he cannot. His skin color.

Ty compliments me on my chicken.

"You know who taught me," I answer and muster a weak laugh.

"What do your brothers do?" my father asks.

"One is a butcher, the other a draftsman for GM. They are both married and have children."

No one is in jail. No one has fathered scads of illegitimate children. No one is on drugs, or alcoholic.

"His family is just the salt of the earth, hard-working, churchgoing, doing what you're supposed to do kind of people." My fork stabs a tomato and lettuce. "Ty's the first one who's gone to a university."

"My brothers both have associate's degrees from the community college." Ty speaks of the importance of education to his father, his father who had to drop out of school in the eighth grade to help support his mother and because they couldn't afford the books or shoes required if he were to attend high school.

Mother serves an angel food cake with raspberries and ice cream. At this point all I want is cigarettes and coffee.

My father shifts his questions to Ty's prospects. Asking him how he's going to manage his football career and his art.

Ty hopes to have a show in Toronto and is painting when he's not playing. He's hoping to save enough money from football this year so his mother can remodel her kitchen.

It would be funny, this grilling by a father, if my life were not at stake. If I didn't care so much that these three people, each of whom I love so dearly, learn to love each other. The prospect of discord lumps in my stomach along with the green beans, the grease from the chicken, the froth of angel food cake. The three of them seem to be getting along okay. They even manage some chuckles as the dinner wears on. But my lump continues to swell.

We retire to the living room. Ty chooses a chair opposite my father. I want to sit with him on the couch, but instead I share it with Mother. Ty sits alone.

My father lights a pipe. "I wonder how much you've really considered this. I mean, if you knew that most interracial couples regret it, would that make you reconsider?"

"Not necessarily," Ty's fingers cup the curves of the swan's head on the arms of the chair, seemingly relaxed.

"I mean, if I showed you that ninety-five percent of interracial couples regret it after ten, twenty years, would that convince you?"

"I know how statistics can be manipulated."

"Ninety-five percent?"

"I would think that we'd be the five percent. The mass doesn't really say anything about the individual. I know full well how statistics don't portray reality."

My father restlessly sucks on his pipe. I know what he's thinking.

"This man is irrational. Stupid. Can't benefit from the experiences of others." I know for Ty this is a word game.

My father tries a different tack. "Most of the great thinkers, writers of your race have been against this. Richard Wright did not believe in interracial marriage."

"Really?"

My father is vague about some article or book in which Richard Wright came out against black-white marriages.

"Mr. Pearlman, Richard Wright was married to a white woman and they lived in Paris," Ty says. He does not sound arrogant, he almost whispers the words.

"I have a deal for you. You two don't see each other, contact each other, call each other, write each other for one year. After that year, if you still want to get married, you'll have my complete blessing. The complete and absolute support of both of us." He nods toward my mother. This was discussed between them.

Ty looks at me. I hadn't anticipated this, but know exactly what my father is counting on. He plays the infidelity card.

"We're already separated," I say. "And will be for a year. Isn't that enough test?"

"I'm talking no contact."

There's a wrenching inside me. I feel myself pulling apart. No contact, no word from Ty for a year? My parents' acceptance and encouragement?

"I obviously haven't talked about this with Ann," Ty says, his voice almost whispers, "but I think I might just be selfish here. I don't want to be without her for a year." He clears his throat. "I want whatever brief contact we can have through our letters, calls, and meetings."

"Not to get our blessing?"

"She and I need to talk about this. I am convinced our love would survive even your request. But I don't want to do it."

"If you really loved her, cared about her separate from yourself, you would let her go. Don't cause each other endless pain, but keep a beautiful memory. You'll end up hating each other. Let her go and don't take her into the Negro world, condemn her and your children to be at the bottom of society. Accepted nowhere."

"She is absolutely accepted by my family."

My father turns away and concentrates on emptying his pipe,

cleaning out the bowl with a metal scraper. "Think about what I've said. Look inside yourselves. Be kind."

My mother starts the dishes.

I walk Ty to his car and hold him until he has to get into the car and drive away. I know I'll see him again, but I don't know when.

CHAPTER 23

It's Halloween, a Sunday night. I am too old to go trick-or-treating and there are no pumpkins in the house. But I am not ready to relinquish the holiday. So I cook a Halloween dinner of rock Cornish game hens, tomatoes stuffed with anchovies, capers, and onions, and genoise cake. While I cook, a football game in which Ty is playing is on TV. After a hard tackle, he lies immobile on the field. I don't see him for a few plays. I hold my breath and then there he is again.

I place burnt sugar mums and red leaves in a vase and then set it on the dining room table.

"A party?" Daddy asks when he sees the setting.

"It's Halloween."

One side of his mouth goes down, a gesture which says he didn't even know.

During dinner Mother tells us about system change in large organizations. I am working on a paper on matrifocality in Negro families as a cultural transfer from polygamous West Africa. The house swirls with plumes of smoke. Great clouds hover near the ceiling. The acidity of the tomatoes is more intriguing than the sweetness of the poultry.

Daddy is researching Freud as a father. He wants to contact Anna Freud and begin interviewing her. Maybe he'll write a book. A wooden ashtray one foot square sits on the table and is filled with crimped and folded white ends like maggots in the gray ashes.

After dinner, Mother retires to her studies. Daddy and I watch TV. He has a book opened on his lap, but the movie captures him. He turns off the table lamp and we relax, Daddy and I, in the TV flicker. This is the first time we have watched TV together. Usually he is too restless to sit that long and, even at movies, he roams the lobby smoking.

The plot is about a married man and woman who meet on a commuter train. As they ride back and forth through the seasons, their love deepens. They share secrets they never told another. They support each others' dreams and hopes. The suburbs fly past their windows. Finally they spend afternoons in the city making love. It is everything they wished it would be. I feel the nubs of the silk sofa, warmed by my body.

During a commercial, we get a second helping of genoise cake. More texture than flavor, it is not delicious enough to warrant the work.

The final scenes of the movie are about to start. What will they do? Leave their families and enjoy the love and connection they have forged? No. They end their affair. Their obligations to their partners and children, their extended families, their communities are greater than their need to be together.

The acrid smell of burning hits my nose as Daddy lights another cigarette.

They will love each other in spite of separation of time and space. As the movie ends in the train station, music welling and credits rolling, they walk in opposite directions.

Daddy's eyes are red, his nose drips. Tears trickle down his face. He wipes his cheeks with his cuff. Never before have I seen Daddy cry. Not when his father died. Not when Isaac died. Never.

I hold my breath at his tears. I say nothing.

"Sad movie," he says.

I, who cry at the drop of a hat, am completely dry-eyed. "Yeah," I say flatly. I'm irritated that he dare cry over two adulterers.

He wipes his eyes again. "Well done, the way they built the plot and characters."

I wonder if his affair with Donna is over. I wonder if they made the same decision as the movie characters. It is obvious he will not leave us for her. Mother has offered him a divorce many times and each time he refuses. His loss is a new thought for me. My anger fades and I am sad for him.

Much later Mother tells me that, when they were in bed reading that night, my father put down his book, pulled her to him, and said, "I'm glad your father had Ruth."

"How can you say that?" Mother asked, thinking of the years of Lala's pain. Is Daddy thinking of himself? Is it men sticking together, rationalizing the distress they cause women?

"I'm glad he had that joy before he died."

Mother tortures herself with the message behind the words. Turns them over and inside out in her mind. Perhaps he's telling her affairs are worth the price and he'll continue regardless. Perhaps he feels there is something so freeing in an affair that it is worth the guilt. Perhaps he's telling her the affair with Donna is over. Perhaps he's telling her men need to revisit impulsive youth before they die. Perhaps that, like it or not, he is a family man.

CHAPTER 24

On an unseasonably chilly day in early November, Mother and I arrive home from Pitt to find Daddy folded over on the edge of his bed. His hair hangs damply in his face. He waves us away. "I want to sleep. Just sleep. Leave me alone." His arms crossed, hands clenching his arms, he rocks slowly. I recoil at his clamminess. He is rumpled in his pajamas. The curtains are drawn. The lights off.

My mind scatters, my fingers tremble as I call an ambulance.

"I want to stay here. Right here. In my own bed," he says. "I'm not going anywhere."

No ambulance will come to the suburb and drive him to Montefiore in the city. Dr. Rosen, my father's doctor, tells Mother to put him in the car and start driving. He'll meet us in the emergency room.

I make sandwiches of leftover Cornish hens. I gather up our schoolbooks. I have a test the next day. I try to do life as usual.

"Comb my hair," Daddy asks.

He, too, tries to do life as usual, always trying to be handsome. I run his red-handled brush through his hair and drape his camel-hair coat over his shoulders. Sweating but cold, he sways and shuffles to the car. So icy and damp I retreat at the feel of him.

"I'm cold," he complains.

It is a wet dusk, maybe that's why he is so clammy. Mother turns on the car's heater. It blows wintry air.

"Turn it off," he whispers.

"But it'll be warm in a minute. It's always cold at first," she reminds him.

"It's cold. It's cold."

"We'll wait till the car warms up." Mother turns off the heater. I listen to the tires on the asphalt and the hush of the tunnel. He feels not human, not alive. I am sick at myself that I cannot fully engage him, use my body to warm him. But I cannot. Another odor I have not smelled before covers his cologne.

"This is just indigestion," he says. "Heartburn. I ate too much at Locante's. Went to a customer's. Felt sick. Came home."

"Maybe it's warm enough now." Mother turns on the heater.

The air surges into the car like a mean breeze.

"It's cold."

"It'll be cold for just a minute," Mother says. "Let the cold air blow out."

Out of the tunnel, we cross the bridge arching across the river and hang suspended over the Triangle's cluster of sparse lights. Around the rivers, night hills twinkle as though nothing out of the ordinary is happening.

"It's still cold," he protests. Mother turns the heat off.

How will I study for my test on the Russian revolution? Daddy knows this subject cold. Maybe he'll quiz me when he gets settled. Hospitals are so boring.

I think of Ethel and Julius Rosenberg. Mother had been a "fellow traveler" of the communists until the Hitler-Stalin pact. How frightened she was at the time of the protests over the Rosenberg executions. She looked at me worried and said, "Poor Ethel. Her poor, poor babies." I sit next to Daddy in the dark cold and think about the Rosenbergs and their parentless children.

We arrive at Montefiore and Daddy moves to a wheelchair. Dr. Rosen, tall and slender with a twitching mustache, meets us. Daddy waves wanly before disappearing in an elevator. Mother goes to the hospital office. I am left in the corridor lined with plastic burgundy chairs. I open my book.

After a while, Mother joins me. "He's had a heart attack," she tells me. "They've given him morphine."

"He'll be okay, right?"

She stares at the green wall across from her. "Right now he's comfortable."

White stuffing, crenellated cotton crumbles out from a tear in the seat. I pull and twist it into a snake. Wind the snake around my finger. Keep trying to read. This is the hospital where Docie worked, where Lala and Docie met. In this maze of corridors painted institutional green. A mustiness under the antiseptic smell of alcohol and Clorox.

Daddy is alone in his room on the seventh floor. He lies under an oxygen tent, the plastic slightly blue. He feels better. He smiles at us.

He'll be fine. This is no big deal, merely a waste of a night, a hassle. He'll come home like after his last heart attack. He smiles. He'll have to quit smoking this time for sure.

"Go call Lala. Tell her to come," Mother tells me.

"I love you," I tell Daddy as I leave.

"I love you, too," he says to me.

I call Lala. Mother and I wait in the corridor. I eat my Cornish hen sandwich and hand one to her which she doesn't eat. I return to my book.

We see Daddy again. He is still under the oxygen tent. He is awake, but not smiling. Blue. I hold his hand. He is not so cold. Good. I try to tell him about my book, but I see he is not interested. He moves restlessly in his bed crumpling the light blue blanket.

"Do you want some water?" Mother asks.

He shakes his head, his mouth a tight line.

Mother covers his feet with the blanket. Then pats his shoulder.

Daddy rocks back and forth and clutches his chest. Moans, throws off his covers. Mother grabs his right hand. We are on either side of the bed. I am by his left hand, the one with the crumbled thumbnail.

His eyes roll in their sockets. He bolts upright. He turns his head from side to side. Rocks. His heart, my heart pounds all around us, beats the walls of the room. Beats in my ears. His eyes search, roam.

Then he stops moving and inhales. His eyes widen. "I'm dying." He says it furious, but terrified.

A drum beats in my throat, my ears. The room has a peculiar blur. He sinks back to the pillows.

"I love you," Mother says.

We are shoved into a lounge with vaguely musty chairs and an upholstered sofa with a coffee table in front of it. The room is foggy, clouds of smoke trapped in it. We pace in separate spheres, my mother and I. I don't know how long we master our routines.

Dr. Rosen enters, chewing the corner of his mustache. "He's gone."

Dead. He must mean. He's dead.

"Two young brothers," Dr. Rosen says. "My God, younger than me."

My father is forty-four. My Uncle Isaac has been dead five weeks.

I wander the room. Its window looks out over buildings still sooty from the steel mills. I lean out.

Dr. Rosen jerks me away.

"I was just trying to get some air." I wasn't going to jump.

He leads me to the grimy sofa and pours a red liquid. I watch it surge like waves at sea and wonder what it is. I've never seen a liquid leap and bounce on its own.

"It's phenobarb. Drink it."

"When it stops jumping out of the glass," I tell him.

He guides my hand to my mouth.

Lala arrives. Her eyes take us in. Me on the sofa. Mother stands immobile in the center of the room, her hands hug her arms, holding herself together. Dr. Rosen slumps in a chair, gazing at the coffee table.

Lala's eyes go dark and wet and soft. Her cheeks sag, her mouth becomes a firm line in her face. She shakes her head slowly from side to side. Then Mother is in her arms, sobbing. The three of us hold each other in the brown gray mustiness wetting our cheeks and each other's shoulders.

CHAPTER 25

I pick David up from the airport . We don't speak, we get in the car and I drive home silently winding through gray freeways and grimy tunnels. Once home, David turns on Porky Chadwick on WAMO and the living room is filled with doo wop music, the Platters and the Flamingos sliding a cappella voices. He moves to the angry staccato. I join him. Silently we dance. Separately gyrating, not touching each other. We move to the African heartbeat slowly. Fast. Furious. Then we get back in the car and I drive him to see Daddy at Schugar's funeral home.

After the funeral, David wants to stay home and run Daddy's business. He hates college anyway.

Mother says, "You need to continue life as though Jake hasn't died. You need to finish your plans."

He returns to college.

The king-size bed swallows my mother. She wants me to sleep with her. I get in the bed. She tosses. She can't bear me next to her, where my father slept all those years. I get out and step on Daddy's red-handled brush. His hair woven in the bristles. His final hairs. Mother relinquishes the attempt to sleep and sits at the pink marble table. "Come sit with me. Come talk to me." The marble feels cool under my arms. We light cigarettes.

"If only we had come home sooner, we could have gotten him there in time."

I frown. "It was probably too late. He was so cold when we got home."

"He was obviously ill after Isaac's funeral. Remember him vomiting and blaming it on bad fish he had eaten? Projectile vomiting, that's what that was. A heart attack. I should have made him go to the hospital then."

"You couldn't make him do anything." We search for a turning point in the details of the last five weeks.

"He shouldn't have had that root canal done. Too traumatic. And that fight with a buyer. So much violence so close to the end. If I had just made him go, he'd be alive. One of those times. Any of those times."

"Don't blame yourself." I wonder if she adds the scene with the cops and Ty.

When I pick up one of Daddy's navy silk shirts and hang it up, I smell his Auvergne cologne heavy in his closet. I stand between his soft embroidered shirts, his gray silk suits, inhaling his aroma. My head buried in him, my sorrow so full that I cannot move. I am stunned. How did this happen? Could happen? With his smell around me, it is as though he's only gone to work, to play poker, to eat at Locante's.

. . .

The next night we begin again. "Did you see Donna at the funeral?" Mother asks. "So upset. Her eyelids swollen."

"I didn't know she was there."

"She should have been with us. One of the prime mourners."

I frown and gently brush the ash off my cigarette.

"Imagine how she felt. Jake was the love of her life. A young girl like that and there she is having to hide her feelings. Her lover suddenly dead. And she had to pretend to the world that he was merely her boss."

Mother retrieves a Sara Lee pecan coffee cake from the freezer and puts it in the oven. "He did a great disservice to her. Seducing that young girl and promising her God knows what that he never delivered." Mother wears a pink flowered robe. I am in a pink velour.

"She is my age, Mother. My age."

"Not your age. Older."

"One year older. And I know not to mess with a married man."

Mother inhales, the smoke a cloud around her. "It's not always that easy." She flicks the ash from her cigarette. The tray fills with ashes soft as feathers. Gentle cylinders grow from the glow of our cigarettes. Ashes joining ashes that must have been Daddy's. I wonder if we'll ever empty the ash tray.

The next night, too, Mother is up wanting me to sit with her, smoke with her, talk with her. "Was it that Donna was young and gorgeous and tall and skinny? Was it that they worked together? Maybe she wanted his money."

I pick a pecan out of the Sara Lee coffee cake, crunch it between my teeth.

"Maybe she pursued him, threw herself at him, seduced him."

Donna as the huntress doesn't sit with me. I say, "Gibbons are monogamous. Daddy wasn't. She wouldn't have had to work very hard."

The dawn is a light streak in the window. "Well," Mother continues, "maybe she turned a little roll in the hay into a big deal. Clutched at him. Wouldn't let him get away. Made him depend on her in the business." Mother picks up a pecan. A thread of icing like an umbilical cord connects it to the coffee cake.

"It's all meaningless," I say.

"What do you mean?" Her eyes are light green. It's as though they lost their depth.

"It doesn't matter." I look away from her pale eyes.

"You don't know what it was like between Jake and me. The love we had."

I am not embarrassed by this, or surprised. I remember catching them kissing in the kitchen, outside the bath. Not the requisite pecks of married couples. Not even the kisses of movie lovers. Mother was hidden by his arms. He bent over her. Their mouths linked them together, their bodies pressed close. Melted. Yearning.

"Maybe it was over. Maybe that's what Jake was trying to tell me when he made that comment about Docie. It was over, but he was glad he had it. " She pops the pecan in her mouth. "A cheap thrill on the side." She picks up the cigarette and instead arches an eyebrow and asks, "I wonder if he was faithful to her?" She inhales, shuts her eyes. "Maybe I just didn't love him enough somehow. I don't know," she shrugs. "Hard enough. Somehow."

"He loved you, Mother. I know that. Donna was a diversion. And you and he would have gone on and been happy. He just died before you could get to that chapter. He died in the middle. Too fucking early."

Aunt Mildred, bone thin, brings me her leftover yarn. I begin knitting. I sit and knit squares to keep my hands busy, to keep myself awake while Mother talks. Dawn becomes my signal to go to bed, then Mother will relinquish me. I drag myself through my classes, trying to complete a paper on anti-Semitism in Germany before 1935.

. . .

David calls from his dorm. The men on his floor complain that he wakes them up. He screams blood-curdling howls, and they bolt awake fearing someone is being killed. He doesn't remember a thing.

"Finish the term out. Finish the year up," Mother orders.

Mother continues to question her life with Daddy. "Donna is just one of many, she just lasted longer."

"Life is meaningless. It's all meaningless." I don't know if I say it or if I merely think it.

"Maybe it's just that we know about her, that this one has a name," Mother says.

"There's no point in our lives if we can disappear at any moment without finishing. No point." I wind yarn into balls, around and around go my hands.

"What do you mean?" Her words lack emphasis.

"It's all meaningless. There's gotta be a reasoned, planned-out end that justifies it all. Illuminates the whole. We can't just go and die right smack-dab in the middle. Without finishing."

"Well, he did." Mother draws on her cigarette.

I knit squares just to make them. Odd sizes. I cast on willy-nilly and quit when the yarn runs out. Just like Daddy's life, but the length of yarn is clearly finite. From the beginning I know that the square I'm knitting is useless.

"He could have had her, he could have left me. God knows I gave him the chance, showed him the door. He must have loved me more. Wanted me more." She inhales her cigarette and the smoke travels out her mouth and up her nostrils.

"He loved you, Mother."

"He did. Must have."

"It's all meaningless. Unknowable anyway."

"Quit saying that. It's not. We just don't know the meaning."

"How can we judge his life when he didn't get to finish it?"

Mother blinks as though startled, "Life is finished when you die. Period. We make what sense we wish to. Or can."

I assumed we would have the chance to happily conclude all the story elements, unmask all the characters, make all the moral decisions finally, tie up the loose ends. I thought I could live a complete narrative and create my role. I thought I could be whatever I wanted to be. He promised me that. How can I, if I might die at any moment? Before I accomplish my meaning?

CHAPTER 26

Mother must decide whether to liquidate or manage Oxxford's Furniture Galleries. She dresses in a powder-blue suit, a pillbox hat, white gloves, Elizabeth Arden Sunny Coral lipstick and drives off in the Buick to work with Donna.

The topics around the marble table change as Mother's problems at the store displace her and Daddy's marriage. She announces small victories. The store was rated AAA by Dunn and Bradstreet, a triumph in view of the bankruptcy five years previous. "He would have been so proud. So relieved." Mother wipes away a tear.

A photography studio sends a notice that Carl Jung's pictures are ready to be picked up. Mother recognizes Daddy's playfulness and brings the photographs home. They were taken the week before he died. A pipe is firmly between his lips, black eyes pierce the future, his smoldering sexuality and vitality obvious. I search his face, the position of his hand, for a clue that death was imminent. None. I study the shadow his ear makes on his neck. None foretell the sudden collapse. No hint of his meager future. He is simply in one of his affected postures, looking thirty, looking as if he still had decades to declare the days singing and the nights humming.

Mother laughs. "No matter what. He was exciting. Unpredictable. Each moment an adventure. He made the humdrum a party." Eyes gleaming, she searches his picture again. "It was worth it, darling. I'd do it all again." Her finger traces his jaw line and then stops on his lips as though she feels moisture there. "I could never have stood a husband who was merely prosaic, lackluster. No matter how faithful."

I, of course, want it all. An exciting husband without the drama of infidelity. I want to win.

. . .

Mother arrives home waving several pieces of paper. "Guess what I found." Her face is flushed. "These are bills from call girls. Jake used them to repay favors. I called them and each of them went on and on about what a wonderful man he was. How much he helped them with their problems. Always willing to listen. An honest businessman. He furnished their apartments."

"Yeah. I bet."

"I can forget the balance due. They were worried about me, about you and your brother. They knew all about Jake's children. He must have talked about you a lot." She puts the bill down. Her eyes shine with tears, but she smiles. "Your father was a kind and generous man. So many different kinds of people liked him."

I wonder if he used the prostitutes himself. Cheating on Donna, cheating on Mother. Infinite cheating. But I say nothing.

"Funny how you discover someone again looking through all the little odds and ends they leave." Mother tilts her head and wrinkles up her nose. "Well, not discover them exactly, but see them from a different focus."

"Pimps and aluminum-siding men and call girls and God knows what kinds of crooks that hung out at Locante's. He was fascinated with the underworld."

She nods, "He liked people." She draws on her cigarette, automatically. "I don't know why you need to diminish him."

"I don't know why you need to put a halo on him," I reply.

"You're angry at him for dying and leaving you." She leaves the room.

No, I think. I'm angry at him for cheating on you, Mother. I'm angry at him for distorting my view of the world. I try to put some balance in your glorification of him. But she's gone before I have the composure to say it.

The next night, she says, "I did something mean," but there's a triumphant gleam in her eye. "I showed Donna the bills from the call girls." I imagine Mother with a sly smile asking, "I wonder what this is?" A picture of innocence as she hands the sheets of paper to Donna.

"Donna got green and left. Gone for most of the day. Came back with red-rimmed eyes." Mother smirks, smoke from her cigarette curls upward in an endless plume. She brings the cigarette to her mouth. "She didn't have a clue."

The trekking to Pitt, sitting up all night with Mother, knitting, seeing Ty when one of his games is a bus ride away, exhausts me. I get a B-minus on an anti-Semitism paper. I've simply spewed out information without synthesizing it. I shrug. I'll still graduate on time and then what?

Christmas is my twenty-first birthday. Mother gives me a necklace of coral cylinders and the card is signed, as her cards customarily are, with her and Daddy's name. I have a sudden memory from a few years back. On my birthday, I received four bottles of perfume from Daddy. Mother didn't know of this present. He picked them out. A first. Each of the bottles was topped by a different colored costume jewel — an emerald, a ruby, an amethyst, and a diamond — circled with small rhinestones. I put the bottles on my dresser and used the perfume sparingly. I loved them, especially because Daddy had picked them for me. I wanted them to last.

Some time later, Donna asked me how I liked them. Was she with my father when he picked them out? Unaware of my cascading mind, she said, "Oh, good. You father asked me to pick something for you and I hoped you'd like 'em." So it was her all along.

I look at the card now. Everyone pretends to give me things from my father. I wonder what he has given me. The jewel-topped perfume bottles are still on my dresser. Their musk smell throbs at my temples, my wrists. I love them too much to throw them away.

Ty sends me a package of presents. I open them in my own private ritual. A white linen dress with bright flowers, a cranberry suede coat, and one of his letters with drawings of children.

After New Year, Mother comes home from work smiling about a deal she made. "I couldn't do this without Donna."

I bristle.

"She knows all about the business and she's teaching me. Jake wasn't a detail man and all the files, all the bills, receivable and payable, are in disarray. Thrown every which way."

"I think you should fire her."

"Fire her? I need her." Mother stabs her cigarette out on a shell. "We need her."

"I don't know how you do it. Work with her. See her. Have lunch with her. Be her friend. Slide in and out of awareness of their affair."

Mother looks at the space on the wall behind me. "Well, he never wanted a divorce. He couldn't be faithful to anyone. And he chose me."

She chews on the corner of her lip.

I think, Oh, Mother. You deserved so much more. So much better.

"Imagine how it must be for her. There's no men in her life. Just work. Just her apartment. Not much of a life for a young girl. We're all mourning. All three of us."

"How cozy."

"Besides, running the store is the last thing I can do for him," she inhales. "And that was then and this is now."

Through the window, I see a chalky stripe on the horizon as another day begins. It is slanted as though the world has slightly shifted. "Do you talk about it? Acknowledge it?" I ask.

"No. Of course not."

I am surprised. My mother irons everything out with careful words and believes that integrity exists between people through self-revelation, communication.

"I don't want to tell her I know and watch her deny it for my sake. I don't want to hear about their relationship." She shrugs. "And I certainly don't want to talk about how he was in bed."

"So you pretend she wasn't his lover?"

"No one's pretending. We know. We both know we know. There's nothing to say." Mother closes her eyes.

CHAPTER 27

Ty is back at Iowa, finishing up his degree. He rents an apartment, a basement room at Black's, where many artists, writers, musicians live. Black's is a rabbit warren, every nook and cranny turned into a dwelling space for students and then promiscuously decorated with Black's collection of stained glass windows, bricks, oriental rugs, lunch booths from a restaurant that went out of business. Ty does not have a phone. Our letters fly across the Midwest.

I am also writing my friend Cassandra, a dark-haired girl with shocking green eyes from Chicago. While studying art and working on writing children's books, she lives in a small stone house next to Ty's basement room.

Her letter arrives before his does. There was a terrible storm. The lightening and thunder crashed around her tiny house. A bolt came in the window and etched a line across a rug. All those weird, dwarfed houses, like something out of Bosch. It was a nightmare. It was the end of the world. She kept thinking the next bolt would hit her house and burn her up alive. So she got up, put her jeans on, dashed through rain coming down in sheets to Ty's apartment.

She opened the door, crawled down the stairs. Ty was sleeping. She took off her jeans and crawled in bed with him. She would have made love with him, Cassandra writes me. She cuddled as close to him as possible. He was nude. She was shaking. The lightning chased her, coming after her as though it had a mind, she told him through chattering teeth.

He said he sometimes still gets frightened of the dark.

He really loves you, Ann, she wrote. He didn't touch me. I mean he held me until I stopped shaking and crying and then he starting talking about you. How much he loves you. How he can't wait until you get to Iowa and the two of you can live together. He longs for you, yearns for you. Finally, I was able to fall sleep.

I've never been nude with a man before who didn't touch me. I have never been with a nude man before who talked about another woman.

I read the letter and think, Just as I thought. A man who can be faithful. A man who I can be faithful to.

CHAPTER 28

During the snow time and the melting slushy time and the incessant rain time, Donna drops by our house. She comes for dinner, or she brings sweet rolls for breakfast, or fabric samples from Drexel, or checks that need signing. In and out unannounced. She treats herself as family.

One night, we broil steak and slather bread with crushed garlic and butter and thyme. Smear our salad bowls with Roquefort cheese. The vinegar and cheese smell refreshing, clean. We eat Daddy's favorite dinner. He is seldom mentioned. The steak sticks in my throat as Mother and Donna discuss a new order. Their voices are lilting. The Queen Anne isn't moving, but the Rococo lamps sell immediately. A window display of paired love seats with turquoise and orange accessories brings in customers. A crazy idea they developed together that succeeds.

There is little room for me. I toy with my salad and am startled to hear Donna call Mother "Nonie," just as Daddy did. I pour a glass of wine and admire the light shining through the purple red. Donna's makeup is newly applied on her poreless skin. Her clothes freshly pressed, she does not look as if she worked all day. Donna is taller than Mother and I. Her breasts are larger than mine, though not as large as Mother's. She watches me with dark eyes tilted down slightly at the corners. Her lips are full and, even when she smiles, they remain sensuous. Her hands are delicate like Mother's. My hands are like Daddy's. Blunt and square.

I shield myself from the retailing language by knitting. A taupe square with vibrant orange and warm beige flecks in it. Their voices excited, they are ordinary work colleagues. I ask Donna nothing. Our talk skips across the surface, avoiding the deeper waters where Mother's and my discussions swim — in the ambiguous space that consists only of perceptions and projections. With Mother's easy laughter and talk of business, they are different than friends, almost like I imagine sisters might be, but without history of rivalry.

After dinner, Donna says, "You look so much like your father. A female, younger version of him."

"Thank you." I will not let her woo me like she has Mother.

"What are you knitting? A sweater?"

"Just squares. I don't know what I'll do with them. My aunt brought me her leftover yarn," I look away.

She asks what I am studying in school. I tell her, but her eyes glaze. She is not much interested in canvassing for human universals in the Cross Cultural Area Files.

"Just like your father. Always reading. Always searching." She adjusts her bra strap, tugging it slightly. Her red red fingernails blood against her white white blouse. "I sometimes think curiosity killed the cat."

A curious cat is better than a happy swine, I think but say, "Yep. Sometimes you learn things you'd rather not know."

Mother's brows come together. Her warning sign that I'm opening Pandora's box. Mother has her boxes firmly shut.

It doesn't occur to Donna that my reference might be to her and Daddy. Perhaps their affair no longer exists. Not in her mind. She sits at our table as though she belongs there. As though history has been obliterated. And I think, maybe everyone is wrong. Maybe they didn't have an affair and they were simply work colleagues. Maybe we made it all up.

Donna swallows and asks me in a gentle voice, "How's Tyrone? Are you two still seeing each other?"

I switch hands and begin another row. The taupe yarn tugs at my fingers. I knit without looking. "Well, he's back in Iowa City and I'm joining him there when I finish Pitt."

"Where are you going to live?" She is careful not to judge. I crossed a boundary that she would not, just as she crossed a boundary I would not.

"There's an apartment available near his. I'm going to live there." This is a lie. I'm planning to live with him, but it is still only 1963.

"What work will he do off season? What's he studying?"

"Art."

I do not make this easy and she retreats to safe territory and asks how will I furnish my apartment. She could get me a great deal on a rug, I could take it with me. "Are you going to graduate school?" she asks.

"Probably. Eventually. But I want to work for a year. And then decide what I want to study. I still love anthropology, but can't imagine being separated from Ty for four years doing research." I've come to the end of another row and switch needles. "I'm thinking of becoming a therapist. A psychologist or social worker. I'm not sure which."

Mother's eyebrows go up.

We fantasize an apartment and decorate it from Oxxford's and her rug connection and for a few minutes I realize how easy it is to put everything in the dark waters and skate on a shining surface. We, the three of us, laugh and joke as women always do and I feel a sense of camaraderie, while underneath I wonder at my duplicity. The ease and power of pretense.

The truth is I am not interested in furniture. I want to put everything I own in a suitcase, board a Greyhound, and take off unencumbered.

Suddenly through the laughter and joking about menstrual cramps, Donna's tone changes. Her eyes are somber and sincere. "Your father was so proud of you. He'd love you to be a therapist, with all his reading of Freud." Her hands are still. "He loved you so much. You don't know, you can't know how important you were to him." I imagine them discussing me. He fumes about my relationship with Ty. He's proud of my scholastic success, my ease with people. Frightened by my exuberance and risk-taking.

Donna's lip quivers slightly and her eyes moisten.

Did he tell her he couldn't be with her because of the trauma a divorce would cause me? Did he use me as an excuse for his inability to commit to her or his lack of sincerity? Were they in bed, with cool sheets covering their nakedness as they spoke of me? At Locante's having lunch? "Of course I know my father loved me."

"I thought you might want to hear it again."

Then Mother and she discuss the Baker chairs. I'm reminded how easy it is to ebb in and out of the recognition of undercurrents.

For Mother's Day, Donna gives my mother jade earrings. "How weird," I say when Mother shows them to me.

She shrugs. "What's weird about it? It's a nice thing to do. Loving."

"Sick." I make a face of disgust. "Fucking Daddy, now acting as your daughter." We stand in the entryway of our house. A mirror on the wall reflects a tree which I see out the corner of my eye as I turn away.

Mother puts the earrings on the bureau under the mirror.

"Incestuous. Well, she's young enough to be your daughter. His daughter, too." I stare at myself in the mirror.

Mother turns me to face her. "Ann. She wasn't his daughter. You, only you are his daughter. Our daughter." Her hands warm my shoulders. She shakes me slightly. "Only you. I love you. Donna is my friend." She pulls me close and hugs me tightly, says hotly into my hair, "I love you. You are the best of us, Daddy and I."

. . .

That night, as I smooth my body into the cool sheets and wish for them not to warm, I think Daddy and I are stuck forever, stuck never finishing since he died in the middle. We will never get beyond this strange knot. I will keep picking at Daddy's threads till I find the answers. I know I want something dissimilar from my family's tangle.

Mother, by loving Donna, completed the story of her marriage. And, with elegance and compassion, had won.

CHAPTER 29

O n one of those white-hot days, Donna drives up in a red truck. Wearing jeans, no makeup, hair pulled in a ponytail high on her head, she looks almost like a teenager. She unloads an object covered with a padded blanket and then another. With a grin, she whips away the blankets revealing a headboard and dresser to match. "The style doesn't fit my new apartment, it being totally modern. Ultra. Ultra."

The headboard is antique white with delicate sprays of pink rose-buds and pale green leaves. Impasto paint forms petals and slivers of stems. The bumps form a gentle texture. Pretty. Virginal. More virginal than my white canopy bed when I was a girl. I imagined Donna's bed entirely different, modern with crisp lines.

"Your father helped me get it and I don't need it anymore."

This is the bed she shared with my father.

"Nonie told me you didn't have a bed. I know he'd be happy for you to have it." Her tone is breezy as though the bed is simply a bed without symbolism.

Crickets hum in my ears. "It's beautiful."

"If you don't like the color or something, just repaint it. Get one of those antique kits and paint it any color you want. Red. Blue. Whatever matches."

Would I be in bed with her and my father, roses on delicate stems arched over my head, ghosts of them on either side of me? In a twist of the Oedipal, had my father been in bed with me all along and is Donna merely recognizing that fact? Maybe I had been the competition after all. Maybe it was Daddy's love for us, all of us, that kept him with our family. In the final analysis, a community man, interested in genera-tivity. A father's love with all its complexity and terror. What would Freud say if I take the present? I stare at the silent bed while my mind races.

Meanwhile, I do need a bed. Maybe this a simple act of mutual convenience.

Just a year before, Daddy spread his arms to embrace the sky, a wide smile on his face. "It's a singing day." He rubbed his stomach and inhaled, preparing himself for yet one more escapade. A flashing world waited for him to seize. "Another singing day."

With all his eager greed, there had never been enough of anything. He wanted more books to read, more stores to open, more houses, forests, cars, women. More singing days. Many more singing days. And I am sorry, so sorry he did not get to have them.

Donna watches me pondering the bed. "He loved you so much. More than anything, he wanted you to be happy. Secure." Her eyes skip past me and she stares at the bed, the graceful Hepplewhite curves and delicate sprays.

I think, Donna and Daddy will be with me regardless.

When she looks back at me, her eyes are moist. "So secure. He wanted you to be so secure."

The truck blows sour plumes of smoke as she waves goodbye.

CHAPTER 30

Lala reads in her garden, her glasses have slid down her nose, her plump feet are stretched out on a garden stool, a cup of coffee beside her. I walk through the house to the garden and give her a hug. The lilies and yarrow are blooming a yellow so sharp it hurts my eyes.

"Well, so you're off to your beau." She always calls Ty my beau. So old-fashioned it seems a stamp of approval, but carries the shock of unfamiliarity.

"Next week."

"I have a present for you. For your new house. It's on the table. There's coffee, too. I'm just going to sit here."

I pick up the wrapped present and bring it to the patio. Japanese rice paper has been glued to the carton, then decorated with cut-out trees, turning the box itself into a present. I slide off the bow and lift off the lid. Inside is a porcelain box. The lid is a figurine of an angel cradling an infant, her wings sheltering it. The clay is white, only a touch of pale green on the baby's blanket and burgundy for his pillow, black for the angel's hair.

"You know its history? Your great-great-grandmother, born on your birthday, brought it from Germany. It's the last thing I have from her."

I reach over and kiss Lala. "I used to pretend I was the baby. I hid bleeding hearts inside."

"I remember." She nods. "Always meant to give it to you. Now seemed appropriate, for this adventure you might have need of a guardian angel."

"Thank you." My eyes fill with tears.

"It has a small crack." Her finger points out the glued yellow line. "It's old, been through lots of our lives. So she's a wise old angel." Lala chuckles.

"I'll miss you. Miss everybody." I acknowledge to myself for the first time my longing for this guarantee of warmth, safety, love. The fountain gurgles. The birds soar through the trees. The smell of the rich earth dampens the sweetness of flowers. Home. The idyllic setting in which we play out our lives.

She nods. "You know, when you get old, society doesn't matter. I don't wear a girdle any more. I don't care what religion or race any one of you marries. Not that I ever really did care. I know with the vast sweep and passage of time things change. Marrying Docie, a Jew, was a big to-do sixty years ago. Now it's nothing. Your great-great-grand-mother married a Catholic who worked in her father's factory. That was such a scandal they had to come to this country." She shrugs.

Lala sips from her coffee. "So I don't care. I don't care for me. I don't care for the family name or any such thing. It's unimportant. Nothing to do with anything about life, not really. Too much real pain and real joy to fuss with nonsense. If you ask me, it's what people occupy themselves with when they don't have anything substantial on their minds. Life itself is what's important."

Lala's toes are still crossed, but they seem right that way.

"I care that your mother worries so and frets so about you and what you're doing. Especially now, when she needs you more than ever."

I shift in my chair. "I've spent all fall, winter, spring taking care of her. Trying anyway."

"I know. I know, dear." She reaches out and pats my hand. And then her hand rests on mine. "She needs a lot of care." Her eyes watch her garden. "Tyrone seems like a gentle man. Nice man." She turns to me. "But I don't care how wonderful he is. There are other wonderful guys too and one who will exact much less a price."

"Doesn't seem to me that my father or Docie exacted a small price."

She sighs. "You're like me. You march to your own drum. The rest be damned, you'll do it your way." She squeezes my hand.

"This is what I learned from twenty years of being unhappy. The more I grew, groomed myself to be a fit mate for him, the more resentment he felt for me. This resentment is woof and warp of the spirit and fiber of a minority group and the real reason why such a marriage has so much more to withstand. You can put that in your guardian angel."

She nods to the statue, then inhales.

I puzzle out her words.

Now, she squeezes my hand tightly. "Tyrone is going to want a colored woman. Like Docie needed Ruth, a Jewish woman, a familiarity I couldn't give him even after all those years living together, all those babies. All that life together." Her voice quavers and her eyes are wet.

She is being sentimental, I think. Just another tactic to keep me from going to Ty. "It'll work out, you'll see."

"It won't matter how much love you give him, how good you are to him. What you've built together. In some form, some symbol or another, he will go back to his mother." She stops, pushes her glasses up to the bridge of her nose. She sips her coffee. "The years have taught me there is security only in self-dependence. Actually very little security at all in life, and even love's fulfillment is only fleeting."

CHAPTER 31

I sit in the stands with the other wives on one of those fall days when the tips of the trees are touched with red, the air crisp but not yet cold, the sky infinite blue. The fullness in my abdomen is welcome. I'm trying to get pregnant. I place one hand over my midsection as though warming a tiny infant and smile.

My other hand holds the game program; Ty's drawing of a lineman is on the cover. The lineman has Ty's bulging forearm, the vein running to the inner elbow. The lineman has done his job and the halfback will explode through the hole and run for daylight, dodging, leaping, charging for a goal. Ty's drawings have been on the program covers and they've drawn attention from the media. An interview of Ty, quoting some of his poetry, is in the newspaper. The juxtaposition, poet/artist and brutal football player, rouses the imagination. It elicits anxiety in his coaches, fascination in the fans, curiosity in the media.

In truth, Ty loves the violence. He loves crashing into his opponent, hearing the crack of helmet against hard pad, his rival's grunt and the explosion of air when he's on the ground. During the off season, Ty's edgy, restless, sad.

Jameson is the quarterback, a good quarterback, but the team is down thirty-four to fourteen. "Shit. What a fucking lead ball," a guy two rows down screams. "Worse than my five-year-old."

"Get that asshole off the field," yells another when Jameson is thrown for a loss.

"He's as fast as molasses in January."

Jameson's wife, Tina, sits next to me, tears rolling down her face. Her frosted hair, varnished in a Sassoon hairstyle, doesn't move as she tilts her face into her hands to wipe away the tears and blow her nose.

"Remember last week? He was the hero." I say while fishing around the bottom of my Cracker Jack box to find my prize. "Here." I offer Tina some, but she shakes her head.

"I'm going to kill them," Tina hisses to me.

"Next week, it'll all be different. We'll win." The offense returns to the bench, and Ty and the defense run onto the field.

"They don't know what he does for the game. For them." Tina juts her chin out, replacing her shame with contempt.

I don't really watch the game, I watch Ty. I watch the way his pants cling to his ass, the flex of hip muscle as he bolts off the three-point position and blasts through the line to the quarterback. Both teams are on him; the pile slowly unfolds. The next play, Ty blocks the end, but the play collapses. Then he grabs the fullback. And then offense is out again, and Ty ambles back to the bench. He gulps some water. He talks to the coach and gets some more water. He reaches into his helmet and I know he's getting the bennies taped to the inside. Benzedrine is handed out by the trainer. Cancels the toll of twelve years of hitting and provides unlimited energy. The defensive end comes over and pats Ty's butt and they stand together silently watching the game. I can tell by the crossing of Ty's arms, the shift of weight from one leg to another, the tilt of his head, his mood, his pain, his thrills.

The offense is stopped. "Jesus, tonight's going to be awful," Tina says.

Ty plays with a broken thumb, afraid to put it in a cast because then he'll be benched. Without him, playoff dreams vanish. So he plays. Each week, he tapes the thumb to his hand, and then wraps rolls of gauze around it, trying to protect it, seeking to fulfill his own ambition. "Well, they won't make the playoffs. Not after this loss."

"Next year," Tina says, as she reapplies her lipstick.

"Not for us. This is it."

"Uh?"

"Ty's going to graduate school. We'll probably have to go back to the States. The best MFA programs are there."

"Quit?" Tina slaps her mirror shut. "I can't imagine it. I mean, we've been doing this since I was fourteen. Shit. Then, he led the team to state championship. I was the cheerleader. The score was thirteen to seven when he broke through on a quarterback sneak and ran forty-five yards." Tina's eyes glisten, her voice raises. "Crowds filled the field. Goal posts were ripped down." She shakes her head. "It was what, ten years ago? I still hear the crowd scream."

"Ty spends all week in the bathtub, soaking in Epsom salts. He's been playing pro, semipro six years. Average playing time in football is what? Three. I told him, if he misses playing next year, I'll put cleats on, stomp up and down his legs, stomach, and back, and throw mud at him."

Tina laughs.

The game is over. I walk down the stands to the railing and Ty walks slowly toward me. He leans slightly to one side, his gait uneven. He hurt his thigh. His uniform is mud-streaked, his helmet dangles from his gauze wrapped hand. His shoulders dwarf his hips, legs. He is the massive muscled pyramidal male. His face, slicked with sweat, reflects the stadium lights and shines like beaten bronze. Near the corner of his eye is a small scratch. Blood glistens on the gleaming brown metal. He is a moving sculpture, carved in relief.

When I kiss his cheek, I taste his salt. He smiles and I am warm honey inside. He jerks his head to the locker room.

The stream of women are in their place outside the locker room. They lean against the wall, some smoking. Bent legs reveal miniskirted thighs. Fake lashes shadow their cheeks with fringe. They are the anonymous women hoping to get laid by a player. I don't completely understand their motivation, though I've partied with many of them. Somehow they hope the man's fame rubs off along with the rubbing. Somehow they think his power will cling with his semen. Somehow they hope to feel loved, protected by powerful arms around them. Or maybe, just maybe, they merely want a great fuck and think a great athlete will have the energy for it.

All of us wait. Tina smokes nervously and glares at the women. "I hate them," she whispers to me.

I shrug. "You'll go home with Jameson," I say.

She pulls out her mirror again and reapplies her eyeliner, wets a finger and smoothes her eyelashes.

"Relax. You're beautiful," I tell her.

Jameson comes out and Tina and he leave.

I wait. Ty's always the last one. He has to undo all that gauze. All that tape. Finally there he is, wearing a suede sport coat we bought in Mexico. He smiles at me and we walk out of the tunnel together.

"Should have won that game."

I nod. "You did okay." Vague cramps begin. I hope this time I'm pregnant. We've been trying for over six months. Then the ache eases. I smile.

"Missed reading that play right before the second half. But, yeah. I had a good game." Ty separates his playing from the loss. His own performance is what matters to him.

"How's the thumb?"

He flexes it and I see the swollen knuckle, the way it twists. He shakes his head. And I know how much it hurts him.

"We're going to the party?" I ask.

"Yeah, but the men are bitching. 'She's going to tell our wives, she sits with them.' "

I'm the only wife who goes to the party.

"I said, 'She goes where I go. And she knows not to say shit,' " Ty replies. Truth is, I notice the men and their other women, but I really only notice Ty. When they win, the party is all night dancing, drinking, playing cards, laughing. Slapping hands over a remembered great play. But even after a win, the relaxation is short. The possibility of a loss lurks for the next week. Anxiety fuels the game.

"I can't sleep anyway." He refers to the bennies. He won't be able to sleep until right before dawn. "We'll just go for a bit. Tomorrow'll be a hard workout."

The party is tame. Hushed talk obsessively reworks the game. Jameson's throw for a loss is blamed on the offensive guard, who missed his block. The men sit around drinking slowly, indifferent to the girls draped over them. A dark-haired girl stares into the center of the room with vacant eyes. A platinum blond slowly trails her fingers up and down the wide receiver's neck. He keeps flinching her away, like a fly. A girl with large breasts has her legs entwined with the tight end's.

The music is Dock of the Bay. I try to get Ty to dance, but he talks with the center, McLean. They played against each other in college. "Yeah, man, if you'd read my eyes right, you'd know we were pulling to the left. You'd have blocked me. Your quarterback would've made his play and you'd have been Rose Bowl-bound," Ty says.

"I don't know how you remember a play from a game six years ago," I say.

"Adrenaline fixes it forever in your mind," Ty says. "Like war."

"Yeah. I remember each and every play from each and every game I played. And now we're friends," McLean picks up his glass, a brown liquid greases ice cubes, taps Ty's and drinks.

"Yeah," Ty says. "Against each other one year, team mates the next, then traded and hitting each other again." The music ends. Silence fills the space in between songs, in between words.

"Except now I know your weaknesses." McLean leans forward, his mouth in a wide smile that doesn't curve. He bolts the rest of the glass.

"Think so, uh?" Ty holds his head back and laughs.

The platinum blond licks the wide receiver's ear, now trails her fingers down the inside of his thigh. He whispers to her and she slides off him, skinny thighs and go-go boots, hooks her fingers in the loops on her waist. She says something to the girl with dark hair, seriously drinking and smoking. Not saying a word, the three of them leave.

The next day, Ty's doctor calls when he's at practice. He tells me that Ty must cast his thumb or it will no longer be opposable.

"Well, we can't make the playoffs anyway."

"No."

"I guess this is it for me." He sits at the dining room table. His head is down as he watches his thumb flex.

I go to him and press his head against me. "We knew it anyway."

. . .

I get off the subway and walk down Bay Avenue, through courtyards lined with boutiques and cafes. Winter is near, red leaves litter the sidewalk and blow in a quick wind. In just a few days, the margin between fall and winter is spanned. I still haven't gotten my period, my heaviness increases, I imagine a baby growing, my lining thickening. We live in a row house in the Yorkville area of Toronto. It's just beginning to be chic, turning from working class to artsy fartsy. Picasso and Arp sculptures decorate the yard of an art collector. A gallery opens up down the block. Next door to us lives an attorney and his opera singer wife. On the other side is a head shop with stoned-out hippies lounging on the stairs. I have to step over them on my way home from work. Sometimes I think I'm the only one working a regular job on the block.

I finished my master's degree in social work and found a job as a social worker in the Toronto school system serving twelve downtown schools. I love it. I love forming groups of kids and doing in-service training with teachers and principals and helping families sort out relationships. I love the therapy with the kids. I love seeing the kids grow and bloom. I can hardly wait to have our own.

The hippies don't move from my step.

I climb over them and they tilt aside for me to pass, don't even shift, as though they own the stairs. I sense Ty before I see him, his gloom in the darkened house. He sits staring at his hand. A thin rod goes through the tip of his thumb. On either side is a rubber band that stretches to a wire about a foot away from his hand. The wire is held in place by a plaster cast around his hand and forearm.

"Holy shit. I've never seen anything like that."

"Supposed to keep my thumb in traction. Here." He pulls my thumb and I feel the bone at the base slip into place.

"Does it hurt? The rod going through the thumb?"

"Not yet." He shakes his head. "But it will."

We are quiet. And then he says, soft and low, "Well, this benches me."

"Yeah." I kneel before him and kiss his forehead. My eyes wet, and when he sees them, he turns away and shrugs.

"It'll keep me out of the draft. Don't have to worry about Viet Nam."

"Yep." I smile. "Guess I'll have you with me for a while."

"Sunday was my last game."

I wonder, would he play it differently if he had known.

"Be in graduate school anyway next year." He says happy words, trying to convince himself. But his voice is sad and I press him to me to make his pain go away.

"But it'll be all right? Won't it?"

"Good as new in a few months." He swallows.

"That's all that counts, really counts, Ty." I feel him inhale.

"More bad news, too." He places his hands on my shoulders and moves me so I face him, our eyes level. His cast is heavy, mashes into me. He wets his mouth. I notice his lip trembles and my heart quickens. He squeezes his lips together and swallows. "I got the results of the sperm count, too."

"Yeah?"

Ty shakes his head. "It's no good, Ann. Low count. Poor motility."

"Low?"

"I'm not sterile. It's possible I can get you pregnant. Possible. But not likely."

I press my lips together. My eyes burn with tears. I try to think of something to say. I wipe my nose. His cast presses my shoulder, hard and heavy. "It's still possible?"

"Doctor says I can try all sorts of things. He can refer me to a specialist, we can try thyroid, vitamins, operations. But he's seen lots of people chase a sad dream."

"I can't have a baby?"

"You could have artificial insemination. You can leave me."

"I want your baby. Your baby, Ty."

He shakes his head. "There's lots of babies, interracial babies needing homes. He says he'll help us adopt. We should think of what we want to do. He'll help us any way we want. There's lots of ways to form a family."

I think of Lala and the paper dolls. I think of the heaviness in my abdomen, the cramping there. I think of how I want, always wanted a baby. I think of the kids in all my schools.

Ty waits. His mouth downturned, a frightened look in his eyes. The warmth of one hand on my shoulder. The bizarre hanger- rubber band-plaster contraption squashes the other. My cheeks are cold, I shiver. I move close to him and nestle my head in his shoulder. I smell his cologne and his sweat and his sadness.

"I have my paintings. They'll always be my children, the children of my soul. You have to figure out what you want."

I feel my face crumble and I'm torn between him and me and my history and my future. Tears crawl down my cheeks.

"I love you. I'll always love you," he says. It's a prayer.

I go into the bathroom, and on my panties, as though summoned by Ty's words, is red the color of fall leaves, the color of zinnias, the color of a red-winged blackbird's wing.

Three scarlet smears on white panties. I think of the thousand times Ty's body has sent me soaring. I guess that's just the way it is. There's sex. There's pregnancy and childbirth. There's motherhood. They don't have to be connected after all.

CHAPTER 32

We live in a stone house at the edge of a forest in Kalamazoo. The forest is weed maples and chokeberry, foam flower, and bittersweet nightshade, but flocks of goldfinch flit through them. My tomatoes are staked behind a chickenwire fence. The eggplant bloom purple flowers and sag with the weight of heavy fruit. An old apple tree yields lots of small and mostly wormy pippins.

Beside the house, so I can see him from the kitchen window, Stone pushes a bright yellow road grader back and forth. We adopted him as an infant. Now he is three, black eyes and hair, café au lait skin, chubby cheeks. All concentration, he smoothes the dirt, vibrating air through his lips to create engine sounds.

Michelle, not yet a year, won't let go of my leg. She hangs on to me for dear life while I stir a pot of mushrooms, ground beef, onions, garlic in my home-grown tomatoes and red wine. It's summer and my small kitchen is steaming. I had planned to have this done earlier, before the day heated up. Michelle releases my leg and crawls to the door, her fluffy ponytail bobbing with her motions. She pulls herself to the knob and says, "Go outside. See Stone." It's the longest sentence she's spoken.

"Heat's gotten to you too, uh?" I scoop her up, bury my nose in her tummy to check that her diapers are still clean, and go outside to the filtered light. My hair has grown to my waist and Michelle grabs a fistful. She's got me now. Our German shepherd, Ghana, is staked to the tree. As soon as I set Michelle down, disentangle her fingers from my hair, Ghana cleans her face with precise licks. Michelle squinches her eyes and mouth and waits for Ghana to complete the job.

I don't want to play with the kids today. I have made pecan buns, rising now under a dampened dish towel in my kitchen. The spaghetti sauce is done for dinner. There are no spiderwebs, dog hair, sticky fingerprints in the house. The dust is gone from the corners. The floors are mopped and waxed and polished. Lala and Mother and Faith should be here any minute. It's the first time any of them have seen the house at the edge of the forest.

Ty's paintings, canvases with sewn and stuffed images, hang on the walls. I do the sewing for him, staying up nights pushing the cloth and canvas through a sewing machine, leaving a pocket and then stuffing it with cotton, rags, polyfoam bits. A life-size nude reclines on a padded sofa. The puffed fabric of the sofa contrasts with the painted mounds of her body on the flat surface.

After graduate school, Ty landed a job teaching at the university. And I work part-time at a child guidance clinic. Our schedules dovetail so one of us is always home with the children. The clinic is the respite I need from homemaking, and family the relaxation from work. We have parent-in-charge days, and worker days. We are smug and self congratulatory in the equal way we set up our family.

Stone shoves Michelle away from his truck, protecting his smooth stream of earth. Michelle pulls at the grass, then crawls to a patch of purple impatiens and pulls off a flower. I begin to say, "Don't pick the flowers." But she just picks one and then crawls back to her small pile of grass and decorates her heap with torn petals. She concentrates as if she listens to her own heartbeat. We adopted her at three and a half months. Sometimes I think she had to learn to be self-focused. "Pretty." I tell her and sit on the grass in my yellow jeans, pulling her on my lap.

"Nonie will be here any minute. Nonie and Lala."

"She'll see nice road I made with the Christmas truck," Stone says.

"Yep. You worked hard on that road."

Stone pats his road. "It's a good truck."

"We're going to the beach, you can make a road in the sand."

He comes and sits on my lap too. My legs are heavy with children, the sweet weight of them. Stone's hair smells vaguely of cheese and I inhale the smoothness of him mingled with Michelle's baby oil aroma and kiss his face, now smeared with dirt, his hair in wild curls and his black eyes dancing with the idea of a road he can make running the whole beach. The length of Lake Michigan.

"Can I take the bulldozer too, and the crane?"

"Yep. You can take them all. All you can carry, how's that?"

Then up the driveway comes the navy sedan. Lala gets out first, using a cane, her other hand massaging her back. Then Mother, then Faith. Ty comes out of his studio, a narrow slice of building that was originally a shed. After the hugs and kisses, after we put away their bags and they change to casual clothes and I toss the tuna into the bowl and pack up bread, peanut butter, strawberry jam, and mayonnaise, a cooler of canned pop, we pile into our yellow van with a black and red stripe down the side. It looks like a Ryder truck except it doesn't have the label. The kids ride in the back in a playpen.

It's a weekday and we're near the Palisades nuclear power plant. The beach is empty enough that when we round a curve, we are alone. Lala walks leaning on Ty, the cane on her other side. Stone and Michelle take off their clothes and splash in the water, too cold even for kids to just jump in.

Ty wears a striped shirt I've made and shorts. On his hands and knees, he crawls along the beach with Michelle; she fits easily under his huge mass. The two crawl along the shore together ignoring the stones and shells. The lake laps as they go. They become smaller until they are lost in the endless sky and seamless lake. After a while, they return. Michelle rests easily on his forearm, sucking her middle two fingers, concentrating on her internal voices. "My little Buddha," Ty calls her.

Michelle sits at lake's edge contemplating the back and forth of water on her toes. Stone works on his road while Lala garnishes it with bits of stones, and shells, landscaping as ever.

We lie in the sun. The children fall asleep, their soft breath accompanies the easy surf. Lala talks of St. Simon's Island. Ty talks of new paintings in metal and draws an aluminum lake, the titanium sky. Mother talks of her job as Commissioner of Mental Health for the State of Pennsylvania. The children's bodies are sprawled next to me. Michelle's arm is over Stone's shoulder, her still wet fingers splayed across his chest.

The sun is warm, the sky only blue, the sand soft, the rolling waves continuous music. We are all together.

. . .

That night, after the sand is washed out of our hair, I read, sing, and rock the children to sleep and ease them in cribs, hand-painted by Ty with jungle scenes for Stone and water scenes for Michelle. Ty,

Mother, and Faith discuss the oil crisis and the price of gas on the trip up in the living room. The living room air is clean. No one smokes anymore. Mother has had two heart attacks and sucks on plastic cigarettes. Faith had precancerous cells on her tongue and managed to quit. I went cold turkey when I realized I wanted to live to see my children grown.

Lala and I are in the kitchen. Lala says, "You need a cookie jar. Remember our cookie jar?"

"How could I forget," I laugh. I visualize the jar on her kitchen counter, a fat lady, her mouth open as though for more food, spoon in her hand, stands ready to cook. I rinse soap suds off a plate and push it in the prongs of the dish rack.

"You should keep it full of cookies. So the kids always have something yummy to eat. Molasses cookies. Tomorrow I'll teach you how to make them." Lala opens one of the drawers and pulls out a dish towel. "It'll make the kids feel secure."

"Think that'll do it?"

Lala's dish towel squeaks on the plate. "Where's this go?"

I open the cabinet for her.

"You know, you're a model for another woman now. How you dress, carry yourself, your neatness, tidiness, character show Michelle how to be a girl, then a woman. She'll be watching everything you do. She'll be the mother of your grandchildren some day."

Right now, Michelle sleeps, her butt up in the air while she sucks on her two middle fingers. "Eventually, yep. Guess so." I pull a plate from the soapy water, suds cling to my hands like warm clouds, but quickly chill. I rinse my wrists and the plate and hand it to Lala.

The spaghetti sauce has burned the bottom of the saucepan. I sprinkle Comet in it, add water, and place it on a low burner to loosen the scorched bits.

"Give me a nice soapy rag, I'll do the counters."

I squeeze out the excess water. Lala looks out the window. I can feel her arranging my yard. "What would you do?"

"Plant fall clematis. Let it crawl up the trees in the woods over there. You'll have fragrant white blooms in fall. And feed those birds, just feed them and they'll entertain you all winter. You've got goldfinch and woodpeckers and cardinals." She places her hands on her hips and rocks back on her heels slightly. "Ummm. Carpets of Muscari in the grass. They'll last forever and you'll have a purple field in spring. Keep it natural. Rounds of trees for steps, railroad ties, just like you've done. Follow your instincts." She finishes wiping the counter and is quiet, standing there, filling my small kitchen.

I oil the salad bowl, watch the oak grain deepen.

"You and Ty have a good relationship. Maybe the best I've seen in this family."

Her pronouncement seems to come from out of the blue. A victory I haven't even known I needed. We face each other. Her lavender and rose smell conquers the garlic cooking aroma.

"I see how you do these projects together. He does his, you do yours, but yet it's all part of a plan, all part of a scheme that you've decided together, but not glued. You're a team. Partners. The love you have for each other is obvious here in your home."

"Thank you, Lala." Pride irons smooth a rumpled corner. I rinse the rag and hang it over the spigot.

"You know, the last few years, I could just be me. Eat what I want to, when I want to. Leave out my decoupage anywhere I wish, schlomp around in my ratty bathrobe. Not care about my appearance. Work in the middle of the night if I couldn't sleep." Lala's dark eyes stare into mine. Her hands are on her hips, gray strands escape her bun, her glasses slide down her nose. She smiles and her eyes crinkle at the corner. "The happiest years in my life have been the last ten. Haven't had to worry about being anyone's mother or anyone's wife. I could just be me."

I hug her. She doesn't see the contradiction in the two messages. Define yourself as Michelle's mother and consider every action in that light. The happiest ten years were when she didn't need to do that anymore. For a minute, I'm confused. But then I know, she would say, you do what you have to do when you have to do it. Life is like a garden, everything in its season. She is a warm weight in my arms and she pats my shoulder, then rubs it in circles.

. . .

The next day, Mother and I are in my vegetable garden. Tomatoes escape from their stakes and crawl among the straw mulch. We grope in hot hay to find them, red and yellow treasures in the straw.

"Marinated tomatoes and green bean salad tonight, uh?" I say. Ty's making his famous fried chicken.

Lala and Faith are in Ty's studio talking about his new metal collages, Lala fascinated by the mechanics and chemistry of it. As I walked to the garden, I heard them discussing solvents, glues, pastes, pigments on various surfaces.

Mother says, "Well, I'm glad you're working again. I was afraid you were going to give up your career and just stay home playing with kids. Being a hippy. Growing vegetables, canning, knitting, sewing clothes."

"I loved the two years I stayed home." The aroma of acid tomato mingles with the sweet pungency of basil growing next to them. I pick some of the basil. The tomatoes and basil are warm in my basket. I hand them to Mother. "Here, smell."

She sniffs them and hands them back. "You're too valuable. You have too much to give the world. Don't shut yourself off in one corner." Mother sits on the mulch, elbows on her knees. She sucks her plastic cigarette, inhales the imaginary smoke deeply, and sighs.

I hunt out the last of the green beans, shooing away buzzing bees. "I was happy. I would have liked ten kids."

"Oh, God."

The bees hum, the smell of hot tomatoes and basil and marigolds pervades the air. My braid is almost to my waist and I lift it and feel the hotness at the base of my neck. When I look at Mother, I see her eyes are wet.

"I'm working. I'm fulfilling myself."

She shakes her head, her elbows on her knees. And swallows. "Lala's been diagnosed with uterine cancer."

"Why didn't she tell me?" I sit now.

"Ironic, it's because of radiation treatments Docie gave her to minimize menopause. The cancer is apparently encapsulated in her womb."

"What's that mean?"

"When they operate, there's a good likelihood they'll be able to get it all. It hasn't spread." Mother's eyes are not as green as I remember.

"So she'll be okay?"

"She's eighty."

. . .

After dinner, we're in the living room. Lala stares at one of Ty's paintings, a mustached, gray man, sitting in a red, white, and blue flowered easy chair of stuffed fabric. It is called *TV*.

"That was on the cover of *TV Guide*," I say.

Out of the blue, Lala says, "I didn't spend much time with Michelle. Didn't really pay any attention to her." She nods her head. "I can't get attached to any more people. Just makes the leaving more painful. Just means another person to lose."

We wait. Mother sucks on her plastic cigarette, lids cover her eyes. The freckles at the points of Faith's cupid bow are dark. Ty's fingers are spread on the arms of the chair, his lips pressed together.

Lala sits with her hands on her knees, her stomach wide and soft as a pillow, her glasses firmly on her nose. She does not look sad; she looks instead as though she just realized something. Then she turns to me, "Please understand."

"I do. It's okay."

Silence is thick as the moist summer air. Then I say, "I love you."

"I know," she says. And she rocks her head slowly, looking at me, looking and Mother and Faith and Ty. Rocks her head slowly as she looks at each of us in turn. "I know. We all love each other."

CHAPTER 33

Wasted by the cancer to ninety-five pounds, Lala leaves her house for the hospital when a sudden breeze sways her poplars. "Oh, look," she says, "They're saying good-bye to me. Bye-bye, trees." She waves weakly. She dies a week later.

Two years later, Mother dies of a heart attack, at the age of sixty-one. She dies alone. A book, Hellman's *Pentimento*, covers her face. The bedside lamp is lit. When Aunt Mildred discovers her, the telephone is ringing. I have been endlessly, anxiously trying to contact Mother. She has been dead for a day. The phone stops. Aunt Mildred arranges for Mother's body to be removed. I try to call again, the phone ringing, ringing, ringing until Aunt Mildred picks it up and informs me.

Mother's death is not sudden, but somehow unexpected. She developed diabetes. She finished her career as Commissioner of Mental Health for the State of Pennsylvania, in Harrisburg. Her life was reduced to work, washing out her underwear in her sink, preparing frozen dinners, getting her hair and nails done, and calling me and David.

Her body was transported to Pittsburgh for the funeral, and then David and I returned to Harrisburg to settle her apartment.

David is suffering the loss of two women. His wife left him for another man, leaving him with their young son. His divorce is final on the day of Mother's funeral. David and his son, Ty and I, and Stone and Michelle sift through Mother's things. David and I take turns picking the objects we want.

After she lost Daddy, she relinquished nothing. Her apartment is jammed with the reminders of life in the large house, the house by the forest, Lala's estate. Stacks of magazines go in the garbage. Her clothes go to the state hospital, enough I am sure to clothe entire units. I throw away her tax returns, but keep her poetry and term papers. I get the sideboard, the Queen Anne gaming table, the glass-topped table where Lala kept her collection of stones. A jade bowl. Lala's sterling. Mother's Limoges. Mother's jewelry except for her wedding ring and a topaz cocktail ring that David chooses.

We make decisions stunned by our orphanage. Ty and our two small children are my family. I no longer have the safety net of a wiser generation. Thirtysome years of family life are dispersed in three hours.

David shrugs off his divorce. "Dates, numbers don't mean anything." He shakes his head, "She's fucking half the men in America and I'm at home taking care of the baby." He squints from smoke traveling from the cigarette dangling out of his mouth stinging his eye. His hands wrap Lala's Spode. "Being faithful."

I think, David married our father. I glance at Ty, boxing up Pup's sugar canister. He stops to wipe Michelle's nose and then plants a kiss on her forehead. I smile at my luck as I tape another carton shut. David and I put our various goods in two separate Ryder trucks. Ty and I drive to Michigan. David drives to Georgia.

. . .

On the first anniversary of Mother's death, I light a Yahrzeit candle and begin to sort through a box of letters and cards from Daddy to her that I have saved for the occasion. The box was made by Lala. Japanese rice paper wraps it and a red silk ribbon ties it closed. I can see Lala nod in satisfaction at the juxtaposition of subtlety and spark. It is as though Mother has prepared this box for me.

I wade through Christmas and birthday and anniversary and Mother's Day cards. Quaint, old-fashioned, art deco, 50s modern, soft airbrushed, and then geometric. Rough paper and smooth and shiny paper. The decades apparent in the changing graphics. I wade through letters written when we were in Chicago and Daddy was on the road. A card from Gary, Indiana, says "Let's go hear Lady Day. GET TICKETS!!!" he writes in huge letters.

He writes on the road in Virginia, *"I want you so much and can't have you. I want to lift you out of your routine work and to grab you and bite you and kiss you and suck you. I want to kiss you completely. I want to devour you with my body, to crush you, to love you. I want to smother you with myself and to liquefy you and me so that there is only one of us left merging together in a*

great wild spurt of flaming liquid which all means I love you.
  Jake

. . .

At the bottom of the box, yellowed and musty, are letters written before the war, when Mother was in Pittsburgh working for the Department of Public Works and he was in Washington working for the War Board. When they were young lovers. *"I miss you desperately. When are you moving here?? When? When? WHEN???? Take the train be here for Labor Day?? Even a long weekend??? Thanksgiving is forever. I want you!!! I love you!!! I need YOU!!!"* Again immense letters so the note covers two sides of a page.

The first one in the box, at the bottom, the paper yellow and the ink a faded blue is carefully folded. I open it and see his impetuous, eager hand on the crumbling paper. *"Darling Nonie,"* it says. *"I want us to share our lives together. I will love you forever. I want you. I will always want to see your green eyes and your crooked smile. But I feel that the way for me is undiscovered. I have not found it. I wonder if you can possibly be happy with me. I know myself how quixotic, unpredictable, undependable I am. I know that I cannot be regimented. I love you in my own way and cannot change that way even if I try. I'm not a man to be faithful to one woman. It's not ME. You have to want ME. As I want YOU. I PROMISE I will love you above all women and ALWAYS honor you. Only you. Build our lives together. I will never leave you. Do you understand? Will you come with me? Please??? Love always and forever, Jake."*

The candle's soft light wavers. The dust of old paper fills the hair in my nose. I read the letter again. A piece has snapped in its exact place and completed the puzzle. I replace the notes, slide on the lid with the fragile, saucy bow. The box is inviolate. My father was faithful to his word and understood himself entirely. Mother thought with her immense love and legendary sex she could transform him. But she knew exactly what she was buying.

CHAPTER 34

I've just completed a grueling stint, twenty-four patients in two days. It's already dark. Driving home, I mull over the people I've seen that day. Janice's ex-husband is suing for custody of their daughter because of her lesbian relationship. She was already depressed. I consider the psychiatrists I know in case I have to refer her for some meds. Rick has the urge to pee during law school classes taught by aggressive male professors. He then reviews his father's suicide. Must be longing for father, or guilt or fear of success issue, or castration anxiety. I shed patients' voices as I drive. Tired. It seems like all I've done is work. Red light. Damn. I can hardly wait to get home, see my family.

Tomorrow is a home day. Ty will be teaching and I'll be parent in charge.

Last week, Stone bypassed the safety mechanism on the Cuisinart and almost severed two fingers. Tomorrow his stitches come out. Then he'll be able to practice the piano. Michelle has ballet after school. Tonight I can relax in front of TV and work on the sweater I'm knitting Stone. A Tyrannosaurus Rex rears on the front. He'll love it.

We live in Madison, in the intellectual ghetto. Around us live other university professors. A Camperdown elm, like an umbrella with a twisted trunk, shelters our deck. There's no room for a vegetable garden. Ty turns the garage into a studio. Stone and Michelle walk through streets lined with sugar maples to get to a neighborhood school.

Sleet falls in bitter drops. Ah, there's my corner. The leaves have mostly dropped and my headlights pick up gold on the streets. Home. Brown with a burnt orange door. Large porch. Naked redbud, but some mums still purple. I smell the chili cooking as soon as I open the door. A small TV plays in the kitchen while Ty tastes the soup bubbling on the stove.

"Hi," I smile. I move forward to kiss him and he gives me a per-functory kiss, his lips closed. "Smells good." I notice then the scowl on his face, his mouth turned down.

I take off my coat and see Stone in the TV room. The TV is on but he's reading a book on military aquatic vehicles.

"Hi, Bump." I kiss him.

He gives me a wet kiss back and opens his arms to hug me.

"How's the finger?"

He shrugs and goes back to his book.

"Tomorrow, you'll get the stitches out."

"Then I can finish my new model." He turns back to pictures of plane carriers.

"Yep." I rumple his clumps of ringlets.

I reenter the kitchen. Ty's back is to me, his hands are on his hips, his shoulders sagging. "Where's Michelle?"

"Let's go in the living room."

Ty sits in the chair with swan arms that was first Lala's, then Mother's, now ours. I sit on the sofa. "What's wrong?"

A muscle moves in his jaw. His legs are crossed. He turns away from me. "I was painting, just conjured up great images. Singing and dancing, putting pieces together. Happy." He spits out his S's.

Ty has unlimited ideas, but he's afraid they will vanish. He stores sketches, photos of colors, images, line curves in preparation for the day his imagination dries up. But it never does. Boxes of unneeded ideas pile up instead.

"The kids got home and made a big pile of leaves in the back yard and buried each other. So I kept on painting. More time 'till I had to make dinner." He clenches his right hand and then relaxes it.

"Then I get a call from some parent. Almost didn't answer the phone. Wish I hadn't. Michelle's terrorizing his kid. Jenny something or other. Michelle's been threatening to beat this Jenny up. Pushes her and pinches her. Makes faces at her. This Jenny is afraid to go to school. Can't I stop Michelle? This guy has talked to the school, but they never catch Michelle doing anything. Can't I do anything?"

"Jenny is, was, a friend of Michelle's. They play together."

Ty's face is turned to mine now and I see the clenched mouth, his arms crossed on his chest. "I can't imagine calling a parent complaining about his child. Kids should work out their own problems."

"What did you do?"

"I was polite to the fucking parent. Then I try to talk to Michelle, but she sits there and looks down. 'I don't know. I don't know,' is all she says."

"Where is she?"

"In her room until dinner. I was so fucking mad at her. Would have spanked her. But you don't believe in that."

"How is using physical force going to teach her not to hurt people?"

Ty scowls at me. "This sure as shit isn't working. The spell, the painting spell is ruined. How can I get back to those images after this shit?"

"I'm sorry."

He doesn't say anything.

"The work will be there. You'll find the space again."

He frowns at me and clicks his tongue, his mouth in a scowl. "No. It's gone." He shakes his head. "I hate having to cook dinner and wash dishes and worry about this kid bullshit. Committee meetings and faculty meetings. It doesn't become me."

"It's just life. Everyday, mundane life."

"Bullshit. I want to paint and this is a plot preventing me."

"What do you want me to do? Quit work and just take care of the kids?" I don't want to quit. I'm giving speeches to professional organizations, I'm writing a book with my partners. I love seeing my patients get better, learn to love themselves.

"No, we need the money."

"We'll live different."

He shakes his head, his mouth rigid. Ty likes to be able to buy what he wants — radial arm saws and aluminum anodizers and sheets of mirror-finished stainless steel and gallons of acrylic paint.

"Hire baby-sitters?"

"Couldn't stand people in the house. Wouldn't be able to paint."

"We could eat out more? Or eat frozen dinners. That way you wouldn't have to cook."

"TV dinners aren't food."

"You don't have to make such elaborate from-scratch dinners. What about if I cook on Tuesday nights, too? And we can start the kids doing dishes by themselves. They're seven and nine now. They could do more."

He nods his head in agreement.

"Meanwhile, I'll try to figure out something with Michelle." If I stayed home and devoted myself to Michelle, she wouldn't have these problems. I would somehow be able to fix them.

"It's my fault. Telling her if someone hits her to hit back. Girls don't hit in this neighborhood. In mine, they were the meanest fighters."

I don't say anything. I don't know what to say.

CHAPTER 35

The sea laps gentle on the sand. Palm trees, sticks with green feathers for leaves, stand stiffly despite the efforts of the ocean breeze. We have been married for seventeen years and lovers for over twenty. As we walk along the beach, stooping to pick up curled shells, Ty tells me of new ideas for paintings. We put on snorkels and float together, holding hands and pointing excitedly to colorful damsel fish and baby octopus waving with water's tide. Day after day, we walk, talk, watch the undersea world until we are cold.

Ty and I lie side by side on chaises absorbing relief from the warm sun, the salt air. He lies there sketching, not the vista, but images inside his head. I picked up *How to Make Love to a Man* at the airport to learn some new sexual trick or escapade.

I finish the book in two hours and close it. "I could have written this book in a week twenty years ago, " I say. "There is nothing here not spelled out in the *Kama Sutra,* only a smattering of new material from Masters and Johnson."

"Let's write an advanced marriage manual," Ty suggests.

"What to do for the second twenty years." I laugh.

"Yes."

Two months after that trip, I get pregnant. I am 40 and my first pregnancy, discovered on Ty's birthday, seems a miracle. We look at each other, happy and scared. We were ready for the parentless stage and instead we're on to a new adventure.

My first book, *Getting Free: Women and Psychotherapy,* authored with two colleagues, hits the bookstores. I toss the idea of writing a book on sexuality around in my mind. I develop some chapters for sexual games — actually some games that Ty and I devised — and mention it to a friend, Mandy, who is a freelance writer.

Right after my amniocentesis, while I am still waiting for the results, Mandy calls from New York: "Are you going to write that book on sex or not, because if not, I already pitched the sexual games for long-term couples to *Redbook* and they are hot to buy. So if you're not going to write it, can I? Will you give the idea to me?"

"Well, I don't know about writing a book right now. Especially on sex. My hormones are all whacked. Besides, I just want to coast, relax a bit." I'm seeing over thirty patients a week.

"I tell you, Ann, this book may be a seller." I imagine Mandy sitting on her sofa, her eyes darting with earnestness.

"God, Mandy. Isn't two kids in puberty, a new puppy, building an addition, working full time, and being pregnant at forty enough?"

"*Redbook* was drooling."

"Well, a proposal wouldn't hurt," I say.

. . .

I am five months pregnant when I begin writing the proposal. I write up a chapter called "*Wholesome Thrills: Sexual Games,*" detailing a game that Ty and I have played called Request Poker, strip poker with the variation of asking for sexual activities. On an afternoon in midwinter, sun patches playing on our flowered bedspread, Ty and I play the game with the tape recorder on. I quickly win at blackjack and he switches to five-card draw. I'm on a winning streak and he is naked except for his underwear and socks.

"You're getting too cocky over there," he says.

"No pun intended?"

"No pun intended." We both laugh. Our cat leaps to the bed, stretches toward a patch of sun, and then curls in a purring ball at the foot.

A few hands later, when he is naked, I say, "You can't beat me. I have a pair of jacks with ace high. Look, almost a royal straight," I say. "But let's pretend you won."

"How can we pretend I won?"

"Because we can. We can do anything we want," I say.

"Well, in that case, take your panties off."

I am just beginning to feel life, soft bubbles, caresses from inside. When I come, my baby responds with flutters.

I edit up the tape, add some more games, a book outline, and concept, and send the proposal to my agent.

. . .

Three weeks after Naomi is born, the proposal is sold. Then every afternoon for nine months, I nurse her, put her down for her nap, and retreat to write the remainder of the book. My Apple IIe, which I buy with my advance, is in the basement, windowless and closed. Only the green monitor, words rolling around in my head, and the bliss of being a mother seem to exist. Characters form under my fingertips. My words create pictures in my mind and carry me away from the windowless basement. I begin to see scenes played out on the cement walls. I get lost in the chapters until Naomi's cries return me to extraordinary happiness with her.

Ty is on sabbatical working in his home studio, fabricating an eighteen-foot curved metal collage wall for a public building. The metallic colors glow from the windows. His excitement radiates through our new addition, our house. Stone and Michelle are enjoying middle school. I am back to seeing patients two afternoons a week.

Near dusk, I put Naomi in her Snuggli and we go for a walk in red and yellow leaves, under sky so blue it leaves me breathless. The streets are quiet except for the rain of leaves drifting to the ground. Naomi's warm body folds into mine, her eyes gaze up to me. I show her the maple branches arching over us. I let her smell pine needles. She stares as though to gather in these new sights. We enter the park and climb the sledding mountain as the sky turns pink. Naomi nurses and falls asleep as we stroll through the red canopy.

This is one of those days, really just an ordinary day, that I want to press like a flower and preserve. To reopen, relive at a future time when I need it.

Donahue picks up a story that Mandy has written on sexless marriages and uses me as an expert. His makeup man thickens my too skimpy mouth. I look lush. The audience claps enthusiastically as I stroll onstage. I am the expert, the celebrity. It's the first time I'm away from Naomi and still nursing. I glance down at my dress, worried that dripping milk is showing through. Donahue is better-looking and more charismatic in person than on TV. I sense his love for the audience.

During commercial breaks, the audience barrages me with questions about their own lives, their own marriages. The makeup man

powders away my shine and enhances my mouth. The lightning inter-
play between me and audience, the hustle of the makeup man, cam-
eramen, producer quicken the pace. When I see the program on TV,
the media has reduced the emotions a notch or two. The trembling and
quivering of the nervous man sitting next to me is not conspicuous. My
exuberance appears only as quick thinking and a slight assertiveness.
Like pornography, it doesn't look as good as it feels.

. . .

My book Keep the Home Fires Burning: How to Have an Affair
with Your Spouse is in the bookstores in a year and I am scheduled for
the author's tour — *Oprah, Sally Jessie, Pittsburgh Today, Detroit,
Cleveland Good Morning.* Radio talk shows in each and every city. I tour
the Midwest energized by the exhilarated audience, the questions they
ask, the connection between us that goes on during the commercials. I
coast from green room to green room, airport to airport. My day is in
the hands of the publisher's escort who drives me from radio to TV to
bookstore to lunch to radio to airport.

I relax in the escort's car until pumped by the nervousness of the
next performance. Constant fussing with my hair, reapplying makeup,
smiling. On radio, I treat seriously call-ins from anonymous people
asking pressing questions. Over and over the same queries: how to keep
a marriage sexually alive in spite of work exhaustion, worries about
children and parents, job and economic stress, weight gain, desire for
new lovers, disagreement about sexual activities? How indeed. I'm
amazed at the instant glibness and smoothness of the talk show hosts.
I love the audiences' questions. I tell everything I know, everything I've
learned from my work as a marriage therapist, everything that works
in my own marriage.

Oprah's makeup man plucks my eyebrows. "See how that opens up
your eyes?" I smile at my wide-eyed reflection in the mirror. "Now your
eyes are huge," he proclaims. I sense Oprah's love for the studio audience. She and the producers generate a palpable excitement. During
commercials, the audience and I hum, the makeup man powders away
my shine, works some more on my eyebrows. I give the audience all
I've got. I give them what I give my patients.

I come home and Michelle and Stone tell me about school and

friends. I am not doing publicity in Madison. "No one will let their daughters go out with me if they know my mom wrote a book on sex," Stone says. Michelle shrugs, her mouth pulled down in a frown, and then rolls her eyes. Nike, our dog, jumps up and down in excitement.

Ty plants familiar kisses to celebrate my return. We walk around the neighborhood, hold hands, and talk about my adventure. My office answering machine is full of new clients, many from neighboring cities. I have to create a waiting list, then fill up my friends' practices with urgent patients.

Still, I put the garbage in a plastic bag and drag it out to the curb for the garbageman. My fifteen minutes of fame, I shrug to myself. Naomi sings *Somewhere Over the Rainbow*. She transports me into her awe with her song. Joy and wonder remain in the filament of moments.

CHAPTER 36

A slam of car door as Ty returns from cutting out metal. I'm loading the dishwasher. And then the Pistons championship game on the studio TV. I rinse out a cup and set it in a rack. The gate of Ty's truck opens and metal scrapes. Tree frogs trill, hyacinths' aroma thick in night air. I put Naomi's scattered Barbies and clothes in a basket.

"Ann. Ann." At first it is so soft, it doesn't register. Then I hear Ty's strangled voice. "Call 911. I've cut an artery."

Where's the phone? There. I dial. I speak as distinctly, controlled as I can. "My husband has cut an artery." I give our name, address. "Hurry."

Ty is in the house, he is gray. The fingers of his left hand are wrapped around his right wrist. "I'll bleed to death. I'm holding my hand onto my arm."

"Hold it up. Hold it above your heart." My heart pounds.

Ty raises his arm, walks to the front door. "Wait for ambulance on the porch. Closer. Get me a tourniquet."

I scan the room. What can I use? The iron cord? Cut it off the iron. I start looking for scissors. Taking too long. Shit. A towel. Read somewhere to use a towel. I grab a purple towel from a drawer and run outside. I wrap it around his arm. It isn't long enough to tie. Hopeless. I'll twist it with a stick. I scan the ground for a branch.

"Use my belt," Ty whispers.

Stupid. Why didn't I think of that? I unbuckle his belt, pull it off. Lay the leather over his thick arm, slip the length in the buckle, and pull.

"Tighter."

I pull harder, leaning my weight away from him. "What happened?"

"I was carrying copper. Just cut. I turned to shut the gate so Nike wouldn't get out. The metal started to slip. I moved my arm up to steady it; it came down like a guillotine on my wrist."

"Shit."

"Harder."

"It's as hard as I can."

"I'll bleed to death. Harder. Pull harder."

If I pull any harder, I'll squeeze his arm apart. "Keep it up."

"I'm getting dizzy."

Sirens wail. "See, that's for you."

I pull the tourniquet. Ty breathes as slowly as he can. He concentrates on slowing down his heart. Mine pounds in my ears. My throat is dry. The sirens diminish. "My fingers are numb. I can't feel anything. I'm dizzy."

"Any minute now."

"Call again." His arm is cold. Left hand glued by blood to his right hand. "Got to get to the hospital. They'll sew me up. Got to come home and finish my show."

"Try to relax."

"I'm getting so cold."

I run back into the house. "Michelle, Daddy's cut an artery. We're going to the hospital. Take care of Naomi till we get back. Just let her sleep." I call 911 again.

"They're on the way, lady. On the way," the voice says.

I grab my purse.

And then the siren sounds. A fire truck is in the driveway. "We went right past ya." He chuckles. "Let's see what we have here." The fireman grabs Ty's hand.

"If you move my fingers, my hand might fall off."

The fireman slides his hand under Ty's and pries open his clenched fingers. A spray of blood arcs then falls to the ground. "Oh, my God, you did cut an artery." The fireman wraps gauze, then tape around the bloody wrist.

The sirens wake Naomi and she's on the porch. "Mommy. Mommy."

"Daddy cut his hand. We're going to the hospital."

"Is he okay?"

"Michelle is here with you. Go back to sleep." I lean down to kiss her. She holds Michelle's hand.

The fireman finishes as the ambulance arrives. They take off the tourniquet. Ty walks to the ambulance holding his wrist. I wave to Michelle and Naomi as we drive to the hospital.

. . .

The hospital is clean white and smells of disinfectant. The overhead lights are blinding. People talk in quiet voices. We're safe. Ty lies on an examining table. The doctor, young, blond hair already thinning, examines Ty. Ty moves his thumb and index finger. "You'll just sew me up and I'll go back to work. Right?"

"Something like that." He listens through his stethoscope. Ty's shirt is cut off. "You've got good circulation. A strong heart." Ty is taken for x-rays. When he returns, an IV is threaded in his left hand. The nurse covers Ty with a light blanket. We are alone in our cubicle. White curtains shut the world away. I place my hand on his arm.

Ty counts the number of completed paintings for his show scheduled to open in a week. "Three still need frames. They all need polishing. Four are not yet put together."

"You can always use some that have been shown before."

He shakes his head no. "I'll need to get a student to help me. A strong one. Frank."

"I'll help you. Michelle will help you. Try to relax." I smooth his forehead, it's damp, but cold.

"How much time do I have? How much? Six days."

After a while, the doctor returns, he says, "We'll be operating in the morning. Prepping you for a general."

"Not a local?" Ty's pants are spotted with various paint colors, and now red blood, turning brown.

"Surgery will take six hours."

"That's longer than a heart transplant," I say.

"I'm an artist. I need my hand. When will I be able to work again?" There's more pleading in Ty's voice than anger.

"It's complicated, delicate surgery. The easy thing was cutting the hand. Our job, sewing it back, will be a little harder. The hard part, the really hard part, is what you do afterward. There'll be a lot of work."

"Shit. I thought you'd sew me back and I'd be fine."

The doctor sits on a chair, his face is level with Ty's. "You're alive. Healthy. You'll still have your hand and the use of your thumb and two first fingers."

Ty moves his thumb across the fingers of his left hand. He pretends to draw and nods.

"You've cut tendons, a vein, the ulnar nerve and artery. We'll try to sew them all back. It'll be some time before we know if the artery will work. Sometimes they just clot off. You'll know because your hand will always be cold. There's enough collateral circulation to supply blood to your hand. The nerve regenerates one centimeter a month. It'll be six months before the verdict is in on that." The doctor's hands are pink, the cuticles blush. Uniform moons lie at the base of each one, the nails cut straight across. Like Ty's metal, I think.

"Six months?"

"The tendons. You'll have lots of physical therapy. If they scar together, we'll have to go back and operate again, scrape off the scar tissue."

"You don't understand. I have a show opening this Friday."

"Amazing things can be done. Beautiful recoveries. Some of it's up to you. Your motivation."

When the doctor leaves, Ty stretches the fingers of his left hand. He makes a tight fist. He crosses his index finger over his third finger. He holds an imaginary pencil. "Drawing on the right side of the brain." He laughs. "It'll take three times as long."

. . .

After his surgery, I find him in his room, the edges of his body softened by pale sheets. He vomits into a basin. "I didn't want to bleed to death. I was afraid I'd lose my hand." He lifts his right hand, a club of gauze, wrapped thickly. "I still have it, for better or for worse."

I kiss him. "I still have you. I love you."

He pulls me to him with his strong left arm. "You know, honey, I had the weirdest image right before they put me under, before I let my mind go." He smells of sweat and fear and antiseptic. "I saw a primeval mammal covered with brown fur. Running, limping. His front leg cut off and matted with blood. His paw lay in the teeth of a steel trap." Ty swallows and wets his lips. "The animal chewed off his own paw to be free. For a second I was him, running, bleeding, stumbling, blinded with pain." His heart beats under my cheek. "And then the drug took me."

I hold my breath, listening to his heart beat, smelling the familiar musk of him.

"I'm just glad to be alive. To have you," he whispers.

"You do," I say. "You do."

CHAPTER 37

Ty's hand is in a plastic cast. Hooks are glued to his fingernails with gobs of epoxy. Rubber bands run from the hooks to a safety pin at the base of his cast. He exercises his fingers by making a fist to pull against the rubber bands, then straightening his fingers. Sweat rolls into his eyes from pain. After two months, his cast is removed and then he must bend each joint to form a fist, pushing past agony. When he has me do it, his mouth coils into a grimace, he stomps his foot in suffering. Brow twisted, he practices picking up cotton balls and dropping them into a bowl. Arthritis from years of leaning in the three-point position stiffens his hand.

Naomi ties his shoes.

I cut up his food.

Naomi buttons his shirts.

I pull on his socks. Then he stops wearing them. Buys Velcro shoes.

But he paints. He can draw. He teaches his left hand to do what it can. Stone is away at college. Naomi, Michelle, and I help. Red slashes across the canvas. Academe is thrown over for primitive. He paints creatures. Angry mother and helpless child. Innocent Adam and Vulvular Eve. Sinuous snakes and howling mammals. Jovial lizards and vicious birds. Potent paintings created under a hegemony of pain.

He is having a show at the Iowa Museum timed to coincide with the 100-year celebration of Iowa football and the first inductions into the Iowa Athletic Hall of Fame. The show is beautifully hung. His paintings are in the venue where the mentors of his youth have hung. Lasansky and Knipschild and Burford.

There's a press conference before the reception. Ty stands at the podium, his voice booms with the microphone, his breath echoes across the seated audience. Smoothly, blithely he discusses his hand accident, how it altered the images that buoy in his head. "Less intellectual," he says. "I'm more interested in life than mere beauty. My work is more immediate, more violent, more universal, spiritual."

Only I hear the slight tremor in his voice, the slight nervousness in the way he shifts his weight.

"Suddenly color takes the front stage, color, not subtle textural change."

TV cameras whirl on. Reporters in perfect nail polish and lined lips ask questions. Reporters in shined shoes and knotted ties take notes.

"The accident unmasked, unleashed a different side of me. Gave me new creativity, a new vision of the world." He smiles his warm smile, white teeth in his dark face.

Tape recorders capture his words. They ask, as they always do, about the peculiar coincidence of football and art.

"Athletes are many and varied in their talents. Sometimes you have more than one interest." He shrugs it off.

Cameras caress his paintings, focus on his hands, knuckles large and knotted, veins like tree branches twisting across the backs. His are the fingers of hard labor, not sensitivity.

"Now we have the really hard question." The curator has the audience's attention. "Who do you want to win, Iowa or Wisconsin?" The crowd is quiet.

"Hey. In that one, I can't lose."

The crowd laughs. Champagne is popped, tables of hors d'oeuvres cheese, and fruit are brought in, and the reception begins.

The next day, at halftime, Ty marches onto the field with other lettermen and is applauded. I saw him play here only once, before I knew him. I sit in a stand once again, once again with other wives. This time, all of us middle-aged. This time, all of us talking about our sons' football careers. This time, comparing the toll football took on our husbands' bodies. Some walk with canes. Many have had knee replacements, hip replacements. A few have stroked out, not from high blood pressure but from too many hard hits in insufficiently protective headgear.

Ty's gait is strong and sure. I know he'd still want to play. From this distance, his hand is whole, complete. At the banquet, the men remember plays from thirty years ago. Fans recall tackles he made, tosses by the quarterback and flash dash runs by the halfback.

It is thirty years ago. We are in Iowa once again. All things are possible.

. . .

In the dead winter, no snow lightens up the gray days, brown plants, and twisted black branches scraping a leaden sky. I pick Naomi up from school, come home to make dinner. Ty returns from teaching and physical therapy. We eat fajitas and salad and in the middle of dinner, I ask Ty how his day was.

He concentrates on picking up his fajita and eating it and then says, "OK." He shrugs. "Same bullshit. Should have tried to get a whole year medical leave."

"Guess what we're gonna do?" Naomi says. "We're going to pretend we're pilgrims. First, we learn all about them and then," her eyes widen, "and then we're going to a one-room schoolhouse where we dress up as pilgrims and eat a pilgrim lunch and learn from pilgrim books."

"Boy, that does sound exciting," I say.

"Like a time machine. We're going to take movies of it. You might have to sew me old-fashioned clothes, Mommy. Okay?"

"Something happened in one of my classes," Ty says softly.

"Oh?" I ask.

He pushes away from the table and clears his throat. "I have this special student in my painting class. She's from Japan. Sakiko's her name. She needed to learn how to stretch a canvas. I had explained to the class, but she didn't understand me, her English wasn't good enough. So I had to show her."

Ty swallows. He tilts his head back and light from the stained-glass shade casts a blue glow on his skin. He pulls the canvas in the air with imaginary tools. His hands collapse on his lap. "I tried to show her, but I couldn't. My hand wasn't strong enough to pull the canvas taut." His voice is strangled.

I reach my hand out to his.

"I tried my other hand. I couldn't do it." Tears roll down his face. "Then my right hand couldn't staple." His head is down and he shakes it slowly. "I couldn't grip the tool hard enough, I couldn't staple the fucking canvas to the frame." He whispers, sighing for air in between sentences, his face now wet with tears.

I'm quiet and then hug him. Naomi hugs him, too. We stand there surrounding him as he sits in the chair, crying silently now. It's the first time he's cried about his hand.

"It'll be okay, Daddy," Naomi says. "Mommy and me will stretch 'em for you."

He shakes his head. "I can't stretch a fucking canvas."

"You're still in physical therapy. It'll get better."

"Maybe."

"You can still paint." I swallow. I rock him gently. "Your paintings are better than ever."

He wipes his cheek with a napkin and then his dripping nose.

There are no pretty stories. I can't say anything to make it go away.

CHAPTER 38

"Sakiko's invited us to a party," Ty says.

"A party?" I tear lettuce into bite-size pieces.

"Yeah, I've been helping her with her collages and she's throwing a Japanese barbecue. Mak and Carol are coming, too."

Mak is Japanese and the assistant dean at the art school. His wife, Carol, is a weaver. I sweep diced onions and halved cherry tomatoes from the cutting board into the lettuce. "What's the dress?"

"Casual. She's wearing a sweatshirt, she told me."

"Ummm. Sounds like fun." I love dinner parties. Lazy eating, good conversation. This time, Japanese home cooking.

"Great."

"Sakiko and I are thinking of collaborating. We have an idea for a series of collages."

"Collaborating?" I drizzle olive oil over the salad.

"A combination of African American and Asian, male and female, her glossy colors, my powerful images." Ty smiles. "A new way to do art. Don't hear much about artists collaborating, though of course in the apprentice system they always did."

I wonder if some of this is about his hand. "I'll always help you, if you need it, you know." I sprinkle thyme and oregano over the salad.

"You're busy with your writing, your patients, and the kids."

. . .

When we get there, Sakiko isn't wearing a sweatshirt, but a hand-knit Italian sweater. She is tall, very thin with a long face, a beauty from a woodcut by Hiroshige. The diamonds in her ears are the size of my pinky fingernail. Not sweatshirt casual. The house is decorated Western rich rather than arty: Waterford chandelier, plush sea green rugs, Queen Anne cherry.

Carol and Mak are seated at the table eating. Dressed entirely in black and white, accessorized by her textured weaving, they are a study in moving minimalist art.

Kenzo, Sakiko's husband, slides a cigarette around his mouth with his tongue. His lips are rimmed like a Benin bronze. Pronounced cheekbones, but not sharp. Sakiko and Kenzo, married for eighteen years, have an arranged marriage, Ty has told me. She brought the money and he is royalty. He pulls the cigarette from his mouth with his left hand and dangles it from the back of his chair.

Sakiko prepares the meal at a grill beside the table while we talk. The conversation flits from Japanese to English. Carol, Sakiko, and I discuss the role of women in Japanese society, the loss of power and control that happened some centuries ago.

The thick slices of beef fragrant with soy sauce, ginger, garlic are so tender I hardly need to chew. Bowls of dipping sauces, sautéed vegetables, and rice are scattered around the table.

Kenzo, who is an international commodity broker, and I discuss the cultural differences in the workplace while we pick up and dip and suck food from ebony chopsticks.

"Ty has saved me from a life of shopping," Sakiko giggles, her hand covers her mouth. "Shopping and mah-jongg." Diamonds on her fingers splash rainbows on the sterling as she places meat in the center of the table.

"Saved you?" I ask.

"Yes. Before he let me in class as special student, all I did was shop, shop, shop. Now, I paint. Painting better." Her voice is soft, almost a whisper.

Kenzo smiles at her. Then talks about his mah-jongg days in college. He brings out his mah-jongg set, lights a cigarette with the glowing tip of another, while watching me out of the corner of his eyes. The acrid cigarette mixes with the pungent garlic.

I admire the set, ivory hieroglyphics in an inlaid mahogany box, soft and slippery leather interior.

"Let's see your new collages," Mak says.

Sakiko passes them around the table. Vibrant colors and torn paper, cut shapes and oil pastels. They have an innocent charm. Some are representations of her and Ty done in pulsing colors. In one, Ty is a large presence beaming at her while she looks up adoringly at him. In another, he is a figure she flits around.

Made uneasy by the eroticism of the work, I check Kenzo's reaction. A slow smile slides from one side of his mouth.

"These are my gratitude to Ty. Showing me how and giving me special paper, what you say, stencil paper to tear." Sakiko gazes adoringly at Ty, just as she does in the collage.

Mak says, "Why, Sakiko, in this one, you have yourself in traditional Japanese wedding dress."

Ty studies a greased background of a winter storm.

Sakiko snatches up the collages, her sharp nails click against the sterling, the diamonds on her Rolex watch flash. "Time for coffee, tea, dessert," she whispers.

. . .

That night Ty and I make love and I snuggle in my place, my head cradled by his shoulder, his arm around me. His breaths still too rapid to synchronize with mine. "I wish you wouldn't collaborate with her."

"Uh?"

"I think she has a crush on you."

"It's about art. We like making art together." His voice has its sleepy sound, slow and mumbly.

"She's in Oedipal thrall with you."

"Don't give me an ultimatum." Ty turns his back and drifts into sleep.

CHAPTER 39

Ty's paintings are hung in Brazil, and he gives a series of lectures in Salvadore da Bahia on his art and African American art to the university. We tease each other in the pool of our hotel, swimming back and forth while drinking caipirinhas — cheap brandy with lime juice and sugar — from a bar in the pool. The sun is hot and the sky blue and the sea beats against black boulders not yet softened by the surging tide.

We wander the hump of Brazil, the faded colors of Pelourinho, visiting a candomble ceremony and remarking how close it is to Ty's family's church. The rhythms of Africa fill the city, fill the dancing beat. We stay in luxury hotels and cheap hotels and monasteries on our voyage to Cachoiera where African-style wood carving is still done.

During carnival, the Fillo's de Gandi parade in blue and white, singing songs with ancient sacred beats that are part of the African Diaspora. Ty looks at the throng, the spreading, smiling, dancing crowd, and spreads his arms. "Ah, life," he says.

"Sweet, isn't it?" I answer.

"So many paintings to paint." He clasps me to him and we dance. "And the whole world to show them in." He has shows scheduled for Toronto, Detroit, Germany, and Kansas City.

I laugh. "Yep. We have fun. More to come."

"I love you," he says. "I'm going to live to be a hundred. I got lots of time to paint, to wander, to see. I thought my hand was the worst thing in my life and look at the great art that's come from the pain and fear."

How lucky I am, I think. The beat in my ears, the sun on my back. My children and the miracle of giving birth, my career, my writing, and this wonderful man. I look at him, vital and engaged, rocking his body to the beat and smiling. Together, we can get through anything.

I know so well the moods of his body, the workings of his mind, the rich images that inhabit his head. He is part of the fabric of my being. His smell is as my smell, his life is as my life. He is as important to me as I am to me. I love him more with each passing year. I can't imagine my life without him. "You know," I say, "I'd still pick you to be stranded on an island with."

He throws his head back and laughs, then grabs me close to him.

CHAPTER 40

We walk along the lake, Lily and I. The sun is warm, the air cool, a few leaves tinged with yellow. Lake Mendota is to our left. Geese stand in a line facing us, guarding the river. They stick out mean tongues and hiss.

I watch my feet tread on the chipped wood trail.

"You seem preoccupied," Lily says. Usually as we walk, we gab away fast and furious about a concert, her cooking class, politics, our families.

"This relationship Ty has with Sakiko drives me crazy."

Lily is an attorney, married to Abraham, a black man who is a psychologist. She's interested in people's dynamics, but not seduced by them. Motivations never serve as excuses. "What do you think?" she asks.

I shrug, "Sometimes I think they're having an affair. Sometimes I think I'm nuts for thinking it."

"Have you asked him?" Lily has a cut-to-the-chase mind.

"Of course. Lots. He says it's about art. Just art, he's not even attracted to her. Too skinny. And..." Ducks glide in the water. The sun reflects brilliant light on the ripples their bodies make.

"And what?"

"That it's just my family dynamics, my father's and grandfather's infidelity, that make me suspect an affair."

Our strides match. We walk a few times a month, sometimes three or four miles. We cross a wooden bridge and a flock of geese fly overhead, their necks stretch southward.

"So, you know me. I delve inside. Wonder if there's some reason I need to think or feel that Ty's having an affair."

"Is there?" Her black hair shines red glints in the sun.

"Do I need to feel close to my mom and grandmother by fantasizing this? Is it a way to have something in common? Do I need some bizarre excitement in my life?"

Lily shakes her head, then turns to me. "I don't know, Annie. Do you think that? I mean it's your field, but..."

"Sounds like shit to me, too." A stark swan stretches his beak to the blue, then sails down the river. "They have a bank account together. When I asked him about it, he said it's just a way for them to buy art supplies, keep track of expenses. He said, Pam and I have a bank account for our office building. What's the big deal? But I shudder when I see their names linked on the statement that comes each month."

"It's a business account. Right?"

We veer away from the river and into a field. Drying thistle and beige seeded grasses, soft as feathers, quiver in the breeze.

"Maybe I should go into therapy and try to figure it out. I'm so jealous of her. All he does is talk about her. Her life as a rich, sheltered Japanese, driven everywhere by a chauffeur, her five houses all over the world, her art. He's fascinated."

"So different than his life. Abraham's life."

"Exact opposite."

"Who could help but be fascinated," Lily says.

"Hey, hey. It fascinates me too, just hearing his version of her life. And the presents. She showers him, us, with presents."

"Uh?" Lily ties her sweatshirt around her waist.

"Well, the first one was a huge basket of food topped by a stuffed collie with an ultrasuede tongue for Naomi. A Christmas present. Ty had run into her at the mall and introduced her to Naomi — supposedly a great honor. The present was a way to repay the honor." My words are fast and furious. "So Ty had me go buy her some canvas stretchers. Then there was a box of Godiva chocolates for Naomi on Valentine's Day. A huge box." I stretch my arms wide to show the size of the box. "Ten pounds of Godiva. A heavy Seiko watch for Ty, and a French designer watch for me. One of their houses is in Paris." The rapid walk and rushed quick speech has made me breathless. I inhale. "But it's not that. It's when she's in town it's like I don't exist."

"She's not still living here?"

"No, they're living back in Japan now. Every four months she returns to Madison to work with Ty and stays, oh, a few months. When they're working together, he's gone. I hardly see him. He's working with her."

"And is he?"

"What do ya mean?"

"Is there work? Art?" We're deep in the floodplain. Shrubbery on our left obliterates the lake.

"Yeah. And some of it's good. Really good. A floating Asian dragon, with a strong Afro improvisational feel."

Lily is quiet. "But isn't that how he is when he's doing his own shows?"

Maybe I'm jealous that I'm not part of his art process while she is. Maybe I want him home working in his studio instead of in her space. So I feel safe. "Maybe I just feel left out."

Lily laughs. "Look, I've seen you and Ty together. It's obvious that you love him, that he loves you. I remember you two playing in the pool in Brazil. Abraham and I watched you swimming back and forth and splashing each other and kissing. And I said to him, 'Look at them, they've been married for more than twenty-five years and they're still in love. What a beautiful sight.' All that passion. I felt like we were spying on you."

Tears fill my eyes.

"Is that still there?" We're the only people on the gravel path. The only people we can see. Fields and shrubs on either side.

"When she's not around."

"When she's in town, are you two still making love? 'Cause a man in his fifties can't satisfy two."

"Yeah." But I don't tell her that our sex is mechanical, automatic, product oriented. He plugs it in and I plug in my favorite fantasy and we both come and that is that. He knows exactly what to do and I am oh so easy.

The dam is ahead of us, our turnaround point. A train blares a forlorn whistle.

"Look, they're working. You're still making love. Don't turn over rocks looking for worms."

When I arrive home, Ty greets me with smiles. "Guess what. We're going to Southern France." He twirls me around. "This summer."

"France?" My eyes open wide as I catch his thrill.

"Just got a call from Gustave. We're set for the entire summer. At least two months."

"How did this happen?" Gustave is a French artist who shows widely on the continent and in America. I shake my head in happy amazement and hug Ty.

"We'll be doing a series of prints. The French are giving us studio space and some equipment."

I frown. "I can't be away that long."

"I know. How 'bout you and Naomi come as long as you can. At least a month."

"Southern France?"

"Small medieval town outside of Nimes." Ty hugs me. "I knew collaborating would open doors. Looks like Sakiko and I have a show in Toronto and Tokyo and now there's a possibility of Paris. Italian collectors will be coming to see the work in August."

I hold him tight. At last his art will get the recognition it deserves. I kiss him, press him close to me. His arms around me, his warmth envelops me. "At last, Ty. At last."

"Yep. New opportunities," he says.

Lily is right, I tell myself. Why do I think everything is about sex? It's something about Mother and Lala after all. Ty just wants to paint. This is his last chance for the brass ring.

CHAPTER 41

"How long have you been having this affair with Sakiko?"

He inhales over the phone. Then, a quiet stretch.
I am vacant in the space. In the silence.
"Not long. About a year," he says.
I have finally asked the right question. After three years of asking, "Are you having an affair?" I have asked the right question. I am cold. Icy.
"Why?"
"I love her."
I stand in our bedroom in the dark, the room half underground. Even in summer the sun is sparse. I can't swallow away the cotton in my mouth. I twist the phone cord around my hand. My mind is racing. Races. My heart pounds. He loves her. He loves her with each beat. But I knew already. I saw her seducing him with the gagagoogoo of the student for the teacher. He needed, oh how he needed that blind adoration.
Then he adds, "I couldn't help myself."
"How could you forget me? Disregard me after all these years?"
"I haven't stopped loving you. I never stopped loving you."
"Fucking me? Fucking her? When you knew how I felt about this?"
He is off in Arizona for a week as a visiting artist. Now I know he took her with him. He asks, "What happened?"
I know he means how did I finally find out. "Sakiko's daughter, what's her name? Yukari? Yukari called looking for Sakiko. Thinking she was dead in the motel or something. It took me a while to get it. I am so dumb. So damn dumb. So trusting. Yukari suspected that Sakiko was with you, and she called in her very sweet voice and left a message,

which Naomi played when we came home from her field hockey game." My words are like fast water over stones. "Which Stone heard. Stone was here for the Michigan State game. Remember?"

After the game, Stone and Molly, his fiancée, and Naomi and I went out for dinner at Sze-Chuan. "What's Dad doing in Arizona anyway?" Stone asked.

Naomi answered, "He's working with Sakiko."

Stone looked at me and said, "Is he having an affair or what?"

I shrugged and absent-mindedly stirred Kung Pao shrimp with my chopsticks.

"I told you they were having an affair years ago, when I saw them driving around in Dad's car."

"No, you didn't. You said the Japanese were too racist for them to be having an affair."

"Why didn't you stop it, Mom?"

"Stop it?" And suddenly I started crying. "How?"

When Stone left to drive to Chicago, he hugged me and said, "Call us if you need to."

"I don't know anything yet," I replied.

"Don't do an O.J. or a Lorena Bobitt."

I mustered a laugh.

Now I know. Amazing how quickly a life can crash. I grip the receiver tightly and sigh. "So, Ty, Yukari said, 'Where's my mama? I've been calling and calling and calling her hotel from here and can't find her. For three days I've been calling and no mama. I'm really worried.'" I imitate Yukari's voice, raising my own two octaves and whispering. I am vicious in my pretense at sweetness. "'Really really worried. Please call and let me know if you know where she is.'"

I pace in the dark room. Our bed fills it except for a narrow passage, but I can't contain my restlessness. I want to run. "Well, I was confused because I didn't know Sakiko was back in America, because you lied to me, you fucking bastard. You left Naomi and me painting the molding and went and picked her up at the airport and then went and fucked her, leaving the two of us to paint."

Ty and I are building a house, which will be complete in six weeks, and living in a small apartment until it is finished.

He doesn't disagree. His silence is my acknowledgment. How well I know this man I have lived with for thirty years. How little I know him.

I swallow and stretch the phone to the bathroom. Water. I need water. "So I was confused. I thought at first you lied to me that Sakiko was here in town. But Naomi put it together."

"Naomi?"

"Yes. She says, 'Mommy, maybe Sakiko's in town. Maybe Sakiko's in Arizona with Daddy.' Then in the middle of the football game, sitting with my heart in my throat and my mind skittering over the field, it finally dawns on me that she's right. Sakiko's in Arizona with you. As soon as I got home, I tried to reach you, but you had checked out. Then I remembered. Saturday. You were going to the Grand Canyon." I had always wanted to visit the Southwest with Ty and the kids. Now he'd done it with her. Without us.

"So did you call Yukari?" He's fishing for Sakiko.

"Yeah. Yukari called back and said, 'I just don't know where my mama is. This is so unlike her. She never, never goes anywhere unless she lets us know where she is. I don't know. My dad doesn't know.'" I talk in her whispery voice again. All little girl and butter wouldn't melt in my mouth. I am the complete bitch. I inhale. "Well, sweet-little-innocent-little-Miss Yukari just blew the whistle on her mom. It took me a while to get it, but I got it."

I try to swallow away the cotton in my mouth. I gulp water. Ty is quiet, listening. I talk a mile a minute, my words racing my heart.

"I didn't want to give her your telephone number. I wanted to talk with you first. I told Yukari I did not know exactly where you were and I would call her back when I found you. I said, 'Oh, is Sakiko in America?'

"She said, 'Yes. Didn't you know?' and I said, 'No, I thought she was coming in November.' 'Oh, no. She came October second. You didn't know?'" I imitate Yukari's baby voice again. "'I don't like that you didn't know my mom was in America. I don't like that she was in Arizona and Mom hasn't told me. I don't like that fact that they may be sleeping in the same hotel. That's my mom.'

"And I said, 'Well, that's my husband.' And she said, 'I'm sorry. So sorry.'"

I gasp for air. I know he's gathering information to give Sakiko so she can protect herself. But I don't care. I only care about myself and Naomi. "So. Yukari let me know." I suddenly realize Sakiko wanted me to know. She knew Yukari would try to call her and then would contact me. Sakiko wanted to force the issue with Ty.

I sit on his side of the bed and smell him – the mixture of cologne and musk sweat that is his sweet aroma — in our sheets.

The silence is violent. I didn't realize the force in my throat. I drink more water. Stay composed. I inhale. "You have a decision to make. Decide who you want. What you want. Let me know." I'm not going to let him waffle. I have seen too many patients wait for years hoping to be re-chosen by their mates, to win, their self-esteem and egos whittled away to sawdust by indecision. Women trying to hold families together at all costs. And then the kids going bananas in the emotional absence of the mother. Sacrificing. Endless sacrificing. When his plane lands the next day, his decision must be made. If it isn't, he'll have made it. I'd be gone. I want to hang up the phone and run.

"I don't want my life to change," Ty says.

"What?"

"I don't want my life to change."

"Why didn't you tell me? I asked you over and over if there was something between you and Sakiko. I made a point of asking before we started building the house."

"No, you didn't."

"What are you talking about? I did." I remember driving in Chicago before we started building. We wandered the museums, made love for hours in the afternoon, and so I felt confident to ask him once again, Do I have to worry about Sakiko? There was silence. And in the space, my confidence and buoyancy sank. "I don't think so. You are life to me. Sakiko is art. Only art." I heard what I wanted to hear.

"No, you didn't."

"I asked, 'Is everything okay?'"

"Everything was okay."

"I said, 'This is the first time we are doing something which absolutely depends on both of our incomes. This is the first time that I am financially dependent on your income for my housing.'"

"Honey."

"The first time." Always, I have followed Mother's warnings and have been able to support myself and the children. Except for now. The house requires both our incomes, and my income is down because managed care requires patients to use therapists in large clinics.

"Honey. Everything was. You think I stopped loving you?"

"You disappeared for months when she was here. I was trashed."

"I always loved you."

"Funny way of showing it. Doing the worst possible thing you could do to me. And lying. Lying. Lying. When I loved you and you telling me I'm just thinking you're having an affair because of my family dynamics." I am thirsty and drink and drink and drink, finishing another glass of water. "Do you know how seriously I took that? Actually thought I'd go back into therapy and figure out why I needed to see you as my father and grandfather?" The thought of his betrayal rips my composure and I scream. "You thought I could have the house and you could have your little rich Asian fuck, is that it? It was a tradeoff, is that it?"

"I thought I was doing the right thing."

"You fucking bastard."

"I didn't mean to hurt you."

"Didn't mean to hurt me? When for years you told me it was just about making art together. And I said, once, if you're lying I'd think our whole life was a lie. That everything was false from the beginning. That you don't know who I am. Can't contain me. Can't hold me in your mind."

"You'd think our whole life is a lie? The entire thirty years?"

"Yes."

"I didn't think you'd be this upset."

Now I twist the cord around my hand, march up and down the alley in the bedroom, the hall, the bathroom, scream into the phone. "Obliterating my reality. Mind-fucking me like that? How could you?"

"I don't want my life to change." His voice is soft. Almost gentle pleading. I imagine his eyes closed and his upper lip twitching.

"Over and over she took precedence over me and the family. Knowing, knowing how I felt."

"I don't want to lose you. I love you."

"You wouldn't have done this to me if you loved me. And did I do anything to deserve this?"

"I don't want a divorce. I don't want to lose you. I don't want a divorce. I don't want to lose Naomi."

"Lose Naomi? You can't lose her, she's your daughter. She'll always be your daughter. But my life. My life is over."

"No. No."

I want to run. Get in the car and drive to the coast. Any coast. "You decide what you want to do. Let me know." I'm not going to be my mother. I did not want to marry an obsessively unfaithful man like my father. I do not want to live with a man preoccupied by another woman for decades like Docie.

"I thought I was solving my own life. Having my freedom. Doing what I'm supposed to do. I've told you how tired I am. Tired of the university. Tired of my hand hurting. Tired."

"I know just what you're going to do. You're going to spend the night, all night fucking. But you know what? This time, I'm going to be on the ceiling watching you, watching the two of you fuck. I'm going to be there and I'm going to stick my fist up your ass and stick my fist up her ass and grab your hearts and pull them out."

Holy shit. Where did that come from?

CHAPTER 42

I wait for him to return from Arizona, peeking through the blinds. It is night. He returns in a taxi. Sakiko is with him. Two shadowy figures. I see them get into his Taurus. He is driving her to Ho Jo's and their car. They own a car together. They have a bank account together. I stand stiffly peering out from between the blinds, stuck in my position, holding the blinds open as though I am frozen. He reappears in his Taurus.

I fly out of the apartment, run at his car. I am a banshee screaming. I bash his windshield with my fist. Scream out my rage, flying through the air at the car, like a witch, like a jaguar. "What's your decision," I scream. "What the fuck did you decide?"

"I told you. I don't want to lose you. I don't want a divorce." He is startled by me.

"What about Sakiko?"

"What about her?"

"Are you willing to never see her again? To never contact her again? To never work with her again?"

He doesn't answer.

"You have to think about it?" My voice is raw with screaming.

"I don't have to think about it. I thought about it on the airplane. I thought about it all last night. Okay? I decided that whatever Sakiko and I had, that relationship is over. It's over. Because I don't want to lose you. I don't want to lose Naomi. She's not going to get a divorce either."

"Why did you do this? What was in your mind? Just a hard on? Art? You loved art so you fucked Sakiko?" I am hot, white hot, my neck pounds with blood. The obscenity leaches my rage.

"I don't know. I don't know," he says.

I inhale the night air, try to gather in the stars through the clouds.

I tell myself, I need to hear him, understand. Calm down, I tell myself. "Why?" I ask him.

We walk around the apartment complex. Naomi sleeps inside. My hand hurts from where I smashed it on his windshield. The night sky is the deep purple of the city without visible stars. I'm hot, though he asks me if I'm cold. I'm thirsty and need to pee and I haven't slept or eaten in two days. My mind circles on itself, devours itself like a dog eating its own tail. Endless whys spiral down to when we first met. Endless how could he do this to me? I've been good to him. I loved him. I trusted him. I thought he was my friend. Is it sex? I thought we had a good sexual relationship. I can't get any air. I can't turn off my mind.

"I fell in love with her. I couldn't help myself."

"Couldn't help yourself?" I spit out the words like spears. Be reasonable, I tell myself. Don't throw everything away out of hurt. Listen to him. "Explain, Ty. Please."

"It sounds crazy. I was miserable. Tired. My hand hurt all the time. I had all this shit stuff I had to do. The kids. Washing dishes. Cooking," he says.

"All you had to do was make dinner and do the dishes three nights a week. Be at home when I worked late two nights. Period." I had taken over all other parental responsibilities because of his complaints. I didn't expect him to go to school concerts, transport Naomi to lessons, arrange her summer day care, go to meetings with her teachers. Nothing. Don't be defensive. "No. I'm sorry. Just explain."

"I thought I was given Sakiko to make up for my hand. Sort of a gift from the gods, fates... I thought we'd continue our relationship. She'd come here from Japan, or England, or Paris and we'd be together. Then when she was gone, it would just be you. She and I would continue making art. Making love. There was this special freedom."

"Forever?" My stomach turns.

"Forever is a long time. She was separate. She had nothing to do with you. She was for me. You and her were in two separate categories. She had nothing to do with you," he tells me.

I shudder. Suddenly I am cold as I imagine living for years, decades with him screwing Sakiko and a sense of that relationship and the vain attempt to convince myself it was all in my mind. Like Lala and Docie. "Why did you have to sleep with her? Curiosity? What sex is like with a Japanese?"

"That was one thing."

"Well, how was it? Was she any good? Better than me?" I'm hot again.

"No."

"No she wasn't any good, or no she wasn't better than me?"

"Yes."

"Why not?" I am vicious in my pursuit, cornering him. Wanting to torture him with my words, salve myself with his pain.

"Because she didn't have..."

"I want to know why not. She didn't have what. She can't come? She's frigid?"

"I don't know," Ty says.

"You don't know? What the fuck are you talking about, you don't know."

"She doesn't have any coordination. She doesn't have any and she's skinny and she didn't have much experience." His hands are in his jacket pockets.

"Give me a break. You didn't fall for that I'm-just-so-innocent shit. She's a married woman with a husband who half the time is off in Thailand or Europe and God knows where else and she's got a grown daughter. She's as experienced as she wants to be."

We walk.

I'm thirsty. "I wish you'd have told me before the house. I could have at least been free to see if I wanted to try to continue some sort of marriage with you. I'm trapped now. I feel trapped."

"I don't see that."

I gather in the air. Swallow away the cotton. "First it's your decision will you give up Sakiko for the family, for me, for our life together. Then it's my decision. Can we go on? Is it possible to rebuild a marriage from these shards?" I have vowed to myself not to get in the car and drive to the sea – any sea. Not to go to a bar and revenge-fuck. I have vowed to try to work on my marriage. One year. One year for me to feel loved by him again, to feel like I am the most important woman in his life. In a year I'll make a decision. "I don't know who you are. I don't trust you. You're my father. You're my grandfather. You're everything I wouldn't want a husband to be." I scream. I cry. I hiss these words out at him.

"No. Oh." Tears clog his throat.

"Are all men like this? And I'm stuck with a quarter-million-dollar mortgage and my dream house. It's the only good thing in my life beside Naomi. My therapy practice going to hell because of managed care."

"Why do you have to give the house up?"

"I'll either have to stay with you or give it up." My words are clipped.

"Honey."

"I don't have a choice here. You got me in a corner. The one time in thirty years when I'm financially dependent on you. Bastard."

"Honey. You don't have to give it up. I have never stopped loving you. I have absolutely never stopped loving you," he says.

My hands clench my arms. The side of my hand throbs. I want to kill him. I smell his familiar aftershave. A Christmas present from one of the children.

"We've been walking and talking about an hour," he says.

"I have to go in and pee. Let me go in and pee," I say.

"Are you cold?"

"I'm not cold. I'm hot." He doesn't believe me.

The cement stops in a clean break, just stops right in the middle. "We've come to the end of the sidewalk."

"I didn't know the sidewalk ended."

"Me either."

. . .

I feel like something died.

It's in his genes, testosterone they tell me. So I'm just supposed to sit there and accept that he's fucking some other woman. Jabbing it in.

I'm a fool. A total asshole. I believed all these years. Trusted all these years.

I hurt my wrist bashing it into the car window. My mouth is dry with a film over my teeth that feels like scum from a pond. I drink. I drink unquenchably, thirsting to be filled with something clear, transparent, obvious, simple, when there is none of that around me. And then I pee, the clarity is yellow and I pee and I pee. I gasp water and sit on the john and wait for the pee to come.

He sleeps, a restless sleep, but he sleeps.

How could he do this to me? I sound like my clients. My life is over, forever changed. I am different. I feel it. A sudden stark drop off a cliff. A free fall.

There was a death. A death of my niceness. A death of my considering him. Considering him always, putting him and his feelings and his needs above my own. Was he comfortable? Did he like the rooms painted these colors? Buy him extra-large towels. Pick the colors he likes. Cook what he likes to eat. Come home so he can work. Always his work ahead of me. Always his feelings. It was putting his work ahead of my wishes. Denying my intuition that allowed this to happen. Putting his desire for artistic recognition above my sense of Sakiko's and his sexuality.

So now what? I don't know. I don't know if I love him. I know I'll miss him, but I don't know if I'll miss what he can give me now.

My wrist hurts. I really did a number on it.

This lack of sleep will kill me. Somehow my metabolism has changed.

He never once put himself in my shoes, looked at it from my point of view. As though I wasn't in his life. I didn't occur to him. He didn't think about how I would feel when he was off with her in Arizona, seeing the Grand Canyon, while I simply worked, painted, worked alone. Nothing mattered but him.

I hate him for that. I don't know if I can live with it.

We women are so used to thinking about others. The moment we give birth, our bodies teach us to think of others. The baby cries. It does not matter if we want to read a book or play piano or go for a walk. No, our breasts respond. We feed the baby.

My husband wants time. It does not matter if I want to go to a movie or spend time with a friend. No. I stay home so he can have his free time. He gains his freedom from my slavery.

Middle-aged women we are. Lined all up, discarded. Unwanted. Men fucking some young cunt, or new cunt. It doesn't matter. Driven. Selfish.

Ty says he's selfish and destructive. Yes. He destroyed me.

And Sakiko, she wants him to get a divorce so that he is free to do art with her. So she can use him to generate her shows. Sex was her bait.

My wrist is killing me when I have to call on it so much. My fury is a small animal underneath my breasts. It rolls in there gnawing. Creating its own nest.

I gave up too much for him. Shit. I suggested galleries suitable for their art, and I was right. They got shows. I helped him knowing it would hurt me.

It's too late.

Now what? Now what? With my life almost gone, over. Complete.

Ah, the conceits, vanities of youth.

I'm hungry. I should eat. I can't imagine what.

I need to pee again. Again.

The big tragedy here is I don't care if he paints anymore. I'm not interested. It's as if I have sacrificed one last thing for his art and I'm done. Finished. This may mean the marriage is over. I don't like him. I don't respect him. I don't believe he loves me. I don't believe he even knows who I am.

I can't imagine making love again. I can't imagine sex without rage.

I never did anything to deserve this. I hate him for what he's done to me. He must not have felt my concern for him, my absolute consideration of him. And that is gone. Dead.

Maybe that is the death I feel. I no longer will consider him. And maybe Lala felt that same death and it ended up being the continual small bickering, the lack of politeness and obvious annoyance between her and Docie. A lack of respect. And of course she hated men. Selfish boys who never learned to go beyond themselves. Maybe she was right. "When it's hard, he's soft. When it's soft, he's hard." Sperm with earning capacity.

I've made her mistakes all over again.

I will not be a victim of this like my mother and grandmother. I will not. I'm not sure how. Not yet.

CHAPTER 43

White glides on, the wood sucks it up. My finger pushes soft plastic into the dimples, fills small holes in the molding with putty, then rubs it smooth. I slick on more White Dove paint. I have made the hole invisible, no one would know the wood was wounded. The paint evokes peace. The irony of peace.

The house is almost ready for us. The tiles I made are set in the bathroom upstairs. Glistening an iridescent green, the snake, frog, chameleon glide, leap, swim across the smooth white. I turn on the brass faucet and a sheet of water eases into the tub. A waterfall.

I don't sleep. I don't eat.

I can't stop moving, restless walking when I'm not painting. The only time I'm stationary is when I'm in my office seeing patients. I shower, carefully line my eyes, paint on my mouth with a pencil, and drive to the office. It is the same as always. Begonias flowering, the faint smell of apple cinnamon potpourri, quiet, unobtrusive paintings. I sit in my leather chair, my index finger rubs the leather already frayed in one spot. My patients' words take me away from my own grief. My life is obliterated by their lives. Blessed relief. I hear with a fresh-honed perception.

Back to the house. I take off my dress and stockings. Matt, one of the finish carpenters, walks in on me while I'm changing. He is mortified. My work clothes are stiffened from dried paint and putty. I can tell Matt's back hurts by how he moves. The men play country and western music. The twang of guitar, sad lyrics of lost love and betrayal, miserable jobs and dysfunctional families surround me and my White Dove. It suits my mood.

I tell them, "You're all going to commit suicide. Listeners to country and western music have the highest suicide rate of any music listening group."

One by one they come to talk to me while I paint. Matt, tall with a cigarette-slim body, is a Viet Nam vet with post-traumatic stress. Dan is in recovery, been sober for five years now. George is on Prozac. "Is it the country and western music?" George is eager to point his finger to the source of his pain.

"None of us escapes life's toxicity," I say. We do our own jobs, moving around each other.

Rob, the tile setter, plays classical music and looks for spirit lines in my floors, aching for perfect angles. He loves my tiles. Wants me to go in business with him.

I paint till darkness comes and return to the apartment. Naomi leafs through a Victoria's Secret catalogue. She is eleven. Black eyes in her light brown skin, hair to die for as it twists and snakes into long ringlets. We stare simultaneously at a woman stretched out in a black lace bodysuit. Her breasts bulge whitely over the wired lace. In the classic odalisque pose, her head rests on outstretched arm, her lips thickly shellacked. Sexy, I think. Maybe I'll buy a lace bodysuit, I think.

"If you looked like that," Naomi asks, "would Daddy have stayed faithful?"

I know the answer to this one. Her other questions I can't answer as easily.

"What's wrong with the women in our family that this happens over and over?" she asks.

"The choice of our men, I guess."

"What do I have to do so this won't happen to me?"

My heart falls to my stomach. I wish I could tell her a pretty story. "I don't know. When I figure that out, I'll let you know. I thought I had, but I hadn't. I'm sorry." I hug her. I would have done anything to protect her from this. Anything. Is this my failure?

"Why did Daddy do this?"

"Ask him."

Instead she throws it in his face. "Did you have to do it with all three major racial groups?" She spits her words at Ty. He walks away.

But this question, the question about Victoria's Secret I know the answer to. "The most beautiful woman I have ever seen, ever, has an unfaithful husband. It's not about how you look."

She looks at me with wide eyes, pleading, "Daddy loves you, Mommy. He loves you with all this heart, he just has a small heart."

I don't know how to respond. Can love be measured? All I need from him is to feel cherished now. He caulks the molding I have painted. He says, I love you, I don't want to lose you.

I tell him "Heal me, heal me. I hand myself to you. You say you want me. Then figure out a way to put this back together."

I wait. I am open to him. I dream up ways he can make me feel cherished, convince me of his commitment to me and our life together. I drink water. I pee. I chew my food slowly and force myself to swallow. Ty can beg my forgiveness, whisk me away to an island somewhere — shit, even a long weekend at the local motel, just the two of us — to find our way back to each other. We can repeat our vows on our thirtieth wedding anniversary under the oak tree in our new house.

Stone writes a script of what he would do in similar circumstances. He would woo me. Ty does none of it.

I ask him what he's thinking and he says, "I'm thinking about a grant I have to write and an executive committee meeting and a student review I have." His mind offers him relief from our drama. He puts me away so easily. So easily.

"I'm thinking about our last trip to Chicago. I'm thinking we should go into therapy. I'm thinking about your hand. I redo every conversation we've ever had over and over in my head. Trying to figure out over and over again why this happened."

He looks away.

"He was faithful to you for thirty years. Maybe that's all anyone can be." Naomi offers her suggestion with terror.

Her eyes are wide, waiting for my reassurance. Tears shine them. Pleading clots her voice. I will try. I will do anything for this child. Finishing my job raising her is the only certainty in my future. I will go on regardless and make myself happy as I always have. My children, my friends, my work, my writing, my art. A full life. I'll move into the house, paint wildflowers, trees, mosses. Write. See patients.

Ty says, "I know you'll probably have an affair. Go on and do it." He wants me to relieve his guilt. He wants me to punish him.

I put chicken and Idaho potatoes in the oven. Tear up romaine. Squeeze lemon on the chicken, sprinkle with herbs. Rosemary is sharp, prickly barbs. Naomi hates this dinner. I'm too tired to think of anything else. I won't eat anyway. She probably won't either. Dinner is an exercise in maintaining the form of family.

I push my chicken breast from one side of my plate to the other. I sprinkle salt and pepper on my potato.

"Are all men unfaithful?" She pours ranch dressing on her salad.

"No. About half," I tell her. "Don't forget, women are unfaithful, too." I smash yogurt in the potato and eat two bites. I pull out the meat with sharp tines and eat the skin.

After dinner, I tell Naomi I have an errand to run.

I drive to the art school. Ty's car is in the parking lot. I get out of the car and search through his briefcase, hunting. I have searched and searched my mind for answers and found only questions. He gives me none. Now I search his briefcase. In his briefcase, I find a small cassette tape. I slide it into my pocket. In his briefcase is our telephone bill, still sealed. Why? Doesn't want me to see all the calls to Japan? From Arizona to Japan? I don't know. In his briefcase is his address book. I write down her address. Tucked and folded in the flap of the cover, I find a slip of paper. Gray paper, white lines. Black writing. Childlike insecure letters. My heart fills my ears. My hands shake. The note reads: *"How are you Ty! Are you ok? I miss you so much and I love you. I had dreams two times of you I was happy that morning. I want talk with you face by face. I miss you. Love Sakiko."*

My heart sinks. A year before he admits they were making love. Obviously they were. "Not so long," he said, "only a year." I hear his voice saying these words. He halved it, at least. Two years maybe three, just like I felt it.

He keeps lying to me.

I keep the note and the tape and return home.

CHAPTER 44

Mandy, now flying between New York and Paris on her writing assignments, has been involved with an Italian lover for several years. Her lover is chronically unfaithful. Their agreement is that he will absolutely not allow her to become sick — i.e., get a STD. At first she slept with additional men in order to diminish her vulnerability. When I tell her what's happened with Ty, she says, "Sleep with two men. That's what men do. Sex doesn't make you closer if there's more than one. Then no one man matters, you know?"

I can't imagine sleeping with another man. I can't even have sex with Ty. It terrifies me. Another friend later tells me that there needs to be three, with three men you don't get attached.

"Come to New York," Mandy says. "We'll go cruising. Get laid by some other man, you'll feel better." I imagine her sitting on her sofa, no makeup, playing with her toes, her eyes flashing. Mandy's hair falls to her waist, she twists it into a bun. Still has a tidy dancer's body.

"Just trying to avoid intimacy," I say.

"Men can't be intimate anyway. Be intimate with your girlfriends." She chuckles over the phone. Her dark eyes always moving. "Too bad men are so much fun in bed though, you know?"

I hear her inhale, then she lowers her voice. "I've never told anyone this, but there's something exciting about being with a man who's been with another woman. An extra charge. You know? It's a turnon." She stops. "Is this perverse of me?" she whispers.

It's the middle of the day. Fall light filters through blinds. I consider her question. "No. There's a theory that explains it. Little girls fall in love with their mothers just like little boys and later identify with their fathers, but are turned away. So they make a great switch, a psychic cross-over, such that their sexual feelings go to their father while their role identification goes to their mother." I stand up and stretch the phone cord to the bathroom for water. Start my pacing routine. "This accounts for the more complicated psychic life of women and the many emotional ties to other women."

"Women are close emotionally to women because women are emotionally available," she says. "Everyone is closer emotionally to women, don't you agree?" I imagine her eyes on her baby grand piano, eager to place her fingers on the keys.

"Yes. That's the point. This is why. So women nurture and it gets perpetuated. Anyway this Electra dynamic also creates a great triangle in the woman's mind that gets perpetuated during sex. The need for another person. Could be you're identifying with the man making love to you, could be you're on the ceiling watching, could be you're thinking about making a baby, or you're pregnant or you have a baby in which case there's always a triangle. Or if the man's involved with someone else — or if you're involved with someone else. Maybe that's why there's such a thrill — it's a vicarious way to make love to another woman. To have a mommy and daddy simultaneously." I'm explaining a dynamic I have explained a hundred times to patients, the triangles in women's minds. The theory usually provides the relief of shared feeling without the change of insight.

"I don't know. It sure is a turnon." Mandy says. "Besides, everyone likes the fantasy of group sex, you know."

"True." Research I did for my book indicated men's most popular fantasy is two women. Women's second most popular fantasy is group sex. I do not tell Mandy all this. I am tired. Our earliest childhood yearnings and fears are material from which we develop our fantasies. Often, we have our childhood triangles of exclusion and adoration, containing our most painful, most terrifying, most joyous potentialities. The possibility of gaining the world of love, bliss, and oneness teeters on the edge of a cliff. Close to winning it all, while close to losing it all.

Suddenly, Mandy laughs, "You know, you gotta see how funny this is. At least from one point of view. You've got a great short story here in your own life. Collapse time a bit. Just imagine. You're on the Donahue show, Oprah, whatever ones you did, talking about the joys of monogamy. You come home from the show and play your messages and discover that your husband is having an affair. You see what I mean?" Mandy laughs. "Perfect postmodern irony."

I manage only a bitter burst of chuckle, as mean as a growl. "Right now it doesn't seem funny."

CHAPTER 45

The familiar smell of turpentine and paint welcomes me to the art school. I have never known his schedule. I never knew what he did when I was not with him. I do not even know his office telephone number. I only knew if he'd be home for dinner, if he were picking up the kids from school or driving them to a lesson or a game. I trusted him.

Now I know his schedule. He has a lunch break at eleven-thirty.

I walk down the halls and see him. There. Standing and talking to Sakiko. Her back is toward me. I am struck by how easy it is to catch them. He towers above her, his mouth stops moving when he sees me. Then she turns and walks away, but I am fast. I intercept her.

"Sakiko. I would like to talk with you. I think we should have dinner. When would be convenient for you?"

Her white shirt balloons over black tights. She has the same huge diamond studs in her ears. She blinks at me. Her hair is pulled in a ponytail, thick and black. She whispers. I hardly hear her. Sounds of walking students, talking students reverberate in the corridor and I crane my neck to hear her. Is she afraid of her own words, or is this a ploy to gain power but remain in the prescribed obsequious feminine mode? I step closer. I smell her. Chanel and turpentine, a stomach-twisting combination.

She whispers, "The Train Track at seven. Be patient with my English. Like Ty." She glances at him adoringly. Is it that even now she can't control her desire or that she is infinitely manipulative?

"See you at seven. At the Train Track." I turn to leave and Ty spins me around by my elbow. I say, "You're still seeing her." I narrow my eyes to pinpoints.

"We were talking about art. She has to finish up some pieces for her show." He has a pleading look to his face. "She's afraid of you. Afraid you're going to hurt her."

"I'd like to kill her."

He stares at me and shakes his head.

"You're still working with her," I hiss.

"I can't make her leave the country."

. . .

My hair smells of coconut. I blow it dry and fluff it till it is satin. My dress has full-blown cabbage roses crowding the black. My lids are peach, my cheeks rose, my lips delicate brown. Mother's pearl earrings emblazon my ears as though she can impart strength. My heart pounds as I drive. The steering wheel keeps my hands from shaking.

The Train Track is next to the railroad tracks, a seafood restaurant that has evolved from genteel to fashionable to yuppie. When Ty and I first arrived in Madison, it was the destination dining spot. Now it has been eclipsed by trendier restaurants serving arugula with dried Traverse City cherries, Amish chicken breasts with pecans and gingered squash.

Sakiko sits smoking on the bench. She, too, has dressed for the occasion — a tunic and pants clotted with gold threads. Her hair shampooed and down. She has told the maitre d' that we need a smoking section. I am not hungry. The restaurant is busy and we are crowded at a small table sandwiched between a wall and a sink lined with glasses. She lights another cigarette — long and thin and very white. Her face is long and thin, her eyes black and luminous in the light brown flesh. There is no rouge on her cheeks. Black eyeliner accentuates her eyes and straight lashes. I note her skin is the same color as was Ty's mother's when I first met her thirty-five years earlier. White people get whiter with age, blue almost. Brown people get darker. As though we all condense. Sakiko is probably careful to stay out of the sun. Her face is horsy-looking and she continues to whisper at me. Tall, but skinny, she is a woman without apparent strength or sinew. She does not know what to order. She hopes I am patient with her English. I disregard the waiter.

I know she is moving to England because of Kenzo's business. I suggest baked Brie in a crust, very continental. I suggest it in all innocence. Later I learn that many Japanese think cheese is disgusting.

I order a salad and shift the mesclun around my plate with the tines of a fork.

"Don't forget to eat," she tells me. "Ty worry for you if you don't eat." Her fingers are bony.

I find her semblance of concern and intrusion into Ty's and my relationship patronizing. "Your English is fine."

"Thank you. Ty help me." I bet he did, I think.

I lean across the table to hear her whispers.

"Tyrone very important to me." Sakiko makes a fist and pulls out her index finger. "First important, my husband, Kenzo." She pulls out her middle finger, "Then Yukari. Then girl friend, Trina. Then Tyrone." Her fingers are knives piercing the air.

I wonder why her mother is not on the list. Then I remember. She hates her mother. Doesn't like being a mother, either.

"Ty teach me about art. Art most important thing in my life. Without Ty, I not be artist. I not paint."

"If you're an artist, you're an artist." I say. "No one stops you."

"I can't paint without Ty. I need him."

She's right. Without the strength of his images, she is glib backgrounds, marbled colors. His figures move her facile decoration to art.

"Ty part of my big dream. Be artist. Have show Tokyo, London, Toronto, New York." She pokes a fork through the crust.

I'm only going to fence so long. I have my own agenda. "Why did you sleep with him?"

She inhales. "I not sleep with him. I not have affair with your husband." Her words are flat.

I blink at her.

She lights another cigarette. "Eat your dinner," she whispers at me.

I nod at the Brie, glistening plastic under the golden brown crust. "You eat, too."

"I eat already."

"Why did he tell me he had an affair with you then?"

"He confused." There is not a ruffle on her face. Not a fragile tremble in her lip or quiver of eyebrow muscle. Her face is polished calm.

"Look. I'm worried about AIDS here. I understand you and Ty had unprotected sex. Your husband spends half his time in Thailand. I'm going to be talking to him."

"Talk to him?" She fishes melted cheese out of the crust. Strings hang from it. She puts her fork down and pulls out a green grape from a bunch and chews it. "Why you want ruin everything? Big beautiful house, marriage, three kids. Why you want to tumble all down?"

Is she threatening me? Will she destroy everything if she is pushed? Can she? "The house is for my family. Not some status symbol." I shrug. "If there's no family, the house means nothing."

She inhales her cigarette and stubs it out. She deals in symbols, glib decorated surfaces.

"Give me a reason why I shouldn't talk to him?"

"No need to worry about me and Kenzo. You not get AIDS from us."

Ty has told me she uses condoms with her husband, birth control pills with him. I find this hard to believe. I frown.

"Japanese women not have affairs. Japanese women always faithful to husbands."

"Always?"

"Always." She stares at me with unblinking black eyes.

"Never, never in all of Japanese history has a Japanese woman been unfaithful?" I stretch her lies to the hilt. How far will she go?

"Never. In all of history." She assures me as though she can actually convince me of this. She continues, "Japanese men faithful to their wives. Japanese men never have affairs. Never never in all history."

I hold back a laugh. Does she expect me to believe this? "That's not true. I have patients who are prostitutes who service Japanese men."

She shakes her head, "Not married. No. Not married."

Case closed.

"You just think we have affair because I woman and he man. If I man, you not think this." The waiter refills our water glasses.

"Of course not. Ty's heterosexual." I eat a blade of lettuce. "He's worked with women before, I haven't thought he was sleeping with them. Besides, he told me he was having sexual intercourse with you. He told me."

"It's just that I woman and he man."

"No. You could be two women or two men and be lovers." How can this conversation be so ridiculous. Stupid.

She laughs, "My girl friend and I go to bar in Japan and we talk. Like this." She motions between us and draws on her cigarette. The smoke is blue when it exits her lungs. "And we spend evening very very late talking. No men send drinks. Usually two women in nice bar get drinks send. But this time, no. So we ask boy — waiter, what you call? — why and he say men think we lesbians." She laughs.

Why is she telling me this?

"Then we go vacation, the both of us. And we on bed, lying, talking and door open a little bit. Like this." She brings her palms together and separates them about a foot showing the door ajar. "We laugh and laugh at idea people walking by, see our four feet, hers and mine on bed and think what those two doing in there? Oh, so silly."

She has come alive. I wonder if she made love with her friend Trina, number three, just before Ty in her enumeration of important people.

"So. Two women, two men can be lovers."

"He just imagined."

'Why would he imagine something that would make me so upset, damage all our lives, hurt Naomi?"

"I so sorry your daughter in this. But." Sakiko shrugs. "Don't know. You ask him."

This is pointless. Her lies diminish my rage. My heart sinks for Ty. She denies him so easily. He was dispensable. Their love secondary. If she had said, I love your husband, he's a great lay and I will continue to see him if I can, and I need him for his art, I will fight for him, I would have respected her. Now I feel sad for the bargain Ty has struck.

I think all this as I toy with my salad. She talks of moving to England. The great trust she has for her husband. Of Yukari in Japan. We push our food back and forth with our utensils, maintaining the illusion of eating. There is no ground that we both stand on.

After more politeness, she looks at me and asks, "Can I work with Ty? Being artist most important in my life. Can Ty teach me, work with me more?"

I meet her eyes. "That's up to him." I do not say, if he chooses to work with you, then I am gone. I do not say that.

"Please don't tumble all down. Being artist my life. My dream." She whispers. Her eyes are wet. "Your dream the big house."

She is so wrong. My dream is my family. "It's already tumbled down," I say.

I know her agenda. I shrug. "Ty makes his decisions. This is not something I give permission for."

She looks away, flicking the ash off her cigarette onto the restaurant floor.

CHAPTER 46

After my brazenness at initiating dinner and my refusal to adopt her face-saving lies – or was she trying to save my face? — Sakiko returns to London. I imagine her telling Kenzo, "Ty is on the executive committee, building a house, too busy to work. His wife is crazy, jealous. Just because we man and woman working together."

Stone and Molly have set the date for their wedding. "Why do you want to get married?" I ask.

"I can't get over Dad being like all the jerks I work with. Thinking about fucking women all the time. Just like all those assholes. All they do is get drunk and run around with women. He turned out to be no better," Stone says.

I don't defend him.

"I love you, Mom," he says.

"Must be hard for you. Us getting married with all this going on," Molly says.

I shrug. Their wedding is the least of it.

Michelle says, "How ya doin, Mom? What a disappointment. He went against everything he taught us. All the values: to be honest, not to lie. I am so disappointed." She turns her face away. "Like my whole childhood is a lie."

"I meant it, lived it. Still believe it," I tell her.

"You've lost a lot of weight, Mom."

"Hell of a diet," I say.

"I had the intact family, the strong values. I feel sorry for Naomi. She has to go through all this," Michelle says.

"Hey. Let's wait and see. Besides. She has me."

"I wouldn't stay with a man who fucked around. What's the point?"

That's her image of a strong woman. "You don't throw away a thirty year marriage that easily. We had a lot of good years. I'm giving myself time to see if we can build a new marriage. Besides, there's what's best for Naomi."

"He doesn't seem like Dad anymore."

On a Wednesday morning, the light dim in our apartment, I play the miniature tape I took from Ty's briefcase. I slide the tape into its port and think, this is probably one of his lectures. Didn't he mention taping them, hoping to edit them into a book?

I push the button and hear droning sounds. I flip the tape over and there is Sakiko's whispering voice. My mind scatters. I cannot make sense out of her words. Ah. Yes. She drives around Paris describing the bridges, gargoyles, the store where she buys food for dinner. "Ah, here is Louvre. Just pass it, see new pyramid. See river with boat homes."

Now she is back. She bought rice, shrimp, and melon, she tells him. Strawberry pie on custard.

I pace the apartment. The tape player in my hand. I stop in the kitchen and pour a glass of water. The blinds are drawn, only one light is on. I walk in gloom, dim dampness. Swallow the water, trying to quench an unlimited thirst.

"Kenzo was out till 2 a.m. My girl friend tease, where is Kenzo? Where is Kenzo? He stop off at hotel, be with woman?" Sakiko laughs. "I trust my Kenzo. I his only woman." She gloats.

"I must go to Thailand with Uncle. Don't want to go. But Mother says must. So must. Too busy to go.

"But you, Ty, optimistic about Ann's trust. You optimistic. Leave all tapes around. Leave all letters around. Assume she never look through things. Too optimistic about her trust. I get nervous about tapes. Too dangerous. We stop."

Even she grasps my trust of him, my partner. How little I plague his life. How stupid my belief in him. I pour another glass of water.

"Even if we not send tapes I have you in mind. You always in mind. I still love you. I still know you. Forever. Even never see you again. Never hear you again. Still love you, Ty."

I walk faster around the bed, into the living room, into kitchen, back to the living room, through the hall, around the bed. I picture her driving while talking into a box and trying to reach out across miles of ocean and a continent to him.

"Still linked one to other. Can imagine right now what you do. You eating dinner and working on Nordic Track. You draw huge animals, abstract, vague. Mix vital blue for large mural. You think about me. I feel you reach me."

My glass is empty. My thirst unsatisfied. I turn the tap and watch the water turn white with agitation. My glass is filled. The water overflows and cools my hand. Water rushes over my fingers, fills the sink. I drink again.

"Even when we old together. You say you love me when my hair all gray. My hair getting gray now. Need to change it. How you say? Dye it. What color? Not black. Too dark. Brown. Brown, deep dark brown. Dye hair color of your skin. I'll dye my hair the color of your skin."

The color of his skin? She's going to dye her hair the color of his skin. The image startles me, shocks me in its absurdity and in its, yes, passion. In her desire for his body, she uses her hair to enact his presence. As she brushed it, would she smell him? Feel the softness of his flesh in the inside of his elbow? Around his navel? His testicles?

"How far you come from small family out into world. First white woman. Now Japanese woman."

How she assumes her replacement of me. I pace. Then give up and sit on the side of the bed.

"So different than tape you send me of singing. The church music at death. Don't understand as death. Sound so happy. So happy.

"Ah, here come street. See top of Eiffel Tower far away. Back home.

"Here I am again. Like talking to you, Ty. Wish we were face by face. Must get ready for Thailand. Next Saturday. So much to do, I tell them. But no. Must go...

"Now I turn corner. Ah, there my store where I buy the pumice stones you love.

"One more month and I see you. You and me in Arizona. You and me away from bullshit of Madison." She spits out bullshit, not whispering, and I know from the display of anger the bullshit she refers to is me.

"Don't feel bad about our studio. Not your fault. Not your fault. Ann's fault our studio ruined by house. Her fault. I love you, Ty." Her voice soft and melodic to comfort him.

I have finished another glass of water and sit stuck on our bed. On Ty's side of our bed. Sakiko had her own agenda. She knew that I was trying to achieve more watchfulness. She wanted me to discover their relationship so a decision would be forced. She was certain he would choose her and freedom. Unlimited wealth and easy mobility, no obligations. No cooking spaghetti for us, no having to watch Naomi's field hockey games, no having to pick her up at school the nights I work. A man can do better, a man needs freedom. The gloaming is thick in our bedroom, the work of the blinds almost complete.

She whispers to him, "Soon, soon I see you. Soon, soon I see you and go to Arizona be with you. You and me. You and me only alone."

And then silence. I know the love she did not tell me at the Train Track.

CHAPTER 47

I paint our bedroom walls hyacinth, the blue of the sky at its most glorious. The walls wick up the color, as though starved for gaiety. Beyond the blue, tangerine yellow aspen dance in my windows, quiver with each breeze. The violence of the consummation captures my breath. Painting is done. Floor is down. Carpeting tomorrow.

Ty brings his students to the house. While I work, he stands, laughs and jokes with them. "This is where my studio will be. 1,200 square feet. A gallery over there for when collectors come." He points to a twenty-foot-long expanse of white wall, he smiles. He listens to them, gives to them, flatters them, and they respond. I am part of his stage setting. He is all the things I used to find so endearing. I know the hole Sakiko wormed into — his need to have people fawning, the football hero, the mentor, the teacher. Now I find his charm silly.

"What are you thinking about?" I ask him in bed that night.

"I'm thinking about what I have to do. All the work I have to do."

I don't think about it. I just do it. He calculates that if he works hard enough, it will prove something to me.

Or does he? Maybe Sakiko waits in the wings. Maybe he'll move me into the house, talking all the time about how much he's damaged us, but giving me nothing. He hasn't committed to me, to our marriage. When she's ready, when he's ready, they'll have their studio, their life together.

"I thought what I was doing was so right. So right," he says.

"I don't know how you could think that. How you could tell yourself that lie." I wish I could sleep. Sleep the rest of my life away. But I can't. Two straight hours is a victory. "I don't understand how you could have gotten so off base. Maybe something to do with your mother's death. Maybe something in the surgery for your hand." I feel his suffering. I can't just forget him. "You need to sort all this out."

"Even now you're trying to help me. Always helping everybody. Quit it. Help yourself. Take care of yourself."

I get up and drink more water and turn on the TV. It's a PBS show on black movies of the first half of this century.

I try to sleep. Useless. I sit in the dark of our bedroom and type with the monitor off. The green glow under my fingers is the rectangle of the on button. But I wake him anyway. It is four-thirty. There is a small sliver of rose gold from the light in the parking lot beyond the venetian blind.

"Tell me what you did. How you fucked her," I say. I want him to tell me every position, every act so that I am there in his mind when he thinks of it. It won't be their secret. I will be there with him. Maybe it will get Sakiko out of my mind.

"No."

. . .

David says, "Don't ask him about their sex life. He'll never tell you the truth. He fucked her for a year. They did everything. Every position. Oral. Anal. Just assume they did it all."

We are talking on the phone. When I tell him of Ty's affair, he says, "I thought you two were the perfect couple. That you had made it."

"Me, too."

"I thought you had escaped." I know he's talking about our heritage of adultery.

"Me, too," I say and then I tell him that I've asked Ty to heal me.

He tells me this story: "There was a very handsome man, a notorious womanizer. He could have any woman he wanted and he did. One day he fell in love and the woman he loved would have nothing to do with him. 'You'll just cheat on me,' she said. And so the man tattooed his face so that he looked like a freak and came to her and said, 'Now I look like a freak. No other woman will have me. You can be certain I will be only yours.' The woman would have nothing to do with him. And of course neither would any other woman."

"I don't expect Ty to destroy himself or what I love about him. I don't expect him to stop painting or castrate himself," I say.

"Think about what you need him to do. Make sure it's possible. He can't undo what he's done."

CHAPTER 48

Empty boxes fill the narrow passageway. I have no place to pace. I dread packing up the apartment. Every item will be a mockery. The Dansk dishes and silverware I bought for our new kitchen. The large towel sheets Ty loves, a deep green to match my tiles. The clock he bought me for my fortieth birthday. A burlesque of the life we had. He goes to the university. I inhale and start wrapping dishes in newspaper.

What should have been the happiest time in my life has turned into a sleep walk. I'd rather be at the new house with the workmen than with my husband.

. . .

We are lying in bed. I'm desperate to get Sakiko out of my head. I want to erase her with my body. I say to him, "Fuck me." I have never thought of sex with him as fucking before, but I can't make love with him. We kiss, but Sakiko watches, licks her lips. I rain mean little bites on his torso, on his groin, up and down the shaft of his cock. He misconstrues this as passion, but it's rage. Hate. I am erasing her. Kenzo applauds. I claim territory. My nails cut Ty's back. Sakiko's hair shields her face. My teeth clench his flesh. I am the one with the cock. I rape him. Sakiko and Kenzo hover over us, roll around the bed with us. I struggle to reach orgasm. but the release is without pleasure. A mean victory instead of a wild soaring. He feels this intensity and thinks it passion. Sakiko and Kenzo stay in bed with us. Ty and I are never alone.

. . .

He touches my shoulder, but I don't respond. I need to work on this, I remind myself. I lay in his arms on a damp morning. His sweat smells of garlic. He asks, "What are you thinking."

I hesitate and then tell him. "I no longer would pick you to be with on a desert island. I am losing myself. I need to figure out a way to take care of my stress. I keep doing everything I can to lift this fog. Exercise, go swimming. Keep a journal. Spend time with friends, do things I used to enjoy. Force myself to eat. I need to figure out how to make my life happy. With or without you."

He is silent.

I ask him, "What are you thinking?"

"I'm not thinking. Just feel sad. Incredibly sad." I do not know if he feels my pain or his loss of me. I do not know if I've been let in or shut out.

Dinner is a prepared lasagna from Produce Place and a tossed salad. Ty is not home. He's at a meeting somewhere. I clear boxes from half the table, two chairs. Naomi and I eat on paper plates with plastic utensils. Boxes surround us. I pour crushed red peppers on my lasagna. Something easily pungent.

"I don't think anybody has a normal life. I don't care about my life. No one has a normal life," Naomi says.

"No one has a pain-free life," I tell her. "No one escapes without trauma or tragedy." I drink my Merlot.

"No, that's not what I mean. I mean, if we had never found out about Sakiko we would have thought our lives were normal. But they wouldn't have been."

"We would have lived a lie. An illusion. We did live one. That's one of the things that troubles me most."

"Even lives that seem normal aren't. Maybe there are no perfect families."

"Uncle David says, 'We paint people the color we wish to see them.' "

"I hate this."

"Me, too."

"I can't wait till we get into the new house."

I eat my lasagna.

"Remember, Mommy, how you used to say, 'I'm sooooo excited about the new house' three times a day and I used to tease you." She rolls her eyes up and places her hand on her chest, imitating perfectly my previous happiness.

I start crying.

"I'm sorry," she says.

"Don't apologize. None of this is your fault." I reach across the table to hug her. "I wish none of this happened to you. I wish I could make this all go away. But I can't."

"It's not your fault," she says. "Sometimes I think we knew without knowing we knew." She squints her eyes. "You know what I mean."

"Yes. Knew it unconsciously. Felt it."

. . .

It's mid-November. Stone comes to help. Michelle and her husband help. We load boxes on a rental truck. Books and casual furniture and dishes. Clothes on their hangers drape over the seats in my Mazda. I hang them in freshly painted closets. Dolls, handmade willow doll beds, crayoned drawings, makeup are shoved in boxes. Food is packed in garbage bags unloaded in the new refrigerator. Rubber bands and Tupperware and curry powder. All the flotsam of family life. I unpack them in the new house, in virgin drawers and newly lined closets. Wire baskets waiting for clean underwear.

We move the things from the storage facility. Items packed when we sold our house and temporarily moved to the apartment. I have not seen these things for seven months. I take out Lala's Majorca dish, the cracked angel hovering over the infant. I feel for all the world like a girl opening another girl's boxes. Votive oil lamps that Ty and I had made love by. Sheets given to us as wedding presents. A marble pear I remember from our apartment in Chicago. The relics of another girl's life. A girl's life. Not a woman's. She was naïve and hopeful while I am not. These familiar possessions have an altered feel and smell and meaning. Leavings long stored, now seen in a harsher light.

I am in my old bed surrounded by my new blue walls. The moon shines first in my bedroom window and then travels silently to the skylight in Naomi's bathroom. Living room and dining area capture the morning sun, the trees steal luminescence from the setting sun. The screen porch is tucked in trees. Birds swoop by my windows. The trees so thick there is no need for blinds. I have built a house cloistered by trees and pitched perfectly to take full advantage. Just as I dreamed.

I try to sleep in my dream house.

CHAPTER 49

He stirs spaghetti sauce and I tear romaine for a salad. It feels like all the other thousands of times we have stood together in our kitchen and cooked. Life is normal. I collapse a box and he reaches for it, swiftly cuts it into neat squares and I slip into the familiar comfort of working together. Life is usual. He brings Naomi home from school and they come in the door and I am happy to see my family. I relax, ease into the ordinary, the customary.

Without provocation Sakiko and Ty whirl in my head, my stomach twists. I am heartsick. I am slapped in the face. My old life is delusion.

That night, the moon hangs outside our bedroom window. Ty says, "I am afraid you'll kick me out of your life."

"You should be. I might." A star blinks next to the moon. I ask, "What are you thinking about?"

"A meeting I have to attend, a reference letter I have to write, a request for a grant I have to review. What are you thinking about?" he asks.

I swallow, the taste of mint toothpaste still faint in my mouth. "Did you kiss her eyelids the way you sometimes kiss mine? Will I ever forgive you?" I push the quilt off me. Lying in his arms, I trace a scar on his shoulder. Small rips have keloided in smooth tissue.

"I was so excited about being with her. We loved each other for years before we made love. It was so free," Ty says.

I try to stay open to him. I say, "You know the saddest thing about all this? You didn't even know how much I loved you. Didn't have a clue." I thought you were better than you are. I thought I meant more to you, that I, our life together, was significant to you. You don't love me enough to overlook my faults. You begrudge me them. I say, "You blame me for not making the world right for you. I wasn't a white goddess after all. You don't take me or my life seriously. And I took yours as paramount."

"This is too much pain. Your words are like knives in me. They rain like thunder in my ears. We should separate. You should be free. Maybe that would be easier for you, less pain."

"It doesn't matter. I have to deal with this pain regardless. You just want to run away."

"You should be free to meet another man. A man who can give you what you deserve. I can't. I'm not thinking clearly. I can't figure out anything and my judgment is poor."

I cry as he talks. I don't feel dead inside. He is locked into masochistic narcissism. "We're at an impasse. I need to talk. You can't bear it. What cures me destroys you." I'm quiet and then I say, "But that's the reverse really of what got us here. What you thought would cure you has destroyed me."

"I don't want to hear your thoughts."

"If I don't tell you, then there will be a wall so thick there'll be no way to chink it down."

I think about other wives and how they demean their husbands, make fun of them, turn them into caricatures. The husbands don't give them much, or they cheat on them. Respect evaporates. Like Lala and Docie. That'll be the best of what we can hope for.

He is silent, then says, "You're right. I love you." Then he rolls over to go to sleep. I stare out the window. The moon is gone now. A plane slowly crosses the sky, leaving a white trail. The sky pales, then transforms. Organdy clouds clot the pink.

I work to convince myself of his love. He chose me. We are stuck together through all eternity. Our genes are mixed, our thrust for the future. All those years together. A lifetime. He loves me enough that he gave her up. I made a great house. Goldfinches already are pecking the thistle from their feeder. I am happy living here. I can paint my wildflowers, finish the tiles, write my books, see my patients, finish raising Naomi.

In the kitchen, mixed in with a bunch of papers, I find a draft of a letter in his handwriting. "Sakiko — Fall is such a good time for collaboration. But you know what a tangle everything is with the house. Maybe some day we will be able to work together."

"You're not finished with her. You haven't given her up. "

"How dare you look through my things. I won't live being spied on. With no privacy."

He's not finished with her.

. . .

The turkey is in the oven filled with wild rice stuffing, dried cherries and mushrooms. Pecan maple pies are cooling on the counter. Naomi brings me her diary. "Look, Mom. This is from last year." I read her entry from the day after Thanksgiving the previous year. "Mom and Dad had a horrible fight because Dad was going to spend the day with Sakiko. Screaming and crying. I thought Mom was going to break a dish. I think Dad's having an affair with Sakiko," her diary reads. "See, we knew."

"Yes, we knew," I say while peeling potatoes. "We didn't always know we knew."

Before dinner, I unpack a box of books and find one inscribed to Ty from me. I was at the Sewanee Writers' Conference. *"To my husband — I have thought about you all this week, thought about your love, gentleness, integrity. To me, Ty, you are a hero. I love you."* The handwriting is mine. The words swim. I turn the book over and close it. My own words haunt me. My eyes burn with tears.

Stone and Molly, Michelle and her husband and children come for Thanksgiving. They enjoy the food and the conversation seems normal.

Ty does not reach out to me. Before I fall asleep that night, I know the sense that I had that everything could slide back in place and be normal is gone. It will never be how it used to be. I have incorporated his infidelity.

CHAPTER 50

I meet Ty at an art opening and he's wearing a tie that had been Kenzo's. He sees my fury and asks, "What's wrong?" Ty's colleagues, the art collecting community, university administrators are dressed in black and arty jewelry. They wander about, form small clusters, hold plastic glasses filled with white wine, look at the beads on mythical creatures. I say, "You're wearing her husband's tie."

"I wasn't thinking."

"How the hell can you wear the tie of a man whose wife you fucked?"

"I just grabbed the tie. It looks good with this suit."

"How can you wear it with me now. Here. Our first night out together?"

"I wasn't thinking."

"You never do." I can't stop myself anymore. I'm out of control.

I follow my own antidepression recipe. I work out. I do things I used to enjoy, shop for Christmas, spend time with friends. My friend Lily brings sandwiches and a chocolate torte to my office and presses me to eat. Alexia and Pam call and talk with me. I hear their anxiety. I lose almost thirty pounds. The loss reveals muscles from years of weight-lifting, swimming, and aerobic dance. Suddenly, I have a six-pack of muscle in my torso. Even my body is not quite mine.

I get a letter that someone is interested in building a house twenty feet from my front windows. Do I want to buy the property and protect my interests? A road will be twenty feet from my new house. Instead of trees, I will see the roof and walls of a house. I stare at the letter. Everything I have worked for seems gone or threatened. Snow falls. The snow is smothering. I count my losses. I count my stupidity. I wish I had divorced Ty in Toronto when we found out about the low sperm count. I gave up too much. I wish I had investigated the possibility of everything going wrong that could, because now everything has. I count. In fourteen months my practice has diminished, my business partner, Pam, has moved away; I didn't sell a novel that I worked three years on, I left a house I lived in for seventeen years, my marriage is ruined.

. . .

White flecks sift through the sky, through the black branches and hit the ground. Slowly the ground is dusted. At first, the earth sucks up the snow. Then it powders the ground. Still I see sand, dried grass. More snow falls. Gradually, all is coated. White. Plants are covered, tree branches frosted.

Next day, my car is stuck and I'm trapped. Cold flakes hit my face like pins. Snow buries, silences the world. I watch it fall. Watch it mound on branches, fold in the eaves. Birds peck through it to reach seeds.

. . .

Ty complains about his day. Too many meetings. A dean who can't make a decision. "I wanted you to be my hands and you weren't. You weren't able to do enough to make the pain go away."

"I didn't solve your life for you." I am resigned.

"No, you didn't."

"No, I didn't."

"You cared for the children too much. I never got that from my mother. That caring." His strangled voice says, "I was the better son."

"Better son?"

"I deserved it more than our children."

"You deserved it, too," I say. "I was not enough." He was jealous of the love I gave our children.

Somehow in the silence we fall asleep.

The next morning, he continues the conversation as though we had never slept, "What is a limited-partnership marriage?"

"Like so many other marriages. An economic and companionate partnership with no expectations of intimacy or closeness. That's what we've had the last three years. I just didn't know it." I say. We lay in bed, each in our own side. "I thought we were special. I thought we had a special relationship. That's what I'm mourning." I need to give up that fantasy, too. Of us being better than other lovers.

"I did too. I still do in some ways," he says.

"How? In what ways."

"I can't talk."

"I realize the reason you could be unfaithful to me is because our marriage didn't mean as much to you. I never could have been unfaithful because our life, our bond was so important to me." This simple realization startles me. "The bottom line is that me and our marriage doesn't mean as much, is not as crucial to you as it is to me."

He does not deny it, but says, "I don't want to know if you have an affair. It would make me too mad."

He could not know because he has no tap lines into me, no fingers, no webs into me. I could easily get away with it. He is so bound up in himself.

"I could never give you enough," Ty says. "My father can't give his girlfriend enough. It's the way of women and men." He lies staring at the ceiling. "They always want more than you can give."

"No. It's the inadequacy of the men in your family. They don't know how to love." My words are harsh, but tears wet my pillow. My eyelids are swollen, transparent.

I ask the questions and supply the answers. I make up the relationship in my mind just as I have always done.

CHAPTER 51

I have lost another pound. I forget to eat. Food chokes and glumps in the back of my throat. I watch the snow fall with all the vigor I can muster. I drive and find myself on an endless street that I do not know. I'm not sure what month it is. I look at the trees and they are bare. November? Snow on the ground. Has Christmas happened yet? January? I am lost. Lost in time. Yes. December. I read a road sign. University Avenue. Which way am I going? Into town? Away from town? I don't know. I don't care. I keep driving. I think about driving to the highway and disappearing into the vapor. I pass Holiday Inn. Right around the corner from home. Home. I'm driving home.

I realize I am so angry at Ty that I'm destroying my own life to get back at him. To punish him. I vow I'm going to stop myself.

Maybe I should move. Start a new life. Do it all over. Be a new Ann. Make up a new name. Pam says move here, we can go into practice together. Start a new life with her. Boca Raton is warm, fun. David says come here, I'll set you up in business, teach you the family franchise. He laughs.

I think I'll go to Brazil and be a candomble initiate. Shave my head. Meditate. Listen to the beat of the drum and be ridden by an Orixa. Worship snakes. Worship iron. Worship water. Worship tides.

What do I do? What? What? Someone tell me. Swim? Run? Do things with friends. Pretend to be happy. Think positive thoughts. I can't seem to do any of them. God, it's been two and a half months and I'm no better. And I am farther and farther away from Ty. I look at him and can't remember why I found him charming or sweet or fun.

. . .

I cook our traditional Christmas Eve dinner — roast beef, in and out potatoes, salad with avocado, grapefruit and pine nuts, fruitcake. Naomi makes my birthday cake. I swim through time. I realize, between tying red and green plaid bows on red foil paper, that I lived with a depressed mother, then a depressed husband, and now I'm depressed. I vow to banish depression from my life. My birthday present to myself.

The presents are under the tree. Naomi trimmed the tree. I wanted clear lights this year. No ornaments. A simple tree whose fresh smell mingled with cinnamon and orange. But I let Naomi trim it as she wanted.

Christmas morning and my fifty-third birthday. I put on my brightest clothes. Red lipstick. I open my presents. Pam sends me a perfume bottle, bright purple with pearl lines swirling through it. I don't like it. Why would she think I would? Too garish. Then I remember, last year I would have liked the bright colors and swirling lines.

Ty, Naomi and I fill up the car with presents and go to Michelle's apartment. Elizabeth and Nicole, her children, bounce up and down to greet us. "Santa came! Santa came!" Their tree is trimmed. Toys are scattered on the floor. Pink and baby blue and yellow and purple plastic. Red and green paper with Big Bird decorating a tree spills out of a plastic bag. Ribbons are on the floor, in Elizabeth's and Nicole's hair, draped on the sofa.

Stone arrives. We take turns opening presents. Stone gives me a brightly striped sweater. Its colors jar my eyes. I want black and white and gray. I want to give everything I have away. I see Michelle's eager smile, anticipating my excitement, when I see the red silk blouse she has bought for me. I close my eyes and bury my head in its softness. Its softness and the spare sheen of silk are all that interest me. Elizabeth and Nicole kiss me with wet lips, scrambling to open their presents. I see my children's eager smiles. But I cannot feel it. I know they love me. But I know it with my head. I cannot receive the love they give me.

I am under a veil. Or thick cotton. Isolated from the world.

That night, I stare out my bedroom window. It is four floors to the snowy sandy soil below. Trees edge the meadow, cut through a fog now rising from the snow. I see myself crash through the window, through the glass. Pointed shards like diamonds cut my flesh, blood flies with me as I fall, dots the snow with garish red. My body lies spent on the ground. Motionless. Over. It would be such a relief. It's over anyway. The rest will be just muddling through. Empty.

. . .

"I hate men. I see them as inadequate. And never being able to incorporate another."

Ty says, "You have to be fed to feed. It's the hunter mentality."

I say, "You didn't feel fed so you fed on Sakiko, but then never fed us." The hate doesn't get smaller.

"I love you more than ever. More than ever."

"Why? How?" He likes me crazy?

He is silent, lying in the bed. I stand by the window, still seeing my twisted neck, my skewed arms splayed out from my body.

"I feel closer to you than I have for years," he says.

He felt far from me because of her. "That's because for the first time I'm dependent on you...financially...emotionally." I want to quit talking and watch the snow, see the fog drift in and out of the trees.

"No. I don't think so."

"Maybe it's because now I need to exploit you. And that's where you feel most comfortable, most secure. Being exploited."

He doesn't answer.

I want to stop talking and watch my blood seep into the snow. The ammonia whiteness. Watch the redness grow like poppies in a field. Like Snow White, I think. "Maybe it's because you know how much you can wound me and that makes you feel powerful."

He is silent.

"Maybe because when you thought you'd lose me, you realized how important I was to you."

"Maybe," he says. I finally get it right.

I'm losing myself. But I'm still making up answers to explain our relationship. Habit, I guess.

. . .

INFIDELITY

I am in the clay studio. I slam the gray clay into a plaster mold I have made. Pound it with a mallet padded with rags, scrape it with a wire held between two handles, rap the mold on the edge of a table till the embossed clay drops. The clay feels smooth and cool. My hands roll out the snakes, careful to maintain even pressure, careful not to form a wedge. I scratch the wet clay with a needle and drip water on the wounded surface. Drip. The water is cooler than the clay. The clay becomes mud, eager to adhere to the snake. The snakes become trees: aspens, twisting together to make a forest, long and slim they wind around each other. The branches of an oak tree shelters the ground.

These are portraits of the trees outside my windows for use as a backsplash for the kitchen. I smooth the edges of the trees, uniting them to the tile. Looking at my work, I do not know if the trees are contorted as they coil around each other, or if they are elegant. I do not know if I am creating hideousness or beauty. I only know that while I make them, I am at peace.

CHAPTER 52

A friend is retiring from thirty years at the university and has decided to throw a luncheon to celebrate. We have the upstairs of a trendy Italian restaurant. On my right is a man I don't know. The second person down on my left is Mel, who was one of the founders of Organization for Investigation of Social Issues. Usually, Mel kisses my hand in greeting with such elegance that the gesture alone wins me. Recently, an article on him appeared in a magazine. He smiles broadly when he sees me.

"Mel, I didn't know you fought in the Spanish Civil War. My mother's lover fought with the Abraham Lincoln Brigade. Paul was his name."

"Paul. I know Paul. A tall and good-looking man." Mel nods.

I laugh. "My mother appreciated tall and handsome men. A poet. I think he was. Or at least I read some of the poetry he wrote her. Not bad."

"Paul. What a figure."

The stuff of romance, I think. A poet who goes off to fight in the Spanish Civil War. "Blond, wasn't he? — a Leslie Howard type. She saved a picture of him. They knew each other in Bucknell. And then he went off and then I don't know what happened. She was busy organizing steelworkers. She met my father. Another tall and handsome man."

"What ever happened to him?"

I shrug.

The woman sitting between us leans back in her chair. "This is going to be an exciting lunch," she says, "in the middle of this conversation." We get her message.

Mel leans behind her. "Oh, do I have stories to tell you. I can tell you so much about him, private stories. Did you see him, ever meet him? Oh, no, of course not. He was before you. We'll have lunch. I'll tell you stories. I always wondered about Paul."

I wonder if they talked about my mother.

The man next to me is tall, thin, gray-haired. He covers his mouth as he talks, as though he has bad breath or is shy. He is friendly though and seems eager to tell me about his research on adultery in Philippines. When I tell him I do marriage and family therapy and have written a book on sexuality in long-term marriage, his interest increases. He runs focus groups in the Philippines to explore attitudes, discover cultural universals and differences. He asks me, "Do you think a woman would be more disturbed by her husband if he were having an affair or seeing a prostitute? What's your perception of what most American woman would feel?"

"I don't know. Probably an affair, though a prostitute would also be a very big deal. Of course there's the fear of AIDS. It changes a lot."

"Yes. But traditional attitudes still exist. Philippines actively fights the AIDS epidemic. Yet a commercial sex partner has relative social tolerance. "

"Is it a male-bonding thing," I ask, "like going to the topless and bottomless bars here?"

"Yes, exactly. Exactly."

Our wine is brought with a flash of label and a taste to someone, male, seated at the table. Seasoned olive oil is poured on plates.

"Exactly. Yes. That's what I've been studying. Male peer versus primary female partner influence on extramarital behavior. An affair is something else. Takes away resources from the family. Especially the second or minor wife. Considered very threatening." He labels himself as a evolutionary theorist regarding adultery. I know he studies it from a demographic point of view. The place where demography, biology, and anthropology meet.

"Not like Mexico where it's expected a man will have a mistress?" I'm about to speculate that the man then helps support two women.

"We're looking at the values from the evolutionary perspective. I have a new article just coming out." He tears off a hunk of coarse bread and dips it into oil.

"Do affairs end in divorce?"

"Well, it's hard to know, the figures are so hard to really get at, hard to get people to talk about these things. They lie and then, after an hour or so, tell you the truth."

"I think here it's something like sixty-five percent of marriages end in divorce if an affair is discovered." The oil darkens my bread. I can be objective about this, even in the midst of my private pain. I know full well the evolutionary thrust for reproduction. First came the woman with the baby. Human babies are unable to fend for themselves, and it takes decades for them to mature. Thus the need for a mate to stick around to help raise the baby. Men ensure more reproductively successful children if they provide food and protection for their mates than if they left their pregnant mates behind and looked for new wombs to fertilize. For the male there is a built-in conflict between raising adequately nurtured children and scattering his genes widely.

"Here's an interesting story," he says between bites. "Two poor daughters come to the city — one works as a bar girl, selling sex to customers. The other meets a boy and begins living with him. Guess what the mother says?"

This is a no-brainer I think. "She's angry at the prostitute."

"Nope. The mother is furious at the second girl — she is not getting anything for the sex and is living in an unacceptable way."

"So it's really about women's pleasure — women aren't supposed to have pleasure. But if you do it for money it's okay." He looks surprised. Pleasure, too, has its evolutionary aspects.

Our lunches arrive. Mine is shrimp and artichoke risotto, his is a pizza of cheese and red peppers.

"Or it's about economic resources to be distributed to the family. Guaranteeing highly invested children," he says. "Of course, in hunter-gatherer villages only two percent of children are the result of cuckoldry. In some industrial neighborhoods, the rate is closer to twenty percent. More anonymity and opportunity."

I concentrate on my shrimp, pulling off the brittle tails. In this restaurant I can be so blithe. I know human sexuality evolved to strengthen the pair bond so that children could be nurtured. My own pair bond ripping apart causes my current agony. Our lives follow a species-specific predictable pattern.

Somehow, the knowledge doesn't reduce the pain of Ty's adultery. Ultimately, I think, my life is important only to me. Mother and Lala are dead.

"I'll send you my articles," he promises. "Are you interested?"

"Yes. Very." I hunt for one of my cards in the pockets of my purse, through the slots and zippers and bills in my wallet. I can never find them when I need them.

"Don't know why I'm so fascinated by this subject," he says.

Maybe it's his way of getting laid vicariously, I think, or maybe there's an adultery of great import in his history. I know why I'm fascinated by the subject — it's the central theme of my life.

"I write with my wife, who is Filipino."

"Are you fluent?" I ask, to help define the boundaries between us.

"No, I'm terrible at languages. I work with translators."

I write down my address on a purple Post-it that I find in my appointment book. "I'd love to see them," I say. "I have to leave, I have a patient in ten minutes." I rise and Mel hands me his card. "Call me. We'll have lunch. I have great stories to tell you. Some never yet public."

CHAPTER 53

Ty wakes and pulls me to him. I'm lying in my place, my head on his shoulder. I try to relax. He is warm, smells familiar. "I know exactly how it was. You're lying in bed together. You have just made love, her head is on your shoulder where mine is now. She is in my place. Your arm cradles her head. Her long black hair is down and draped over the pillow. You tell her how much you love being with her. How exciting it is to work with her. How you look forward to it. It is the most exciting thing in your life. You dread having to get up and go home and cook dinner. You hate it, hate having to leave her."

He has a shocked expression on his face and I know I've gotten the scene and the dialogue exactly correct. "That's the outlines. That's part of the truth."

I know. I know. Oh God how I know. If it's different tell me. Tell me, please tell me.

We go into Chicago and roam the market. The stores are closing, but we buy bottles of Italian wine and good cheese. The streets are littered with scraps of paper, cans, garbage bags. We eat at a Chinese restaurant. We sip our tea. He's having a sabbatical next year, he talks about setting up his studio. Maybe going on some short trips.

I turn away. "Trips?"

"You're not going to chain me. Imprison me."

"If you can't do the time, don't do the crime." My mood is venomous. He is a glass half empty: selfish, depressed, mired in disorganization. No. This is a hard time. He's trying. He organized this day for us. Don't give up. What will you have if it doesn't work?

The waiter brings egg rolls. I pour on hot mustard and the sweet and sour sauce. The hot mustard cleans my sinuses. Burns my brain. Feels refreshing.

"I shouldn't be making the rules, Ty. You make the rules. Figure out how to live to assure me of your fidelity. So I can trust you again."

"I can't think about that. Too much to do." He sips his soup.

I work on my egg roll, watch him dip his spoon in the soup swirling with egg.

Lobster in ginger and onions is uncovered by the waiter. I dish out some for me and some for him. I stir the sauce into rice and begin to eat. "This is good." The sharp sweetness of ginger is like the color orange.

"Yes."

"So where would you go?"

"Just short trips — New York. Florida. Phoenix. Mostly I want to work on a series of paintings about Icarus."

"Ordinary things are now all suspect."

"I know."

"I totally trusted you. You should have been accountable to me in your soul. Carried me there and always considered me. You shouldn't have put me in a little box."

"It wasn't like that. You don't understand. I was accountable to you. It was just separate." He tries to explain.

"Did she ask you what my reaction would be if I found out?"

"I told her you wouldn't find out. But that you and I would work it out and she and I would still be able to work together."

He thought I was my mother and my grandmother. I put my chopsticks down and close my eyes. "That's what you believed?"

"I just told you."

"That your infidelity would be no big deal to me?" I labor to keep my voice even. I have to remain reasonable so he can tell me and I have to remain open to his words. I want this marriage to work if we can put it back together.

"I thought Sakiko and I would go on forever, working together. That that would be one part of my life. I didn't want anything to change our relationship, my life with you. I keep telling you this. And telling you this." Although his voice his soft, his words are clipped.

An affair without end. Another lifelong partner? "Ty, I can't imagine anything worse. Thank God I found out. To live year after year feeling something wrong and thinking it's all in my head, living an illusion. And then more of my life down the drain."

"Not an illusion. I love you."

"You mean you love me, too."

We fall silent and eat. The tang of the ginger is a fine foil for the sweet lobster. I say, "She is so different from me. Opposite in every way. Shy about sex and unassertive. Uninterested in talking about feelings. A terrible mother and an unfaithful wife. Hardly able to speak English. Manipulative when I'm a straight shooter. Reed thin. I can think of no common trait and that troubles me."

"Maybe that's why. She is so different," he says.

"Yeah." We finish our meal.

"She didn't love me," Ty says.

"Why do you say that?"

"She only knew a part of me. She never really knew and understood all of me." He sips tea, but it is cold and he pushes the small cup away. "She loved the idea of me, but not me."

The waiter brings our bill and our fortune cookies.

"I know you love me." He picks up his fortune cookie and opens it. "Your power to lead men must be held carefully," he reads.

I read, "You can walk a long way with a good friend."

"I don't want to be accountable to anyone. I'm not even sure I want to be married," he says.

"I'm not either, anymore." I reply.

We drive home. Lights twinkle along the lake. This is the part of Madison that reminds me of Pittsburgh. At the Alligator Club, the music is Motown, the dancers a mixture of black and white, young and old. They play "Dock of the Bay" and Ty takes me in his arms. And for a minute, I am back home. "I never noticed how sad the lyrics are, " I say.

Ty twirls me away. "Always were. You never listened before."

I hear the lonely futility in the lyrics. "I guess not."

The music switches to "I Gotta a Woman" and we move into a smooth twist. We dance to Ray Charles and James Brown. We twist and jerk and do the fly and the mashed potato. I drink too much. I don't want to stop dancing. I am back in the River Room in the University of Iowa student union. I want the drum, the percussion to swallow me, the beat to seize my dancing body so I fly again.

On the way home I say, "I remember something Lala said. She said you'd have an affair with a colored woman because you'd need to go home to Mama." Over the years, I thought how wrong she was and never have I defined Sakiko as a colored woman. But her skin tone and value is the same as Ty's mother as a young woman. Sakiko has that Mommy comfort of giving him food and washcloths and pumice stones as though she is bathing and feeding him. She adores him without demands.

"There's all different ways of going home."

I watch signs flip by. Hanging on to the drum still in my ears. Hanging on. The highway is almost empty.

"I love you. I know how much I hurt you. When will this be over?" He wants me to stop talking about it. He wants our life to go back to what it was. But when? During Sakiko? Before her? Before his hand accident?

"I'm not who I was," I say.

CHAPTER 54

Thirty years. Thirty years of my life have been gifted to this man. How do I prevent making the rest of my life testament to his infidelity? If I leave him it's because of this. If I stay, I will always think of it. It'll be less painful with passing time. Maybe. He isn't giving me enough to make up for it. How do I make my story different from Mother's, from Lala's? How do I make it right for me? How?

Ty stirs in the bed. "What are you thinking?"

"I'm thinking no matter the dynamics, the truth is your dick was hard and you had to stick it in, and you didn't love me enough to stop yourself."

"You're right." He says it casually as if it's nothing. This small love he has for me.

"Did you ever turn it around? Did you ever imagine me doing with another man what you did with Sakiko?"

"That's one of the reasons I feel so sad."

I hit him, clutch him, bite him. I'm out of the bed and he grabs me, I fall on the floor and he drags me across the floor and I say, "Go ahead and hit me. Hit me."

His fist is raised as he towers over me.

"Go ahead and hit me. Kill me. I don't care." Oh, God. How did I come to this?

He turns and walks away.

I get up and go the bathroom. Turn on the water to smother my cries. I stand in the shower and scream. Scream till my throat is burnt with anger, scream till the sound reverberates in my ears.

I can't keep trying to work on this. I gasp for air, hold it in deep, and howl. Hot water pricks my back, sheets over my hair, face, open mouth.

One year. You promised yourself one year.

I wish I were dead. I can't die. I need to take care of Naomi.

My screams intensify, increase in pitch. Screech till my ears sting, ring from the timbre of my own voice, until my throat is ragged. I'm destroying my life to get back at Ty. I'm destroying my life so he knows how much he hurt me. Enough.

There's no one else to take care of her. My Naomi. I must finish my job raising her. There's no more sound in me. Enough.

Naomi is ready for bed. I come to kiss her and she wraps her arms around me. "Mom. I love you."

"I love you, too." Her arms are warm and she hugs me tight. Her girl smell thick in her sheets, soap and sweat and toothpaste. My eyes are wet.

"Why were you screaming? I heard you screaming. I heard you say you wanted to die. I hear you crying all the time, wailing and screaming. Even when you're not here, I hear you crying. Like the house is haunted."

"I know. I know. I'm sorry." I hug her.

"It's not your fault. But I hate living here. I hate living like this." She talks into my hair.

"Me, too." I'm doing the best I can. I am.

"I want to go away somewhere." She looks at me, her hand is on my arm now as I sit on the side of her bed.

"Away?" My eyes are wet. I wipe my dripping nose with my hand.

"Yeah, maybe go live with Michelle for a while."

"No."

"I don't think it's fair for an eleven-year-old to be living with two such depressed people."

I kiss her, hold her in my arms. I don't know how to shield her from this. I don't know how to shield her from me. I rock her. I make a vow. I have to get it together. I will get it together. I will pretend to be happy at home as well as at work. "It'll get better. I know it will. I promise. We're going through a rough time."

"Will it be like it used to be?"

"Daddy and I are trying to try to figure out a way to move on from the affair. We're seeing a marriage counselor. You can come too."

"Maybe I will."

"All of us are doing the best we can." I kiss her and turn out the light.

. . .

That night, I dream I pick up two men at a bar. A young one and an old one. The young one says to the old one, "This is the kind of woman that could drive me crazy."

In the morning, I get dressed and go to the clay studio. The clay captures me. The cool snakes, the sharp slashes from the scratching tool. I can join the clay so smoothly, so evenly it is invisible. For a while, I become the clay. Smooth. Malleable. My mind contains only clay, my trees, my dream for each tile. Sakiko and Ty are gone.

Swimming, I count my laps. Listen to my breathing. My body moves effortlessly in the water, smooth surges, like a whale, like a shark as I glide. Back and forth, faster. Aluminum bubbles churn around me. My arms whirl me through the blue. I regain a sense of being a piece of the world.

. . .

I go to lunch with Alexia. We sit at the booth and order wine and mussels and pasta. Alexia has her hair in braids, small gold leaves dance at the end of each one. She wears a jean dress and her emerald ring.

The waiter comes. He has dark hair and flashing eyes. "I'm here to serve you today."

"You are, uh? Serve me?" My eyes meet his.

"Can I get you anything. Anything at all?" He does not remove his gaze from mine. His mustache is thick. An Omar Sharif.

I raise my eyebrows. "Well, now, how about some more bread. The crusty kind."

"Be right back." He draws out the right as he moves away.

I watch him walk away and then turn to Alexia. "Am I wrong to even think of working on this?"

"You two had a good marriage, at least it seemed so from the outside."

"Ty doesn't give me anything. Says he doesn't want to lose me, but doesn't recommit. Sometimes I think he's just waiting for his exit, after we've settled in the house. Sometimes I think I'm so nuts that he can't do anything."

Alexia pours herself more wine. "You have nothing to lose by understanding what's happening. By working on it."

The waiter returns with the bread. I slide my index finger around the curve of my wine glass. He places the bread down and gives me a slow smile. Then pours me some wine. "Anything else you need, anything at all, I'm right over there. My name is Michael."

"I'll certainly call you if I need anything." I say it slow and low. He hesitates a minute before he walks away.

"You need to understand the dynamics so you can undo them or not repeat the same mistake," Alexia says.

"Yeah. Yeah. The party line. Like understanding is going to cure shit." I sneer as I rip apart some bread. "I think about it all the time. When I don't have visions of Ty and Sakiko in bed, I think about the great why. Why did it happen? What did I do to contribute to it?" I dip the bread in oil. Then leave the bread on the plate to gather more oil. "Thirty years ago, I thought Ty would be faithful to me. I thought I was his fantasy. Without admitting it, he thought I was the white goddess that would show him how to master the world. But I didn't provide absolute safety. I didn't, couldn't, make sure nothing bad happened to him." My words rush out, my hands shred the bread.

"And you?" Alexia's eyes are as green as her emerald.

"I guess I could be safe as a Jew and still have his fidelity. A variation of the old oedipal dilemma. Not marry a Jew like my father. But not marry a white Christian either. Not go into the enemy camp. He tells me he feels enslaved. "

Michael returns with our plates. He moves behind me to put down the mussels and when he does, his arm grazes my back, rustles my hair.

I meet his gaze. "Thank you." We stare at each other. He opens his mouth slightly. And says, "Here you are." His eyes fastened on mine. "Enjoy." And then he leaves. Alexia watches him walk away.

"You've just raised the temperature in this restaurant twenty degrees," Alexia says.

I laugh. "Yeah. Suddenly I'm flirting again." It's my father waiting inside me, I think. Helping me test whether other men are possible, even exciting. "Thought I'd forgotten how. But I guess not."

"Not indeed." Alexia slides some of the pasta onto my plate. I wind it around my fork.

"What were we talking about? Oh, yeah. I figured out that Ty feels enslaved because I've been a caretaker. He feels like an inadequate parent because I enjoy being a parent. He needed all my attention and adoration all the time. He had the hand accident, his mother died, Sakiko came along. For the first time, my art, my writing was more important to me than his art was to me. He felt abandoned."

My fork is in midair. The pasta wound tightly in a ball. I look at it and put my fork down and shrug. "When I discovered his affair and went nuts, his fantasy collapsed." I pick up the fork and eat the pasta. "Well. What the fuck. Relationships. Shit."

We concentrate on our food. The mussels need more garlic. But not much tastes good to me. "You know, it's weird. My grandmother, Lala, had four daughters. They all married addicts of one kind or another. Two sexual addicts, one gambler, one booze. Once I asked my Aunt Faith, Why? She thought for a minute and then said, almost angrily, 'Because they're exciting.'"

"And you?"

I shrug. "Well, Ty was exciting. And this shit is certainly exciting in a chaotic way. But do I want it? No way." I dab some bread in the mussel juice, the too faint garlic and tomato and wine. "I don't know. Maybe it makes us feel important. Like these guys have a great need for us and we are certain with our strong love we can solve anything. Sort of like climbing mountains."

"You'll get through this. You're still working and treating patients."

"Not enough, though."

"Everyone's practice is down. You'll figure that out in time. Still taking care of Naomi. Still working out."

I concentrate on prying open a mussel. And then say. "If I stay in the marriage, it'll be for Naomi. Ty means less to me with each day." My eyes fill, hot tears pool at the corners. "The saddest thing, I won't be able to give someone everything I have to give."

Alexia puts her fork down. "Look. Sexual betrayal is the hardest thing that you would have to cope with. Give yourself time."

It is? I list the tragedies of the world. Your child being molested and killed. Being in a concentration camp. A slave. "No way."

"The worst thing that someone *who knows you* could do *to you*. With *your* history."

"Oh." I fish out another mussel, a pink-gray lump on my fork. "So what do you do when the worst thing possible happens to you and you're fighting for your life?"

Alexia sips her chardonnay. Her lids cover her eyes. Her mouth is still.

"Don't tell me I'll learn a lot. Whatever lesson I learn won't be worth the cost. Don't tell me that shit." I finish my glass. "I won't ever be the same, the same person I was."

"No." Alexia eats some pasta. "Maybe you'll be better."

I sneer. "Right. But first I have to figure out what the fuck I'm going to do."

"Give yourself time. You're always in such a rush about everything."

"Gotta get it all in before I pop off."

"See? Hear what you just said?" Alexia raises her glass. "There's life."

"L'chaim," I laugh as I lift my wine glass.

. . .

After lunch, I return to my office. It is quiet and peaceful. The chenille plant blooms fuzzy pink, silly flowers. If I were one of my patients, I'd suggest Prozac. I make an appointment with my doctor.

I place an advertisement for my practice in a local newspaper.

I contact a group of therapists banding together to deal with managed care. They're having a meeting next Friday.

I contact a friend with whom I've done mediation around race relations at University Hospital. "I have an idea for a new consulting business. With our track record already, we may be able to get some work around racial and sexual harassment in the workplace."

"Let's have lunch on Tuesday," he says.

"Great."

. . .

After I pick Naomi up from school, we put on an Aretha Franklin CD and we dance. We dance until we sweat. We dance until we laugh. After dinner, I go to the clay studio and welcome my time with the clay. My trees are graceful, not contorted.

CHAPTER 55

My patients replay Ty and I as so many variations on a theme. Betsy walks into my office, sits down, and begins crying. She has responded to my add. She pulls Kleenex out from her bag and blows her nose in it.

She is slender, late thirties with long blond hair, wearing a brown dress and a dark coat. "Oh, God. I haven't talked about this before. I've been alone with this for six months." She grabs more Kleenex. I place my box on the leather ottoman between us. "I don't know where to begin."

"Begin at the beginning. Begin in the middle."

"My husband is having an affair."

Is there no way for me to avoid this subject? Over half of my current patients are dealing with some issue of adultery. Men having affairs, women having affairs, women dealing with their husband's affairs, men dealing with their wife's affairs, children dealing with their parents' affairs. It keeps slapping me in the face, like a cosmic joke.

"That's just the beginning. He's a legislator, the woman was his legislative aide. She seduced, chased him, sent him letters, followed him. Finally he started the affair with her and she purposely, it seems, got herself pregnant."

Betsy's tears redouble. "And he got her pregnant in my, our, bed when I was away with the children. Visiting my dying sister. Oh, God. I could smell her in my sheets — that awful musky oil odor — when I got back and couldn't figure out what it was. I'm so stupid."

My empathy apparently shows because she says, "That's not all. That's not the worst of it. Or maybe it is." She turns her face away. "God. I haven't told anyone this. I've been so ashamed."

"You've been alone with all this for six months? You haven't talked with your friends? Your women friends?"

"No. I'm too embarrassed." She blows her nose, then continues. "I couldn't believe he'd do this to me. I trusted him. I never checked up on him. There must be something wrong with me."

These are my words. She could be talking for me.

"Did he tell you why?"

"He said we didn't have sex enough. Now we do it four times a day. I'm so tired. And there's more." She hesitates. Turns her face away. She has a perfect profile, pretty under the red nose and blotchy face, tired eyes.

"What else? You said there was more." She starts to tell me and then veers away.

"Yeah. The aide thought, once she was pregnant, that he'd leave me and the kids for her. But he didn't. Then she tried blackmailing him. So he told me what was going on. Is this a fatal attraction? Am I part of a scene in some awful movie, some terrible soap opera and don't even know it? Is someone writing this horrible script and acting it out against my will?" Her voice cracks and for a split second cheeps like a baby bird.

She grabs another piece of Kleenex.

"So then what happened?"

She blows her nose. "I'm sorry. I'll use up your whole box."

"That's okay. That's what it's there for. I have more."

"Oh God. So she threatens him with a sexual harassment suit. And so now of course, if it gets out, he'll lose the next election and, and he won't even have a job."

"Oh, no."

"If he loses his job, then I don't know how we'll support the kids. I mean, this was his life. All he planned to ever do. And I dropped out of school after I fell in love with him. And now, all he wants to do is have sex, four — five times a day. I'm working full time, running around driving the kids to swimming lessons and art class and violin. Cooking. Trying to deal with this. Trying to keep my marriage together. "

"Do you want the marriage?"

"I shouldn't, should I?"

"Not necessarily. You two maybe can get through all this. It'll be rough."

"I love him." She stares straight at me and says without any emotion, just defeat, "I hate him." She stops for a minute.

"There's bound to be lots of strong feelings at a time like this." I say it softly.

"He was my boss. I was his secretary."

"So this follows a pattern for him."

"Well." She stops crying. "I never thought of it that way. But yes. I am seven years younger than him."

"So is she much younger?"

"Yes. She's younger than me. So she's fifteen years younger than him."

"He needed that adoration? That display of Oedipal thrall."

Her face lights up. "That's it. Exactly. You understand before I even say it."

Yes. I think to myself sadly. Yes I do.

"I told him that. That he loved the attention while I was busy working, raising his kids, washing his clothes, cooking his food, cleaning his house." She shakes her head. "No, ours."

"Yes. Yours, too."

"I haven't told you the worst yet. This is the worst. Or the hardest yet. She's going to have the baby next month. He's going to be in the delivery room. He wants to be a part of the baby's life. He can't ignore his child." She sobs.

My eyes are wet.

"So now everything special, sacred between us is gone. Over. Now he'll even see her give birth, share that with her. Just like he did with me, with our children."

She tears another piece of Kleenex from the box, and says, "I don't know even how to think of this. I mean he's doing what he's supposed to do with the baby. Taking responsibility. But I hate him for it. But I'd hate him if he didn't do it, too. You know what I mean?"

"What will happen then? After the baby's born?"

"He wants the baby in his life. I've begged him not to be involved with the baby. She's such a loon, I'll probably end up raising the baby. Including it in our kids' lives."

"Can you do that?"

She shrugs.

"You haven't told him no to any of this."

"I'm afraid I'll lose him."

"You're still trying to make him happy." I tell her what I should tell myself.

"Yes. You're right."

"God, how have you gotten through this? Handled this for six months alone?"

"I go to work and pretend and it's a refuge. For a while, everything is like it used to be. Or like I thought it was."

"Ah, yes."

"And at home, I'm just trying to figure out what to do. What we can do. And being fucked to death." She is silent for a minute. "I should have killed him. That's what a reasonable person would have done. I want to run away."

"Yes. But that wouldn't solve anything and would disrupt the children's lives."

"Yeah. That's why I don't. Am I crazy trying to make this work?"

"No. But you can't let it make you crazy."

"I've lost fifteen pounds. Everyone at work says, 'Betsy, you look great. How did you do it?' I smile and say thank you. What a way to finally become fashionably thin." She manages a smile. Then the tears start again. "I'm trying so hard to be there for him. Be what he wants."

"You have to make sure it's what you want, that it's for you, you and your kids, not just him. You're important, too." I tell her and I tell myself.

She stops crying. "I keep forgetting that... the kids and him."

"Don't. You're important, too. "

She wipes her nose and turns to the clock. She straightens up in the chair and dabs at her cheeks with her fingertips. "I was just happy. Just doing my developmental stages and suddenly a tornado destroyed everything."

Another new patient, Tom, comes in because he started having disturbing thoughts after seeing a violent movie. A well muscled man, who works out with weights and jogs and plays the guitar, Tom's thoughts became increasingly violent. He couldn't get them out of his head and they were accompanied by crushing anxiety, pounding heart, sweats, chills. He thought he was going crazy, afraid he'd end up in the mental hospital. He calls me and I see him the next day. He's never had violent images in his head before. I prod him about his thoughts.

I question him. "What are these thoughts of?"

"Death," Tom says. "Very violent. Images of blood and gore. Just like the movie, but now I'm in it and it feels real. As though I'm doing the killing."

"What exactly happens?" Sometimes describing a fantasy diminishes it.

"I'm killing, knifing someone. Over and over. And then I see the body parts strewn everywhere. It's so real, as if I've actually done it. My hands feel wet with blood." He shudders. Then sits still, his hands on his thighs, watching me as he talks. He wets his lips, "I'm not a violent person. This is so unlike me. I've never had anything happen like this before. I'm scared shitless. I mean I don't like violent movies, or even watching football games."

I take a shot in the dark. "Who are you killing?"

"My wife."

Bingo, I think. "Your wife?"

"Yes."

He isn't elaborating. I shake my head slowly and ask the obvious question. "Why her? What's your marriage like?"

"Good. Great." He goes on in glowing terms to describe how the relationship is just the right mix of closeness and separateness, how much they trust each other and have worked at building a life together. They fell madly in love seven years ago, moved in together after a year and have been married about four years. She has a new job. She is sometimes insecure.

I find this peculiar. Is the wife a surrogate for someone else he's angry at? I start exploring by asking him questions about his mother? His boss? What's happening at work? I'm hunting for the problem. We spend several sessions talking about work. His anxiety decreases. There's no more thoughts of murder and mayhem. No more images of bloody knives and body parts floating through the air.

It's not until the fourth session that the precipitating incident for the anxiety attacks becomes clear. He and his wife go golfing with another couple. The wife has become his good friend. She plays the flute, they practice duets together. While their spouses are working nights, they go for long walks, a movie, read the same books and discuss them. "She may be the love of my life," he blurts, stops a minute and swallows. "God. I'm addicted to her smell of almonds and vanilla."

"Is there any connection between her and the attacks?"

He shakes his head. "Not really." He sits still. I can feel him thinking. He shrugs. "Well. We were planning to spend a night together that weekend. The weekend I went nuts. But the anxiety attacks stopped me."

I can't help thinking, Good, but say, "So what do you think? See the connection?"

"Well, maybe."

"What's the message from the anxiety attacks?"

"We're still planning to start the affair." He stares at the Egyptian tomb print hanging on the wall behind me.

"Are you still scared about starting it?"

"The anxiety attacks are gone. They were probably because of that movie. We – she and I — have talked about this for months. We're in love with each other." He says this with emphasis on the word love. "We've looked at all the sides of it. This is our decision."

"Your decision?" I stop myself. My job is to help him think it through. Help him understand why he's doing what he's doing, and make a free decision. Maybe cut through the denial to see the fear and guilt underneath.

"She may be the love of my life." His voice has a husky, almost tearful pleading quality to it. "Our affair will continue forever. I have no intention of getting a divorce. I wouldn't want to put my wife through that. I love her. We have a good marriage. This is separate. It's none of my wife's business."

I blink. I can't get away from this. Ty in another guise.

CHAPTER 56

Trees are sharp white against the sky. Light reveals them, etches them as they flip by me. The white dotted line snakes in front of me. Farm houses are off in the distance, in glimpses of fields beyond the trees. Naomi is in the backseat, her Walkman in her ears. I glance at Ty. Both his hands are on the steering wheel, his eyes on the road. Is he merely judging the traffic, studying cars ahead and judging their velocity, deciding whether to pass the Ryder truck trudging up the hill? Is he thinking about me? Is he aware that my hand is on the car seat so, if he wants, he can hold it, touch me?

Yesterday when he picked up his canvas bag to leave for work, I waited for him to kiss me. He did not. When he came home, he scanned slides on his light box for this trip to Chicago. He did not kiss me. "I love you," I said while I was cutting veggies for stir-fry. Will he say it back? Will he kiss me? Will he acknowledge me?

"I love you, too, but saying it sounds hollow," he said. He's thrown me away and is uncertain he wants me back.

My hand waits for his acknowledgment. I need to win something from him. But he withholds. No, he is merely oblivious. It produces a desperate hunger for him. I'm hanging on a cliff waiting for his rescue. I hate it. I hate my obsession.

I glance at him. He turns on the radio, searching the static for a talk show, needing to fill his mind with strange voices. He is in his own shell, isolated from me. I look out the window at the stiff trees, the bristling fields. I never wanted to get married anyway. I was too much like my father; I never thought I'd be faithful and never thought anyone else could be either. I should have stayed true to my childhood self. Maybe my childhood self can guide me now.

The highway curves, *Come to State Farm and Be Secure,* a sign reads. As long as Ty was faithful to me, I felt loved. That's all he had to do. I was the complete low-maintenance wife. I made as much money as he, I didn't demand anything from him, he had whatever freedom he craved, I trusted him. I didn't want a big house, fancy clothes, expensive cars, lavish entertainment. Didn't want to spend money like my mother. Didn't want to be fucked imaginatively. As long as he was faithful, I felt loved. Tears stream down my cheeks. I turn my face closer to the window.

Ty listens to the radio. Naomi listens to her tapes. I cry.

I'm not the giving tree. I'm not. I'm not.

Tears blur the landscape, the colors merge into a black white abstract of jagged edges, floating twisted bars. I am alone, crying unseen, unheard, surrounded by my family.

I think, this will be our last trip to Chicago as a family. My sweater is damp. Suddenly I am cold.

David has said, "You keep writing scripts to separate. Write one to stay together."

I do. I try. I go to therapy. I try to understand all this from Ty's point of view. I keep counting what we still have: the years, the friends, the understanding — no, cross that off — shared experiences, the love? common interests, easy familiarity. I count.

We arrive at the Art Institute. A Magritte show. Illusion behind torqued reality. I see my image in the wine bottles, in the clouds behind his windows. Ty is sullen and quiet as he strides through the galleries unattached to me, to Naomi, to the paintings. I try to explain to Naomi the quirky view of substance as though seen through a prism, through a microscope.

. . .

After she is asleep, Ty and I go to the hotel lobby. The restaurant is closed, there is no bar, and so we sit in the lobby. Ty asks, "Why was your father unfaithful? What was going on inside him?"

I am quiet for a minute. "Two things," I say. "He had a great thirst for life, a life which…" I swallow, "it was almost as if he knew he had to fill to the brim, every second, before it ran out." How would he help me now if he could? "And he had this great need." I stop and search to find my father, "He was, I guess, underneath it all a little boy who felt unloved, insecure, lonely behind the charisma, charm, and brilliance.

He desperately tried to use any woman's body to get home safe, close to a oneness he once had and lost."

Ty shudders.

We sit quiet. A couple enters the hotel. An older man with a mustache and younger woman with red hair. His hand is on her back. She looks up at him and laughs.

"Did he love your mother?"

"Yes. He loved my mother. My grandfather loved my grandmother, too." For a second things slide back into place.

I am in bed trying to sleep, Naomi in the bed, snoring gently on the other side of the room, Ty a huge weight beside me.

I remembered when we were in southern France and attended a Moroccan boy's circumcision ceremony. Naomi and I and a friend, Lorna, were in the women's room. Ty and her husband, Gustave, and the men were somewhere else, drinking tea, smoking cigarettes, and gambling. This is a culture that practices polygamy. Women entered, took off black robes to reveal sexy dancing gear. Long light dresses, flowered, some heavily and beautifully beaded. Bare and bejeweled bellies, veils and glitter and heavy makeup. The room was hot, ringed with tables. Music started, sinuous as a snake. We must get up and dance, we were told in Arabic, then in a French I could not understand until translated by Lorna.

"But I don't know the dance," Naomi complained.

More women joined the dance floor. While dancing, they tied a fringed scarf around their hips. The rapid hip movement shook the fringe, amplifying a small movement to a frantic one. Women approached each other, lips wet and open, brows moist, arms outstretched. Barely moving their feet, their hips stirred in little trembles as they offered their abdomen toward their friend, eyes eager. Heat rose. The smell of incense — patchouli and musk. Roses.

Naomi whispered, "Are these women all lesbians? What is this? Shaking their butts at each other."

"A different culture. No, they're not lesbians. This is how they party."

It was a clitoral dance, not vaginal, not the long stroking motions of the twist, the jerk. The dance form of a vibrator, the kind of movement that on the clitoris brings a woman to orgasm.

Platters of food were carried to the men.

We were served coffee in little cups.

I was moist from the heat.

"Where's something to drink? Some pop. Some water," Naomi demanded. "The men are in an air-conditioned room, probably. Being fed. And drinking pop. This sucks. What's wrong with these women? They need to rebel."

I took Naomi to the bathroom and wondered if it was safe to drink the water out of the spigot. Probably not.

Orangina was served. Naomi swilled hers down. "Thank God."

Later, picked-over platters were brought to us, sweet pastries, grainy and sugary. And the dancing continued. The music faster, the fringes quivered, trembled.

"I hate this. I want to get out of here," Naomi said.

"Come, let's dance." We joined the women. I caught the dance easily enough. It felt as I thought, sexual, erotic. The women laughed, talked, touched each other. Gestures and behavior exactly the same as couples at a bar, couples on a date, couples at a nightclub. We were adhesive from the heat.

"These men don't know what they're missing. How little they are getting of what women are able to give," I said to Lorna busy eating pastries. "Men seem relevant for money and sperm."

"I feel faint," Lorna said. "Too hot."

"The emotional significance for these women appear to be each other," I said.

"I gotta get out of here."

When I wake up, I do not have the picture of Ty making love to Sakiko. Images of the women of my family cooking in Lala's kitchen fill my mind, Lala and Mother and Faith and Penny. Images of the women's dance. When a man commits adultery, the family becomes a matriarchy, I think. He is closed off and becomes emotionally less relevant.

I live on numerous levels. On one level, I work and cook and clean and eat and drive and watch Naomi in a play. Just the same as always. On another I am fundamentally changed and something about me is destroyed. And on still another level, the relationship with Ty is irrelevant. I am who I am. I will do what I do. I exist and love and do and die and Ty is nothing but moments of pleasure and moments of pain in my life. I move between the levels, the skimming of the first one, the pain and loss of the middle one, and, at the core, a centeredness and quiet. In the final analysis, no one else cares about my life as I do. No one can do what needs to be done for me, but me. I am alone. Intact.

Two days later, back in Madison, I have a mammogram. There's a lump on my breast. They quickly do more mammograms. An x-ray plate is on the light box. "Is that mine?" I ask the technician.

"Yes," she says. "Turn this way. And inhale."

My left breast is clamped. On the x-ray, I see a lump the size of my fingernail, two and a half cm, caught in a network of gentle veins.

My ex-partner, Pam, calls. She's being audited and needs my tax return to prove to the IRS that we co-owned the office building and that I paid half of the taxes. "Just photocopy your tax return, or at least the Schedule E, and that'll take care of the entire matter."

"No."

"No?"

"It might trigger an audit of me. I won't risk it. There's too much shit in my life."

There is silence on the phone. I am behaving uncharacteristically. In the past I would have Fed Exed her my return, more concerned about her anxiety than any negative possibility for me. I am putting myself first.

"They might make me pay $3,000 more in taxes," she says.

I think, better that than additional worry or shit for me. I am resolute and without guilt. "I'll write a statement and send copies of canceled checks, but I won't give them my Social Security number. I'll check with my accountant first and see what she says."

"OK, then."

. . .

When I hang up, I am surprised by my lack of guilt. I had sensed that my guilt had vanished, but this is the first episode that proves the change. I wonder what made it dissolve. Guilt had always determined my actions with others. Is guilt a self-punishment that is a contract with authority? Did Ty's affair end the contract? Did the fates welsh on their bargain?

I try to remember when I first felt guilt and, with a flash, remembered trying to kill David. What's the connection? Yes, of course. I was replaced by David. I was replaced by Sakiko. Left out. Second. No longer the one and only. The same sibling rivalry issues. Cain and Abel.

I am filled with a sense of soaring. Lighter and able to fly. I feel freer than I have ever been.

. . .

There's a call from the radiologist. I had the lump, a cyst, on my mammogram from five years ago. I don't even need a biopsy. I am healthy. Life awaits me.

. . .

Wandering in my woods, I find under a patch of snow new strawberry plants growing among moss. I bring some inside and take out watercolors. Faure's *Requiem* surrounds me.

I rub my brush over a green that is soft, yet new. The color dissipates in swirling clouds in the water. I am the green leaves. I am the delicate moss, each strand tipped with an ochre spear. Earth's blood runs in the stem, etches the veins in the new green. Delicate tracery. Lace in the woods. Leaves, in fetal position, emerge from tight nests. I am lost in the leaves, the velvet moss, the rich earth smell. I am lost in minute splotches on the leaves, a small hole already eaten by some animal. I am lost in the slight yellow stripe marching beside the blood ochre as the newborn red sucks in the sun and becomes green. I am lost in my brush the size of a hair, and the green and yellow I mix on my pan, the pigment diffusing in the water until it becomes the color of unborn leaves. So subtle only its difference from the paper reveals it. The voices singing fit the mood of the beginning of life. Tender. Fragile. Inevitable. It's a singing day.

CHAPTER 57

John's office windows overlook the city. I see the roof of my office building when I stand up. Now, I am in one of his plush chairs, Ty sits in the other. Naomi is on a fold-up chair between us. The chairs remind me of ones in my parents' house, the same fabric, almost the same color, the same square lines. Naomi wants to come to this session.

John's long legs wrap around each other. He tells Naomi he's glad to have the chance to meet her. Often, when I am with Ty and one of the children, I have a knot of anxiety inside me as I try to ensure that events proceed smoothly. Today the knot is there. We broach the subjects gently. Naomi complains about how upset her parents are, how I'm always crying or screaming.

"It's a hard time for your family," John says.

"I'm a terrible father," Ty says.

"No, you're not," Naomi says.

"I'm too angry."

"All dads yell. Look at the *Simpsons* on TV. That's just being part of being a dad. Every dad gets mad sometimes."

"I'll damage you."

She shakes her head. "No one thinks you're a terrible father. Not me, or Stone, or Michelle, or Mom."

Ty looks away.

"My friend's father has a colostomy bag and he dumped it on her head because she was talking on the phone. That's a bad father," she says.

"I never should have been a father. That's why my sperm count was low. I should have listened to the gods."

"What about me? I'm here," Naomi says.

John turns in his chair. "Yes, indeed," John says. "I've asked that question myself."

"I love you," she continues.

"You're a great kid. Your mother raised you, that's why. I knew to stay away."

I shake my head. "She's so much like you, Ty. Don't you see? She even plays field hockey like you played football. The same conception of the field and movement, same attack."

"You're not hearing me. That's not the point. I'll just cause her trauma."

Naomi turns to him, tears down her face. "I haven't had any trauma in my life. Not until now. This is the only trauma. If you leave, that will be trauma in my life."

Ty shakes his head. Deep creases run from the corners of his nose down to his mouth.

"I love you. You're a good dad. You take me to movies and watch my field hockey games and teach me to draw and talk to me. And I love you. I like being with you. I want everyone together."

"I'm a toxic father. You don't know what's inside of me. "

Ty and I have had this conversation a hundred times. John's told him, I've told him, leaving will cause her more trauma than staying. He keeps referring to demons which will destroy her, that he must stay away from her. Nothing we've said deters him. Now nothing she says deters him, either.

She turns to me, "Is this going to happen to me, too?"

"I don't know." I inhale and shrug. "I guess that about half of marriages break up after an affair."

"No, that's not what I mean," Naomi says.

"It won't happen to you because you have her for a mother." Ty jerks his head toward me.

Naomi nods.

I get her question. She's afraid she'll go nuts at midlife, toss all her cards in the air and let them come down helter-skelter, regardless.

I think Ty attributes more power to me than I have. I don't feel I can prevent or predict anything.

CHAPTER 58

It's a Friday night, and the graduate students and faculty in painting are coming to our new house. I wear a tank-top denim dress that shows off my waist, trim from thousands of situps, and a necklace I have made. Ty tells me he needs to talk with me after our party. One of the male students sees me and kisses me heavy on my lips. I spend the evening flirting with him, feeling him watch me. I show off the house, sculptures I made out of trash from Ty's studio floor, my ceramic tiles. Except for the work I did under Ty's direction, which he regularly claims as his own, my work has always been diminished by Ty as mere craft. The comments by artists suggest that I have made art and that my art is vibrant and original.

On Saturday, Ty is busy, unavailable. I spend the day shoveling mulch, the sun-fragrant earth overpowers the fishy fertilizer smell. When he returns, I ask what he wants to talk about. "There really isn't anything," he tells me.

"I thought you wanted to talk with me." I wear overalls and a tank top. The shovel is still in my hand, dirt embedded in the webs of my fingers.

"We did already." His mouth is set.

"We did?"

He disappears into his studio.

On Sunday he goes to a meeting and gets home after I'm asleep.

On Monday evening, when I come home from work, there are three messages on my answering machine. The first one is from Pam. She received my packet of information and her accountant said it should be sufficient. The second is from Alexia suggesting we go to the poetry slam the next night. The third is for Ty from Mak. They are all set for the trip to Japan. His plane, his room and expense funds are allocated for the six-week trip. The plane reservation confirmed. They'll be leaving in two months, right after Ty returns from Holland.

I replay the message. That's the meeting he went to last night. I play it again. He's going to Japan without discussing it with me.

I play the message yet again.

Oh, well.

I fix on the trembling of the leaves in the breeze and the cluster of sunlight. There's a small pattern of webs in the screen and a reflection of the window molding in the glass. A drip of paint is caught in the middle on the woodwork and the echo of wood grain is discernible under the paint. Birds twirl around me. Their songs drown out cars on the freeway. A robin picks hungrily at the sand, probably eating up the wildflower seeds I scattered yesterday. No. Robins eat worms.

I pick a spring beauty and open my watercolors, focus on the faint pink in the petals, the slight cilia on the stems. Enough. It's time to make my decision.

When Ty gets home I tell him he has a message. When he returns from the study, I say, "So you're going to Japan?"

He turns away, his twisted hand resting on the counter. Then he faces me and says, "It's an opportunity that presents itself."

"An opportunity." I hiss out the word between my teeth. "I need an opportunity to present itself to me. An opportunity." I pick up a knife to cut up some onions and for a minute imagine plunging it into his belly, watching the bright red spurt. I clench the handle tightly between my fingers and throw the knife on the counter. Instead I ask, "When did you decide?"

"John said I was supposed to think what you mean to me. I told him I love you, admire you, and feel bonded to you. This trip came up. I decided to go on Saturday and made it final on Sunday. Now all the arrangements are made. I wanted to talk with John about how to tell you. Choosing this trip reveals what you mean to me, too."

I get the message. I thought I meant to him what he meant to me. Now I understand. You never know what someone else feels. You only know what you feel. I say, "Exactly. A three-week trip to Japan is chosen over a thirty-year marriage."

Naomi walks in. "What's wrong?"

"Dad is going to Japan."

"What?" She screams. She stares from him to me, him standing there resolute, me crying while sautéing onions. "You're going to see

Sakiko? Don't you see how hard Mom is trying?"

Naomi's face is purple and wet with tears. "Please. Please. Don't go. How can you go? Do this? See Sakiko now?"

I hold her tight with my arms as her tears wet my shirt.

"I'm not. I'm going to Japan with art students."

"You're going to see her." She has red eyes, a rivulet of tears and snot streaming in her open, screaming mouth. "I don't want you to get a divorce. Don't get a divorce. Don't. Please. Please. I don't want to be a divorced kid."

Her shoulders quake between my arms. Or are they my shoulders? My shirt is wet with her tears. Or are they my tears? Her howls are in my ears. Or are they my screams, my words? I can't stay on center. I yawn in air, but still am empty, breathless, I can't get enough.

. . .

Ty asks me to help him with his brag sheet, a list of his accomplishments during the year that partially determines the extent of his raise. Annoyed, I agree. I quickly type up the words he dictates. When we come to the part about future plans, he asks me to add a line about a collaborative project one of his students is doing with him. "But leave that be, I'll finish that part later."

The next day, I decide I'll make a romantic dinner, a set piece for the final act. Naomi is away for the evening. I buy a lamb loin roast and napoleons for dessert. While the potatoes are roasting in rosemary and olive oil, I decide to check his computer to see if the brag sheet is finished yet. I flip it on and, lo and behold, the notation for the collaborative work is gone. Instead there is a new notation. He and Sakiko have a commission in Kent, England, to do ten metal murals. Ah, so she figured out a way to sweeten her pot. They have been working on the murals during the winter and are excited by the project. He is spending the summer in Japan and then the fall with her in England.

. . .

Dinner is my last try. I say, "We have more to lose by breaking up than we gain. I've worked hard at understanding your affair. But I need some help here, Ty. What can you guarantee me?"

"I haven't thought about it." He resumes eating the napoleon.

I sip my coffee. Should I tell him what I need? I lick the custard from my fork. The flavors of the napoleon are not distinct and are too creamy sweet. "This is what I need. I need you to promise that you'll be faithful. I need you not to travel without me. I need you not to collaborate with another woman."

He stands up. The chair rasps on the floor. Shudders flinch my spine. He turns his head away, knuckles on the table.

"Those three things." My voice is firm.

"Those are my shackles," he says.

"Those are my bottom lines. That's the least I deserve."

"Do you see how this enslaves me?"

"I see that any request that comes from me will enslave you."

"Yes." He sits back down and shakes his head. "I won't promise you those things."

I will not be unhappy for twenty years just to stay married. "That's it then."

"I'll move into the basement."

"How's that going to work, Ty? You're going to sneak up in the middle of the night and fuck me?"

"If you want. If you need me to."

"And how will it feel when I have another lover?" I will no longer accommodate myself to him or to his art.

"I won't bother you."

"I need my own life."

. . .

That night I dream that I meet a man, tall and lean and with an easy smile. Then I start having trouble walking. I look at my legs and discover they are rotting away. Flesh hangs in huge hunks. I see my bones and my tendons. White and stringy. Blood runs through blue arteries. Naomi is with me and she too begins to have trouble walking.

We return to the hospital. The nurse tells us it's a toxic infection and gives us pills. We'll be healed in a few days. I look at my legs and can't figure out how that could be. There is no blood, just bones and tubes. The flesh has fallen off. I am perplexed that I can still walk. The nurse says Naomi is amazing, that a ten-year-old child could suffer so without crying. Her legs are already healing. I get into bed to rest. Naomi is beside me. Meanwhile the romance with the guy continues and sure enough in a few days my legs are healed and seamless.

. . .

I've been handed a new life. I don't know what will happen next.

CHAPTER 59

We have one last bit of business together. The two of us have contracted to escort a group of alumni on a tour of the Netherlands. Ty will lecture. I will make sure everyone's needs are being met.

Something about the age of the buildings lining broad streets in Amsterdam reminds me of Barcelona. The red light district has a fresh-scrubbed look that is less seedy than Hamburg. Wisteria vines bloom along the windows. The women wear Day-Glo lingerie. It is purple under strobing black light. Groups of young men stroll the streets and look in the windows. It reminds me of fraternity rush at the art fair. The men make comments about the wares — great tits but a shitty ass and wonder out loud what she charges, probably ten dollars. I want to say to him, great ass, but the dick is too small. And half soft.

Ty and I are going crazy. It's like a honeymoon. We're up till three a.m. fucking trying to override the Prozac to come. We do sex in every position, every variation, as though it's the last time.

At the Tropen museum, I see a wooden relief sculpture of a man with an erect penis. The penis extends to his navel, the vein on it exquisitely and tenderly done. It's carved in wood the color of Ty's skin and suddenly I want to trace the ridge of his penis with my tongue. I visualize the vein that snakes down his shaft and try to remember the exact placement of the twist, the way the foreskin covers it.

"I wonder if I'll ever have another lover," I say.

"Of course you will. You're beautiful."

"I am? You never told me." The face on the sculpture does not smile, as though the erection is serious business. I guess it is.

"Any man you sleep with will fall in love with you. You do this bonding thing in bed. I don't know how you do it, but you do."

"Yeah. It's worked so well for me in the past." My teeth are clenched.

"If you can be your free self."

. . .

He cries in my arms. I lick salt off his neck. He says he must save me from him.

"I'm not afraid of your demons."

"I am. I want to retreat from them, crawl into a dark corner and scab over. My hand is getting worse. I will only continue to damage you. You and Naomi."

"Don't kid yourself for a moment that you're doing any of this for me."

I straddle him, stare into his eyes, feel him deep inside me. My tears drip on his chest. He says, I love you I love you I love you.

I feel more bonded to him than ever.

And we're breaking up.

During the day we walk around with all the other seemingly happy couples, the fraying of their relationships only slightly visible at the edges. Older couples, children raised, proudly sharing pictures of their grandchildren, great grandchildren. They brag about their spouse's accomplishments. They remind each other to take pills at breakfast.

I say, "Do you realize what we're giving up? Helping each other as our bodies disintegrate. The sense of a whole life shared? Helping each other to die?" We're on a green field. Blue washcloths hang from a line. Herring, raw and salted, is being cut in great chunks. The fish house is the color of rain clouds. The sky is caught in the canal.

"I don't want it," he replies.

"Tell me how it was, Ty. All these years where part of you hated me. Hated when I left a coffee cup or a knot of dirty underwear on the floor, or asked when you'd be home for dinner, hated me for the evidence of the phlegm of my humanness. And wanted to be free."

"When I cut my hand, I thought the gods had honored me. Now I feel unwanted, evil, unworthy of living with another."

"You're not Jeffrey Dahmer. You're not the worst thing in the world." We approach the fish house and are handed our chunk of fish.

I can't stop the one-liners, the silly attempts to latch my mind to an understandable reason, to end my own bafflement.

He hated washing dishes, so he wanted out of family life.

He couldn't deal with his hand, the art school, his painting, and the family. He couldn't cut off his hand, so he cut off his family

"Your mother died and you discovered you hated her, so you dumped me," I say.

"You work out the financial settlement," he says. "You may want to kill me, but I know you won't cheat me."

"Money is not what I'm talking about."

"Want to see what being dumped is? I'll show you, if you say it again."

"People will think that leaving me is worse than having an affair."

He is surprised. "They will?"

. . .

Holland is green fields, furious green from the low sea level and all the water. Fields dotted with black and white lambs and black-and-white cows. Sky-blue canals cut through as if it were color coordinated by Martha Stewart. It is almost too picturesque. Trees are pruned to nubs. I get lost in the green. I am afraid to die alone. I'm not afraid to live alone. What will happen to me next? When I stop, the green smothers me and burns my eyes.

One night we work out the settlement agreement. Or rather I work it out. He doesn't want to be bothered. It's like Monopoly. Trading small wooden houses. I try to cover all future contingencies. Naomi's college. Retirement. Houses.

. . .

We resume our unfucking. Each time, I say good-bye to his body, his smell, the feel of him inside me. His voice. I imagine him in the world and not hearing his voice, not making love with him. I imagine him in the world not knowing how he is. I still haven't learned to breathe fast enough to keep up with him.

We have dinner in the Kastel Denewith, only candlelight playing against stone walls, harp music. Dancing between courses. More food, more courses, more dancing. The candles grow dim. We see our faces glowing in the velvet flame. So romantic. Shadows of couples dance on the cool softened stones. This is the most romantic place I've ever been. Who will I dance the twist with when I'm seventy? I think about mated lions and their pride. I think about Lala's dolls stretching from the past to the future. I think about the pair bond. Ty plays with my knee and I feel heat between my legs. He holds my hands and my breasts tingle. But he does not invite me into his head.

I dance with Kevin, a retired dentist from Delaware. He twirls me in a slow waltz until I'm dizzy. "How does it feel be married to a father-son all these years?"

"You think so, uh?" is what I say, but I think, son maybe, father no way.

I return to my seat and think about Georgia O'Keefe alone in the desert. Margaret Mead in Samoa. My childhood dream of being a strong single mother. Lala. The happiest ten years in her life were the last ten. Alone. No one's wife. No one's mother. Untangled.

. . .

I dream I drip blood from the backs of my knees. The blood is very red and shaped like elongated triangles with a ruby bead at each tip. I drip blood from the palms of my hands.

. . .

Ty gives his usual lecture on the effect of his hand accident on his painting, the sudden rush of bright color, the shedding of academic intellectualism for raw emotion. I hear the half-truths. I wonder what he's going to say five years from now. What myth will connect changes in his art to our separation.

. . .

That night, when I undress, my dress clings to my body, it slithers, rustles as I take it off. He picks me up and carries me to the bed. I will always love you. I will always want you. I love the way you feel. The warmth of your flesh, the heat in your crotch. How you fit next to me. I love to watch you, to look at you when you bend over.

I didn't know.

I said it. I told you a long time ago. You catch me watching you undress. You must know. This evening when you dried your hair with a towel tied around your hips. When you stretch to pull a weed in the yard, your ass when you bend over. The expression on your face when you saw the green fields, held the chrome blue fabric.

You didn't tell me.

I didn't think I had to.

When he's deep inside me, he says, you get lost in the flowers, I get lost inside you, in your waves, your gentle waves. I will miss your waves.

I get lost in the flowers, white daisies and white roses, small with yellow stamens, organs trembling. Time stops and slows or hastens, I don't know which. I am still, quiet inside myself. Pick flowers forever, wander through my daisy fields. Snip. Snip. They fall to the ground and I crush them in my arms. The scent of boldness surrounds me, the scent of sun and bees and earth and greenness. A bird calls and I am with her and I am alone and in the flowers and not alone all at once and I am lost for a moment, away from myself.

The Kroller Moeller Musseum captivates me. It is spare and modern. A freeform object floats on a shallow pool. A stainless steel inverted pyramid, half buried underground and half planted with grass, merges industrial modern with the earth. I think about how to make it.

We wander the Royal African Museum, walking in the sculpture garden. "All you have to do is let yourself go and you'll be in love," he tells me.

"You think people are replaceable." Topiary trees shaped into balls and pyramids and crisp columns encircle a pool. A savage jungle behind it. The sculptured trees hold chaos at bay.

Fetish figures with handmade nails, mirrors for bellies, grimace at the fury of life. Sharp breasts suckle babies with rage and pity. "I love this exhibit. It goes right up there with the Picasso exhibit in New York."

"Tutankahmen in Chicago," he says.

"Fauve in Washington." I sort through our years together.

"Musee D'Orsay."

"The Haitian exhibit in the Petit Palais." Rushing through the decades, the cities.

"Munch in New York."

Thirty years. A hundred different cities.

We walk back to the hotel in a downpour. The rain slicks my T-shirt to my skin, outlines my nipples. During our honeymoon in Mexico City, we were drenched after seeing *Sound of Music*. That night, all night we walked to our three dollar hotel. My dress was transparent. Then, we ran laughing, holding hands. Splashing in the warm rain. Now we hunch down in thin jackets. Not speaking. A circle. Beginning to end.

The week started out feeling like an upside-down honeymoon. Now it feels like when I said good-bye to Lala. She was dying of cancer and I knew I'd never again see her. I mourned her then. Now, I mourn Ty, mourn my own life.

I dream of men with hard shoulders and thick necks, rimmed lips and veined hands, soft hair on torso and arms, wanting me, telling me that they can't get enough of me, complaining they want more. Sometimes the greatest safety is no safety at all.

. . .

We have the final banquet, pictures and movies of University of Wisconsin's glory. Old football games. Professors receiving honors. The couples are all glitter. Jewelry, makeup, suits, styled hair. One woman hugs me good-bye and says, "You know, we've been on these before. And we decided, Harv and I, that you and Ty were by far the best couple that's led us. His lectures were terrific. And you were available and easily approachable. You two were the best couple."

We were, I think. I thought so, anyway. I blink. I don't want her to see my tears. "Thank you," I say.

. . .

On the flight back to Madison, I make some sketches for a sculpture, a hermaphroditic scarecrow for my garden. Aluminum hands with titanium claws. A snake penis and stainless cone breasts. Pointed ears from rusted steel. Black slits for eyes. A demon in my garden.

I fall asleep and wake over the edge of the United States. I wake with the thought that I can't tell what will happen next. I can't predict the consequences of any event. But there's life waiting. Always life, quivering and coiling as glittery and unpredictable as mercury, until the end.

EPILOGUE 1998

Latitude: 46∞01' N. Longitude: 81∞41' W.
The Pool at Baie Fine

We sail, Dan and I, north by northwest. The sun shines a silver path in the water for us to follow. Mists cloud the land's edges, the water pink from the morning sky. As we cruise up the Detroit River, smoke spews in fluorescent hues from steel mills and chemical plants. I wildly capture colors of rusted buildings and pyramids of eggplant sand in my sketchbook. America's industrial might is squashed between sky and water. We go under a bridge and before us the lake stretches, vacant under an empty sky.

Dan says, "I love this, sailing in open seas with only instruments. It's like life."

"Except in life you don't have instruments," I say, the breeze blowing my hair.

"Your parents and they're faulty." His hat shades his rugged face.

"And they're liable to blink off at any minute," I add.

We continue through easy seas, a white sky, stopping at quaint villages along the eastern edge.

And then, around Cape Hurd, seas start. Eight-foot waves pitch us like a cork. We tilt toward cold steel water and swing upright to a clotted sky. Water surges us forward, sprays us till we're soaked.

I go below and am slammed into a wall. I think I broke my jaw, my hand instantly purple with a hematoma that expands before my eyes. My fingers still move. I crawl to the couch and am thrown off, pummeled by cushions. I lie on the floor unsure what to do and feeling sorry for myself. Books and nautical charts fly above me and skate across the floor.

Enough, I think. And crawl to the fridge to get ice for my hand, the purple red flourishing. Dan comes down to take a reading from the GPS and goes back up to the bridge.

Ice numbs my hand. My jaw throbs. Blue spreads down my forearm. Shit. Dan beeps the emergency signal. He needs me. I have to climb the ladder to the upper deck. Maybe I heard wrong. But there it is again. I roll across the floor with a sudden pitch of the boat. I have to go. My left hand useless, the boat twisting, surging, I grab railings. Pull myself up with one hand. The water appears dangerously close to me, my thighs clench the bulkhead bars. I crawl to my seat, blinded by fog.

"I don't know where the fuck we are," Dan screams. He points toward a dark mass tilting not far from us. "I thought I saw rocks and breakers." Dan tries to stare through the fog. "But they're gone now." The boat surges to rocks. "Take the wheel. Head for sea. I'll check our position."

We spin toward the smashing sea, white frothing water. Then heave back again to the rocks, closer.

Then the fog lifts. Just like that. Something wipes the sky clean and exposes a sunlit coast. We're on course. Only my purple hand, blue jaw and arm to show for my terror.

A few days later, we wind our way through a shallow river littered with serendipitous rocks. Sheer white cliffs plunge into the ribbon of water. We round a bend and there is a deep lake, surrounded by granite mountains with pine trees growing in the rock crinkles. The Pool at Baie Fine. We anchor, tie to a tree, shed our clothes, and dive into the black water. Its warmth rushes over my body, slips around my limbs, breasts, crotch. Encompasses me. Dan and I swim together, talking, laughing, splashing. The fresh air redolent with the astringency of pine.

Then we walk the land. Soft pine needles and jagged white stone, forests of aged trees gnarled in their struggle for soil and water. We pass a Massasauga rattlesnake coiled in a patch of bright sun, brown diamonds slide down his length. He stares at Dan through elliptic pupils, his rattle at attention.

"A handsome fellow," Dan announces, and we continue on our way. Reaching the top of the mountain, I paint a picture of the island at the mouth of the pool while Dan wanders the cliffs. Trees are black-green on white rocks. The water shimmers in the sun, captures crystals on wavelets.

The colors, the sun prisms send shivers through me. I can lose myself in the infinite cobalt sky, the blue floating on puddles in my paper. I am more content than I've ever been. Living with Naomi in my house in the forest. My house is filled with my art, my and Naomi's friends, music, an occasional drum circle. New loves. When you survive the worst possible thing that can happen to you, there's an exhilaration about life. Now I know the answer.

I did not realize how much I had accommodated myself to Ty, to making him happy. Now, the TV is hardly on. When I come home, there's no longer anxiety as to his mood. I paint brown-black trees against my sky. Guess I always lived with a depressed person. First my mother and then Ty. Funny, I think, as I blot the black-green, see it seep into my paper towel. Ah, perfect. I am free to be me. My skinny brush slides black-blue across my paper, revealing the ruffles each rock, each bit of wind makes in the water. Life. You never know what's going to happen next. A sudden storm or a glorious sunset.

Just then Dan returns with a small pine tree extricated from a crevice. He hands it to me. My hands cup the dirt ball. Its trunk and branches are thickened and twisted, the needles miniaturized by hardship.

"Already a bonsai," I say.

"Could be."

"Or we could plant it and let it grow as big as it can."

He sits next to me. Shadows fall on his arms, his hair illuminated gold in sun patches.

"You know," I say. "You never can tell from an incident what its consequences will be. I mean, I thought Ty and I splitting was a negative event. Hell, the worst thing in my life." I add dry dots of yellow-green to my trees. "And it turned out to be positive. He did me a big favor."

"It's the difference between history and journalism."

"Perspective, eh? We just learn from events. And grow."

"You have to run the experiment. See the results." Dan's a scientist. His hand is soft and warm on my knee.

I watch the sun play tag with ripples. I inhale the piney air. "Yep. As long as there's life, there's possibility."